LEGAL AID LAWYERS AND THE QUEST FOR JUSTICE

This book examines the state of access to criminal justice by considering the health of the lawyer–client relationship under legal aid. In the largest study of its kind for some two decades, ethnographic fieldwork is used to gain a fresh perspective upon the interaction that lies at the heart of the criminal justice system's equality of arms. The research produces two contradictory messages; in interview, lawyers claim a positive relationship with their clients while, under participant observation, there emerges quite the opposite. Paying more heed to what was seen than what was said, it is supposed that these lawyers were able to talk the talk but not walk the walk. The lawyers treat their clients with wanton disrespect; making fun of them, talking over them and pushing them to plead guilty – despite protestations to the contrary. The evidence is damning for this branch of the legal profession – and tragic for the clients who depend on them. What is responsible for this malaise . . . inadequate financial remuneration? Increased time pressures? Lapsed ethical training? Whatever the origin, this book is intended to show the profession that there is a problem – one that could get worse unless they choose to learn from the mistakes made by the lawyers in this study.

Legal Aid Lawyers and the Quest for Justice

Daniel Newman

HART PUBLISHING
OXFORD AND PORTLAND, OREGON
2013

Published in the United Kingdom by Hart Publishing Ltd
16C Worcester Place, Oxford, OX1 2JW
Telephone: +44 (0)1865 517530
Fax: +44 (0)1865 510710
E-mail: mail@hartpub.co.uk
Website: http://www.hartpub.co.uk

Published in North America (US and Canada) by
Hart Publishing
c/o International Specialized Book Services
920 NE 58th Avenue, Suite 300
Portland, OR 97213-3786
USA
Tel: +1 503 287 3093 or toll-free: (1) 800 944 6190
Fax: +1 503 280 8832
E-mail: orders@isbs.com
Website: http://www.isbs.com

British Library Cataloguing in Publication Data
Data Available

ISBN: 978-1-84946-433-8

Typeset by Hope Services Ltd, Abingdon
Printed and bound in Great Britain by
Lightning Source UK Ltd

FOREWORD

For the diminishing number of often-disheartened lawyers who, like me, work in the Cinderella world of criminal appeals, Daniel Newman's book is both timely and important. Many of us have suspected for a long time that criminal defence lawyers are (with of course some very important exceptions!) in general, 'not fit for purpose'. Daniel Newman's book sadly proves this to be the case.

There can be no argument with the basic proposition that those who are accused of a crime need effective and fearless representation, and the more serious the offence then the greater the need for the very best defence. However, many appellants having been wrongly convicted say that their lawyer didn't listen to them, wasn't interested in them, didn't understand the evidence against them or the case that they wanted to run and, generally, did a bad job. We have to explain that, however true this may be, it's bad luck because as a ground of appeal, incompetence, laziness or the downright stupidity of their defence team will almost certainly not succeed as a ground of appeal.

Daniel Newman's research, put bluntly, tells the story of a criminal justice system that is populated by and large by a collection of lawyers/paralegals and gophers who would not survive in virtually any other branch of the law. In their defence, they point to the scandalously low fees that they receive from the LSC and how criminal legal aid is an easy target for politicians to cut to the bone; knowing that forcing down standards will not produce an outcry from the media, from the public or by and large from the legal profession. Victims of legal incompetence and error are a marginalised and disenfranchised group with no voice, no public sympathy and no political clout. They have no money to pay for a decent service and their lawyers know that they will rarely face a negligence claim and are unlikely to be the subject of a complaint to the SRA or the Legal Services Ombudsman for poor service.

Adding to this, having established the CCRC, politicians are now no longer interested in why our criminal justice system produces miscarriage after miscarriage and refuse to address the fundamental issue that it is impossible to deliver a first class criminal justice system on the cheap. The introduction of fixed fees in criminal cases is just one example of a cost cutting measure that has made the situation worse. What is the point of an uncommitted defence lawyer doing anything to challenge the prosecution case when their fee is based on the page count not on the work done? Doing hundreds of hours of work challenging the prosecution at every stage gets you precisely the same fee as if you do absolutely nothing – the logic of inactivity is overwhelming.

By using ethnographic methodology and having observed at close quarters three criminal defence firms, Daniel Newman's research shows, in a vivid and colourful way, that, although defence lawyers by and large talk the talk, they don't walk the walk. Daniel Newman's research illustrates brilliantly that such lawyers are not delivering the service that they should and as a result the adversarial system – which relies on equality of arms between the prosecution and the defence – is failing. Even when the CPS is as incompetent and as flawed as it often is, it still succeeds in cases where it should not.

In my experience, defence lawyers often fail to do even basic things to investigate or put the prosecution to the task of proving beyond reasonable doubt that the person they have charged is guilty. In one of the cases I am currently dealing with, the appellant was charged with murder following a fight with his friend through a broken kitchen window. Expert evidence pointed to the fact that the victim had impaled himself on a shard of glass while he was trying to hit the appellant with a squeezy mop. For reasons that still remain bewildering, the jury were never given the opportunity of considering the self-impalement option, which, from all the available evidence, appeared the most logical explanation for what had occurred. It was put to the jury that the appellant had either stabbed the victim with a shard of glass or threw a shard of glass at him. There was no evidence to support either contention. The legal team responsible for this particular outrage (that led to a life sentence) obviously failed in their duty to the client and to the court. There are a frightening number of similar examples where a more thorough investigation and a more informed and competent defence could have produced a fairer and more just outcome.

Although we cannot change the criminal justice system (and sadly it is difficult to imagine how it can be changed for the better) some of us who are deeply worried about its many deficiencies have recently established the Centre for Criminal Appeals, which, if it secures funding, will focus on investigating miscarriage of justice cases and will attempt to do some of the work that should have been done before trial.

We know that this is shutting the door after the horse has bolted and we know that some of the cases we will examine are old and important evidence will have been lost or destroyed and memories will have faded. What we are hoping to achieve, however, is to establish a core methodology of best practice that we hope will influence defence practitioners who may learn from the very many mistakes that are continuing to be made daily in the criminal courts. By doing this, it may at least be possible that one innocent person will get a better defence, and it may well be that this will encourage those committed defence solicitors to continue to do a good job and if so it will be worthwhile. In the meantime, everyone who is interested in and cares about criminal justice in this country should read Daniel Newman's book. It can only be hoped that it stimulates a debate about this vitally important subject and that things begin to improve for all those who face criminal charges, particularly those who are innocent of the crime for which they have been charged.

Glyn Maddocks
31 January 2013

PREFACE

This work was inspired by the time I spent as a student volunteering with a campaigning group for miscarriages of justice. I was responsible for corresponding with the prisoners; men and women claiming wrongful conviction and writing to us more in hope than expectation. At this time, I gained a small insight into the awesome power that the state wields in its operation of the criminal justice system and the devastating effect this power can have on the individual if it goes awry.

While volunteering, I came across several lawyers who had also given up their free to time to engage in pro bono casework for these prisoners. I was inspired by the passion they displayed and became enthused at the zeal with which they presented the need for a strong criminal defence profession. They raised the rhetorical question: who else will stand up for the most vulnerable groups in society against the might of the establishment? In so doing, they forced me to query the common stereotype that lawyers are greedy and only out for themselves. I wanted to prove them right, highlight this noble cadre of lawyer. No matter how much of a minority they were, I intended to hold up their practice as a beacon of what the profession could be and, thereon, of the need to encourage more crusading lawyers and not decry them all in one fell swoop.

It is to my great regret that I could not find such lawyers in the research I subsequently conducted. Indeed, it revealed quite the opposite as I found that lawyers who would regale me with grandiloquent statements of themselves and their profession failed to back up this bluster with actions of substance. They let me down and, more importantly, they let their clients down. As a result, I fear that what I have depicted in this book will only add fuel to the fire of those who already dismiss lawyers as contemptible. While I am critical of the poor lawyering that I encountered, I hope that my findings will not be used in this way. Rather than drawing any firm conclusions about the hopelessness of wanting integrity and honour from the legal profession, I desire that my research can represent a starting point for a renewed debate about just what exactly we want from our criminal process and how we can use it to achieve justice.

Whatever reforms or public spending cuts take place, it is likely that lawyers will continue to be central to upholding the rights of those suspected, accused and convicted of crimes in the criminal justice system for the foreseeable future. So we must find a way to work with them, rather than against them. And we must make sure that lawyers work for justice, rather than against it.

Daniel Newman
Dinas Powys
Christmas 2012

ACKNOWLEDGEMENTS

This book is based upon PhD research conducted at the University of Bristol School of Law, between 2007 and 2011. The work was supported by a grant from the Economic and Social Research Council [PTA-031-2006-00092].

First and foremost, I want to thank my PhD supervisors, Richard Young and Michael Naughton. Throughout my research, they provided invaluable expert and pastoral advice and I owe them a great deal in helping me to realise the potential of my funding. I could not have hoped for a pair of more knowledgeable or understanding supervisors.

I also need to thank my partner, Rhian Wilson – hopefully, Rhian Newman by the time this book is actually read! She has always been there for me and supported me throughout the various trials and tribulations that accompanied the research. I know she will believe that she is owed a particular debt of gratitude, being the one person (victim) I subjected to reading over my drafts, despite it being far more boring than one of her beloved travel guides.

In addition, I would like to thank my parents, Carl and Dawn Newman, and my grandparents, Norman and Gloria Cook. In so many ways, they put me in the position to do the research in the first place. They made sure that I had the wonderful opportunity to spend years rattling around in the cosy confines of university, a luxury they never had themselves. And they supported me throughout, so I could never have got here without them.

Finally, I must thank the lawyers in this research for granting me access to their professional lives. Though on reading my account, they may rather wish they had not, perhaps even feeling as though I have abused their good faith, I hope they realise that I fully appreciate their grace and generosity. As patronising as it might sound, I only do this because I want to help them reach their full potential as lawyers working for justice. I know that, by and large, they were good people with lofty ambitions that deserve to be realised.

CONTENTS

1

Access to Justice and the Lawyer–Client Relationship

This book is about lawyers, criminal defence lawyers. In particular, it focuses on how they treat their legally aided clients – ordinary people, suspected or accused (even convicted) of committing offences.

As the author, I realise that neither lawyers nor criminals are the most popular groups in society. Does anyone really love lawyers, apart from their mothers? And even some mothers may struggle to love their offspring when they are career criminals. All the same, I want to establish the players in this little drama from the outset – if the thought of spending the next few hundred pages reading about lawyers and their clients strikes you as pointless or even fills you with dread, this book might not be for you. However, I believe that if you have even the most basic interest in living in a truly democratic society then perhaps you should read on. As repulsive as lawyers and/or criminals might be to your palette, it is important to understand them as a measure of the strength of our democracy. In a democratic society, justice should mean fair treatment for all under the law, the ultimate test of which is the criminal justice system – the arena in which individuals and the institutions of the state collide. If those suspected, accused and convicted of crimes are not treated fairly, then society is on rocky ground. Every miscarriage of justice, such as the Birmingham Six or the Cardiff Three (or the hundreds of routine and mundane miscarriages that pass by without fanfare every year), where individuals are wronged by the state, poses a challenge to society, and should act as a reminder to question whether the criminal courts are working for justice.

This book contributes to that process, addressing the state of access to criminal justice through an exploration of the lawyer–client relationship under legal aid. In so doing, I question whether the nature of that relationship puts the client's access to justice in jeopardy. Are defendants in the criminal process able to receive justice – of a level that we would be happy with our children, partners, siblings or parents receiving if they ever got into trouble with the law?

First and foremost, there is a need for a terminological clarity when looking at matters of justice. Within the bounds of this book, access to justice has a necessarily restricted, though highly potent, meaning – relating to the basic ideology of the criminal process as it currently operates. It tests one of the system's key claims to fairness, perhaps the foremost principle: that it functions justly. The book will not engage in wider philosophical debates as to just what constitutes justice but, rather, restricts the definition to the elemental aspects of greatest relevance to the study at hand. This work is, at root, a practical study of law in action.

Accordingly, I posit that the key mark of a just criminal process lies in its ability to distinguish the guilty from the not guilty in its application of law and through its fact-finding. In England and Wales, accurate fact-finding and correct application of law is premised upon the adversarial theory of justice, where competing prosecution and defence accounts are permitted to do battle, within procedural limits, before an impartial adjudicator. In the light of the conflicting arguments and evidence advanced by each side, the court is expected to determine whether the prosecution has proven guilt beyond reasonable doubt. This situation presupposes roughly equal resources and expertise on both sides of the argument: the *equality of arms*. In these circumstances, Young and Wall (1996: 6) have established that, fundamentally, 'access to justice seems, therefore, to imply access to legal aid and lawyers'. Implicit within this statement is the notion that these legal aid lawyers should practise active defence – systematically taking the prosecution case apart to expose its weaknesses and investigating the case for the defence. Access to justice, then, requires a lawyer who appears fully committed to their client and who always puts their client's interests first. All that follows is presented under the supposition that this notion is crucial to fairness and upholding the presumption of innocence, thus contributing to avoidance of the wrongful conviction of the innocent.

Considering these elements, it is important that the administering of justice is recognised to involve both process and results. While results are ultimately crucial for the long-term impact they can exert on individuals and communities, this research highlights the importance of process, which can exert equally significant effects along the way. In so doing, it seeks to ensure that those suspected or accused of crimes are not subject to arbitrary or oppressive treatment within the criminal justice system. The actions of these legally aided lawyers are deemed crucial in determining whether or not their clients are exposed to such harms.

The stance taken in this study reflects a particular left-liberal position. It seems important to recognise the specificity of such beliefs, in light of Lacey's (1994: 34) assertion that criminal justice can only be properly understood with reference to its 'normative implications'. Debates around criminal justice are necessarily enthused with an array of values, ideologies and interpretive frameworks. Accordingly, any discussion of criminal justice requires that the speaker articulates the choices they have made regarding its purpose. The standpoint of the interested party is crucial – they cannot be assumed to approach the subject impartially and neutrally. Matters of criminal justice are not merely theoretical; they are firmly located within real life situations – social contexts and personal implications. There is a great deal that is essentially contestable in criminal justice, and meanings will vary for different people depending on their particular perspective and position. Modelling the criminal process can play a useful, if not imperative, function in socio-legal research. It provides a ready means of identifying the normative position held by the researcher. In the process of establishing my own standpoint, then, I need first to discuss the most iconic models of criminal justice, those offered by Packer (1968).

MODELLING CRIMINAL JUSTICE

In framing his work on the criminal process, Packer (1968: 149–73) constructs two models to describe divergent value systems: 'crime control' and 'due process'. These models are supposed in competition to dictate the operation of the criminal process. However, the models are not intended to represent reality nor desirable ideal; they are neither what *is* nor what *ought* to be. They share much common ground – such as the contention that there should be some limits on state power – but each stands for extreme points on a spectrum of doing criminal justice. This device allows for the identification of where the institutions of the criminal process sit at any particular moment and, thereon, predicts future trends.

Under the crime control model, the central function of the criminal process is the repression of criminal behaviour. It relies on the efficiency of the criminal process to capture and convict a high proportion of offenders as swiftly and definitively as possible. This evokes the image of an assembly line conveyor belt, with an endless stream of cases flowing down it. What follows is an essentially managerial system, with routinised practices working to pass cases along through each successful stage, screening out those likely to be innocent as early as possible while quickly moving on those likely to be guilty.

This system operates under a factual presumption of guilt. In this process, the centre of gravity lies in the early, administrative, fact-finding stages. Here, the police and prosecution are invested with much trust so that those who progress through are assumed to be guilty. As much as it represents the prevailing attitude, the presumption of guilt is a prediction of likely outcome. Once the police have decided upon a suspect, this individual can be believed to be guilty even before they actually become a defendant. The model, therefore, sees nothing wrong in organising affairs so that pressure is put on the defendant to both confess and plead guilty. This pressure is usually effective, rendering many of the later stages of the process largely perfunctory.

The raison d'être of this model is to repress crime; conviction of the guilty is the key tenet, with the mistaken conviction of some innocent defendants an unfortunate but acceptable price to pay. It seeks as few restrictions as possible on the fact-finders, and stands in opposition to rules restricting illegal arrest or coercive interrogations that might lead to the exclusion of otherwise credible evidence of guilt. To these ends, defendants should only be allowed access to representation in a minority of cases and, then, only at court. To encourage wider representation would needlessly serve the defendants at the expense of the court's ability to discern the defendant's guilt, running counter to the ultimate aim of the process: to secure conviction.

In contrast, due process is more concerned with upholding the rights of the defendant, so much so that the criminal process comes to resemble an obstacle course. The due process model lacks confidence in pre-trial fact-finding enterprises.

In this model, a great emphasis is placed on the possibility of error. There is an undercurrent of doubt, questioning the reliability of individuals to observe events and recognising the opportunity for inaccuracy in recall, influence of bias or the possibility of coercion. Informal fact-finding processes are, thus, rejected. Instead, this model champions adversarial processes, with the case against an individual considered publicly in a formal hearing with an independent tribunal. As such, decisions are only made after the accused has been provided with the opportunity to discredit the case against them, which they should be able to do at each stage. Defendants are presumed factually and/or normatively innocent until the evidence against them has been properly tested.

Central to this model is the right to representation, in order to allow the remedies and sanctions that check this process to be properly enacted. Furthermore, this position is premised upon the notion of the equality of arms, so that each individual should have the ability to contest a charge against them. This necessitates that – where the system allows the right to be represented by a lawyer yet the individual cannot afford to instruct one – the state should provide one for free.

This model challenges the finality of the crime control model, championing the essential right to appeal a decision. The due process model also harbours a deep scepticism about the morality of the criminal sanction – a device typically used against those deficient psychologically and/or economically. It is considered hypocritical to condemn individuals for their choices to breach the law, while concomitantly failing to provide for their humane treatment within the criminal process. As such, this model favours limiting the ability of the state to catch and punish alleged offenders. The end result is that, while crime control prioritises convicting the guilty, due process is primarily concerned with the acquittal of the innocent. Adherents are willing to allow the frequent acquittal of the guilty to meet its aims.

Of course, Packer's (1968) models have been critiqued and augmented, though against his own understanding, premised upon what is (Choongh, 1997: 35–42; Bottoms and McClean, 1976: 226–39) and what ought to be (Griffiths, 1970: 410–17). For Choongh (1998: 625), Packer (1968) fails to appreciate the significant minority of police arrests unconcerned with establishing guilt. The complementary model of 'social discipline' accounts for cases in which the police have no intention of charging and simply seek to control hostile elements of the local population (Choongh, 1998: 627–28). In his original study, Packer (1968) provides legal models that bear no relation to such work, which is conducted solely to achieve police-defined objectives. In addition, Packer's (1968) models have also been found deficient by Bottoms and McClean (1976: 228), who offer a 'liberal bureaucratic' model. They suggest that humane and enlightened court clerks act in a manner differentiating them from both crime control and due process. This upholds the protection of individual liberty over the repression of criminal conduct but is practical enough to realise that there must be a limit on the protection offered.

An alternative critique is presented by Griffiths (1970: 367–71), dismissing Packer's (1968) two models as one, monolithic, 'battle' model. By this line, Packer (1968) is condemned for adhering to a dominant ideology that positions the defendant and state in opposition, assuming disharmony, conflicted interests and encouraging a state of war. In contrast, Griffiths (1970: 371–86) supposes that there might be a state of love as in his 'family' model. Under this, disputes are settled in the manner of a stable family; everyone recognises that they are inexorably bound together, seeking to resolve their differences as amicably as possible. Any punishment is ultimately accepted for the greater good.

All three of these alternatives, though, continue to talk in Packer's (1968) language of *models*. That approach is criticised by MacDonald (2008: 269–89), who believes that the resulting models are inadequate, conflating strong and weak ideal types as well as failing to properly differentiate between empirical and evaluative research. He suggests that, rather than models, socio-legal studies can only move beyond Packer (1968) by developing a multidimensional framework. Accordingly, MacDonald (2008: 289–303) proposes a reconfiguration of the due process model into an ideal type based on a defensive criminal law that aims to protect individuals from abuses of state power.

In this light can be seen two sophisticated frameworks, with broadly due process concerns, centred on 'rights' (Ashworth and Redmayne, 2010: 19–61) and 'freedom' (Sanders et al, 2010: 47–58). These approaches share a common foundation in their intention to overcome two further crucial deficiencies posited to inhibit Packer's (1968) theory: that his models are incomplete and that they do not offer aspirational ideals (Sanders et al, 2010: 47). As such, Ashworth and Redmayne (2010) attempt to overcome these difficulties by insisting that individuals be seen as rational and rights-bearing, with state power subject to limits that treat them with dignity. These authors adhere to a retributive rationale for punishment, where censure is morally appropriate but need be proportionate to the offence and must follow a fair conviction. Their criminal process is concerned with authoritative determinations of guilt, but only in a way that protects human rights. This perspective pays particular reference to the European Convention on Human Rights as enshrined in the Human Rights Act 1998. In the position set out by Ashworth and Redmayne (2010), these rights need be developed so as to offer a reliable constraint on the criminal process. Rights become a concomitant aim of their system.

This approach requires the balancing, and prioritising, of certain rights weighted against others. However, Sanders et al (2010) problematise the manner in which that process is inherently vague, while establishing and enshrining particular interests at the expense of others. In contrast, they offered an approach that conceives of the criminal process primarily protecting and enhancing freedom. Their framework encompasses all who come into contact with crime or the justice system: victim, suspect or offender. In the name of a free society, maximising the freedom of each must be prioritised. This ranges from the freedom to enjoy one's possessions or walk the street without fear of attack, to the freedom from having one's life arbitrarily invaded by state officials or being wrongfully convicted in a prejudicial tribunal.

Human rights are considered but a basic minimum, a safeguard that the state should respect. However, they are not considered enough in and of themselves. For

Sanders et al (2010), state institutions have much leeway to behave in a manner consistent with human rights but antithetical to increasing freedom. The authors invoke the example of a police stop–search policy whereby powers could be used whenever the law permitted. While this would not impinge human rights, neither would a more restricted use of those powers. The latter approach, though, would be better suited to protecting and enhancing the freedom of the community at large. Greater credence should be given to the role that rights, and other safeguards, play – or fail to play – in promoting freedom. Paying attention to the interplay of rights and freedom is important because a large part of the reasoning behind having such rights is to enhance freedom, but this is too often subsumed by a focus on the rights themselves: their wording, technical interpretation and associated litigation. The daily application of the rights, as they are experienced in the real world, is obfuscated by a concentration on the abstract legal principles contained in the letter of the law as written or argued in court. Rights are normal and banal – they are lived and not just confined to the domain of occasional and special formal pronouncements. To gain any real value from these rights – and ensure that they work to protect people from harm (as is their intention) – the implications for freedom must be considered and this involves engaging with ordinary life.

In this research, I follow the freedom approach. As such, the book is more interested in the everyday reality of rights – how they are invoked, used, subverted or ignored in practice. Proceeding with the insight of the freedom approach allows a greater appreciation of the individuals involved and their ordinary experiences. It calls on the criminal justice system to be tasked with the role of enhancing the freedom of all: accuser and accused alike. While Sanders et al (2010: 42–47) are keen to reinstate the place of the victim – missing from Packer's (1968) models – this research focuses on those suspected and accused of crimes. In this manner, it can be described as promoting due process values, with a concern that these individuals are justly treated within the criminal process. The particular approach to access to justice underlying this research is one which Sanders and Young (2006: 29) label 'pro-suspect'. As loaded a term as that sounds, rife with *loony left*, anti-establishment sentiment, I will take it on as an apt description; I am devoting my time and effort to fighting the corner of those who are forced to defend themselves against the accusations of the state. It would be reductionist, though, to suppose that I seek to promote defendant rights at the expense of victims; despite the pigeon-holing promoted by our adversarial system, I do not believe it is this simple as justice, if it works properly, should be made to work for all. This research, then, evokes Eleanor Roosevelt's (1947) noble epitaph that 'justice cannot be for one side alone, but must be for both'. Victims deserve justice; but this research is concerned with ensuring that the other side also attains it. In the legal process, the police and prosecution support victims; but as this study looks at the other side of the criminal case, it is somewhat inevitable that a focus on those suspected and accused of crimes brings attention onto the role of criminal defence lawyers.

THE NEED FOR LAWYERS

It seems easy for socio-legal literature to proceed with the implicit assumption that the values of the author are those routinely accepted. By this line, the author expects the audience to hold the same view as they do – whether because the author feels that they are intrinsically correct or because they are simply preaching to the converted. As such, I could well just thunder ahead with this book assuming that you, the readers, are all as *wet* as me. In this manner, Travers (1997a: 359) suggests that:

> Academics are simply out of step with British society, which has moved increasingly to the right . . . Much research has a liberal or left-wing political bias, whereas users of research, such as the British government, and rank-and-file members of the police – as well as a large proportion of the British electorate – hold very different assumptions about . . . the purpose of criminal justice.

Indeed, from the 1980s onwards, popular debate around criminal justice policy can be identified to have taken a more punitive turn (Garland, 2001). While judging public opinion on socio-legal issues is notoriously difficult, it can be noted that my research was conducted in a political climate infused with populism and attempts at hard-nosed political posturing when it comes to crime and criminals. The term 'populist punitivness' aptly describes this situation – as coined by Bottoms (1995: 40) – 'to convey the notion of politicians tapping into, and using for their purposes, what they believe to be the public's generally punitive stance'. People who are caught up in the net of criminal justice are now increasingly portrayed in media reports, political rhetoric and in actual policy statements as belonging to an undeserving, feckless underclass. Accordingly, the New Labour Government adopted tabloid-centred, 'anti-crime politics' (Tonry, 2004: 64); they were 'banging the law and order drum' (Young, 2003: 41). From the 1997 general election campaign onwards, the Party proffered a hard-line stance unprecedented by a supposedly left-wing British political party and quite at odds with any other government in Labour history (see Brownlee, 1998). This was encapsulated in a speech made by, then Justice Secretary, Jack Straw, celebrated by the rabidly right-wing *Daily Mail* as 'Liberals who push criminal rights drive me nuts' (Hickley and Slack, 2008). Within it, Straw (2008: 12–13) can be found to criticise these 'liberals' for becoming 'lost in a fog of platitudes', so much so that:

> I am concerned that it has retreated into language that doesn't chime with the public . . . When I hear phrases like 'criminogenic needs of offenders' it drives me nuts . . . I profoundly disagree that we should describe someone's amoral desire to go thieving as a 'need' equivalent to that of victims or the law-abiding public.

Without accurately exploring the notion of *criminogenic needs*, deploying the phrase becomes a quick and easy tool with which to mock those who argue for human rights – it just sounds shot through with painfully woolly, wildly do-gooder overtones, ensuring that Straw is able to depict himself as far more sensible and on the side of the ordinary, law-abiding citizen. Despite the fact that New Labour infamously created a new crime almost every day it was in office and offered something of a tour-de-force in cracking down on civil liberties (Morris, 2008), the lead-in to the 2010 general election reflected the clamour for ever harsher treatment of those implicated in the criminal justice system (see Mille, 2010). Accordingly, Theresa May's (2010) first speech as Coalition Government Home Secretary saw her promise that this new administration would be 'tough on crime'; by implication, tougher still than New Labour. She effortlessly dismissed New Labour as far too soft on crime, describing them as having been 'bowed to the lawyer lobby' (May, 2010).

In conducting this research, I may be inviting similar, likely greater, criticism; I acknowledge that the plight of defendants is not the most fashionable of good causes. While others may disagree with my defence-minded perspective, it is a cause deemed legitimate within the bounds of this book, wherein they are considered inherently vulnerable by taking on that status. The defendant can be faced with an alien, oftentimes bewildering, environment once drawn into the criminal justice system. In the face of this, defendants can quickly find themselves very much out of their comfort zone – left inarticulate and overwhelmed. As such, it seems necessary to provide them with a helping hand to guide them through: an expert. It is at this point that the notion of the equality of arms assumes its significance; our adversarial system depends on there being powerful arguments on both sides of the question of legal guilt (see Fuller, 1978). On their own, defendants would face a permanent, and telling, disadvantage against the might of the state. To avoid this, they should be provided with access to criminal defence practitioners: lawyers. Accordingly, Goriely (1996: 26) asserts the 'unequivocally' held principle that 'in the adversarial system which prevails in the courts in this country, representation is needed on both sides'. Indeed, McConville et al (1994: 2) view the desirability of this provision to be self-evident:

> The need for defendants to be legally represented in criminal cases is perhaps so obvious that the fact that solicitors may be seen giving advice at the police stations to suspects who have been arrested and advocating their cause in Magistrates' Courts hardly seems to require explanation.

The reality is that most defendants simply cannot afford to hire a criminal defence lawyer privately. Lawyers have expensive hourly rates that quickly add up. For those with an average wage, it seems fair to suggest that even paying a lawyer to read a letter would represent a bit of a luxury, let alone the lengthy periods that can be accrued over the life of a case as it progresses through the courts. As such, access to justice does not simply require access to criminal defence lawyers but, specifically, access to criminal defence lawyers funded by legal aid. This principle has been ardently advocated by Ashworth (1996: 56–57) who identifies four strands underlying its necessity: complexity of the courts; police and Crown Prosecution Service resources; the potentially devastating impact of a conviction upon a defendant, and; that the ability to defend oneself should not depend on financial resources.

The first two of Ashworth's (1996: 56–57) strands highlight the relative weakness of the criminal defendant when compared with the agents of the Crown. The criminal process involves convoluted procedures and unfamiliar linguistic conventions, resting on a mass of highly technical, interlocking and overlapping laws stretching back centuries. The state prosecuting has, near enough, unlimited access to the necessary expertise required to properly navigate the system. In order to retain any pretension towards equality of arms, the defendant must be in the position to draw upon such expertise of their own. Understandably, individual defendants are highly unlikely to posses such skills so this requires the services of a criminal defence lawyer. This lawyer must support the defendant through the inherently alienating criminal justice system.

In *Magistrates' Justice*, Carlen (1976: 19) offers the thesis that the main function of the Magistrates' Courts is to operate as a means of social control, through 'superordination and subordination'. Both the physical arrangements of the courtroom setting and the behaviour of magistrates, court staff and police work to alienate defendants. Defendants become *dummy players* in the process of criminal justice, ignorant of exactly what is going on and excluded from the games that those in charge play. While Carlen (1976) focuses on the practical playing out of criminal cases, McBarnet (1981) locates defendants' alienation within the law itself. Her study, *Conviction*, duly addresses official legal, police and formal rules. These have been established in a manner that precludes defendants from being able to take on active roles in their own trials. Again, defendants are silenced in the criminal process through their lack of understanding over what is happening to them. All this contributes to a sense of 'confusion' and 'exclusion'; incomprehensibility that feels positively threatening (Bottoms and McClean, 1976: 55).

Those studies were conducted at a time when defendants were largely unrepresented in Magistrates' Courts. However, even with – to some extent, because of – increased levels of representation, this process of alienation can still be identified. While it is easy to become lost as an individual within the strange and self-contained world of the legal system, even greater levels of detachment follow the appointment of a lawyer with the individuals, invariably, taking a backseat while the legal professionals go about their business with one another. In large part, this can be attributed to Magistrates' Courts' business becoming increasingly complicated over recent years, with regard to both legislation and bureaucratic procedure. Successive governments have attempted to professionalise the criminal justice system. This has seen the introduction of measures such as bad character hearings, reforming the right to silence so that inferences can be made, admitting hearsay evidence in criminal proceedings and the regimentation of sentencing guidelines. There has been an explosion in the variety of hearings and personnel involved in the processing of a case through Magistrates' Courts. As a result, there seems far greater need for defence lawyers to be involved from the outset. Represented or not, greater complexity serves to further remove the defendant from active engagement in the criminal process; their alienation is ever increased. For the ordinary man or woman in the street, there is no shame in admitting that they find the whole court process absolutely bewildering – despite being theoretically primed with ensuring that justice is publically accountable and able to be democratically scrutinised, the reality is that the legal system does not work for outsiders. It is a member's only club, the world of lawyers and jurists.

This alienation seems amplified with regard to the place of the defendant in police stations and the Crown Court. In these arenas, defendants have greater access to representation but, concomitantly, even less of a role to play themselves. The police station is explicitly the territory of the constabulary; defendants temporarily lose their liberty as it is entrusted to the officers. At the same time, the Crown Court is the more daunting step up from the Magistrates' Court with increases in seriousness of case, waiting periods and means of sentencing. In this grander setting, sometimes in front of juries, experienced judges and legal representatives – adorned in wigs and gowns – play the games. Both settings alienate defendants.

As such, all three locations remove the defendant from the criminal process in significant ways. The defendant becomes definitively a *client*. Their ability to comprehend, let alone conduct, cases themselves are diminished; they are reliant on lawyers. As such, they are entered into a process of 'legal dependency' (Ericson and Baranek, 1982: 92–100). So it is that Bourdieu (1987: 828) identifies such clients to be separated from their cases as:

> The establishment of properly professional competence, the technical mastery of a sophisticated body of knowledge that often runs contrary to the simple counsels of common sense, entails the disqualification of the non-specialists' sense of fairness, and the revocation of their naïve understanding of the facts, of their 'view of the case' . . . the vulgar vision of the person who is about to come under the jurisdiction of the court.

Defendants are, then, locked into a 'self-referential system' (Moorhead et al, 2003: 7). It is in this context that they are encountered in this research; the book is necessarily focused on their status as clients. While I approach the topic looking to empower suspects and defendants by telling their stories, it is a necessary evil that I reduce them to dependent clients, as this is the best way to make sense of their actual experience; effectively, they operate within the legal system as the *plus ones* of lawyers. As such, I address the lawyers and the role they must play in serving their clients; lawyers represent something of a proxy.

By Ashworth's (1996: 57) third strand, lawyers have great responsibility in these circumstances because the convicted defendant faces serious consequences, which increase the moral and social significance of the first two points. Clients might have their reputation tarnished, lose money, have their liberty taken and be privy to all manner of physical or mental ills. The importance of this consideration informs Ashworth's (1996: 57) final point that the ability to defend oneself should not depend on financial resources. This consideration is premised upon fundamental notions of equality and such provision can be regarded as a human right. Within the European Convention on Human Rights, the need for legal representation is clear:

Article 6.1

> In the determination of his civil rights and obligations or of any criminal charge against him, everyone is entitled to a fair and public hearing within a reasonable time by an independent tribunal.

However, while Article 6.1 offers an equality of arms, Article 6.3(c) shows the matter of funding to be more ambiguous:

> Article 6.3 Everyone charged with a criminal offence has the following minimum rights . . .
>
> (c) to defend himself in person or through legal assistance of his own choosing or, if he has not sufficient means to pay for legal assistance, to be given it free when the interests of justice so require.

The relationship between these two Articles, then, is rather murky. Problems are created by the open-textured phrases by which they simply refer to the defendant's not possessing *sufficient means* and, thereon, the qualification when the *interests of justice so require*. The European Court of Human Rights has refused to identify any base level of income to tie into the former, while the latter is conditioned upon the complexity of the case and the potential consequences for the accused.[1] As such, the European Court of Human Rights has granted much discretion for individual governments in when and how they provide this legal assistance.

In the criminal justice system, duty solicitor schemes ensure that all accused are eligible to receive police station representation, though the advent of telephone-only advice can be considered to somewhat temper this right (Skinns, 2009: 68–70). Most Crown Court appearances involve legal aid, though New Labour introduced means testing. Although a large amount of Magistrates' Court first appearances automatically receive legal aid, the routine mass of cases rely on both means and merits tests. While these satisfy the letter of Article 6.3 of the European Convention on Human Rights, Ashworth (1996: 68) concludes that, normatively, this is not enough as the clauses 'appear to be trial-centred, and . . . they fail to insist on proper standards of fairness and equal access to justice at the pre-trial stage'. This raises serious questions about the quantity of service that defendants receive. Legally, access to justice might be challenged by a lack of representation.

My research is concerned with those who were represented and so goes a step further. In doing so, rather than simply looking at matters of quantity, I am concerned with the quality of the service those clients receive. Lawyers are, surely, not inherently good – as human beings engaged in social interactions, their performance and, thus, value to those they purportedly serve will inevitably vary. If legally aided representation is considered a right, it seems legitimate to insist that this representation should be sufficient to enact the adversarial principle the right is intended to support. Indeed, McConville et al (1994: 295) warn that we can no longer take it for granted 'that legal representation is an end in itself and to be

[1] *Imbrioscia v Switzerland* Series A no 205 [1994] 17 EHRR 441; *Artico v Italy* Series A no 37 [1980] 3 EHRR 1; and *Pham Hoang v France* Series A no 234 [1992] 16 EHRR 53.

valued . . . on that basis alone'. Representation should not necessarily be taken to confer access to justice upon an individual. Discussing recent research, Moorhead (cited Baksi, 2010a) suggests that there is an increasing amount of evidence to the effect that some lawyers do not operate at an acceptable level; they are 'not really up to the job'. As such, this book takes the line that even those who are represented might not receive access to justice if the service they are provided with is of a low standard. This position is guided by Felstiner's (2001: 191) contention that, 'the production of justice might be defined as a dimension of the relationship of lawyers to clients'.

This vision of access to justice, then, depends on the health of the lawyer–client relationship. Access to a legally aided lawyer is not enough of itself. If the lawyer appears committed to active defence and displays due process values then they may facilitate access to justice. Within this research, that is judged to constitute a healthy relationship – providing the greatest opportunity to the client, and so working to their benefit. If lawyers do not show such values and, rather, appear to practise passive defence, they then fail their clients. This would constitute an unhealthy relationship – one that has the potential to cause the client harm. It is my contention that access to justice can be gauged through addressing the relation of lawyers to their clients. In order to appreciate this dimension, we must first consider the legal profession itself.

THE LEGAL PROFESSION

Criminal defence lawyers are, rather self-evidently, members of the wider legal profession and, as such, the sociology of the professions provides a rich resource to aid in understanding their position. In particular, it can be seen that the fabled public service ideal forms a central part of professional ideology – whatever the practical reality.

The definition of a profession is difficult, and essentially contestable. Much of the early literature in the sociology of the professions utilised the idea of trait theory to distinguish professions from other work; however, there are so many traits that it can be difficult to know where to stop (see Leicht and Fennell, 2001: 25–27). Indeed, Millerson (1964) notoriously documents as many as 23 traits posited by 21 authors, in something of a 'checklist' approach best summarised by Atherley and Hale (1975: 323). These traits, though, can be considered to represent little more than, 'an uncritical reiteration of "professionals'" statements of pious hopes and self-interests' (Atkinson, 1983: 225). They tend to include bureaucratic features such as assessments for entry, codes of ethics and professional associations. However, the most emblematic element is the moralistic notion that professionals posses a principled commitment to serve society; accepting a responsibility that extends beyond their immediate clients. The professional supposedly pertains to Pythagorean standards, eschewing any connection between work and wealth, occupying a privileged position above the pettiness of the class systems and the division of labour that taints the masses (Jacob, 1999: 116). Professional justification, then, may be found in their supposedly possessing an ideology of public service (Freidson, 2001: 122–23).

Until the 1960s, Freidson (1994: 13) suggests, sociological writing on the professions seemed to take this high standing for granted:

> Most sociologists have been inclined to see professions as honoured servants of public need, conceiving of them as occupations especially distinguished from others by their orientation to serving the needs of the public through the schooled application of their unusually esoteric knowledge and complex skill.

Those academics emphasised the positive functions of the professions and legitimised the notion that professionals were disinterested servants of the community. From the 1960s onwards, there was something of a watershed as the sociology of the professions became increasingly critical. These studies associated the professions with political and economic elites (see Freidson, 1988; Johnson, 1972; Larson, 1977). In contrast to the previously sympathetic professional portrayal, there emerged a more judgemental one, identifying contradictions in the public service model of professionalism. Perhaps, the key issue to consider is professional autonomy. For example, Larson (1977: 5–14) locates the professions at the heart of the class struggle. Far from being independent and disinterested, the professions are said to collude with governments, ensuring state protection and guaranteed markets. As such, while the professions claim a form of universalism – to serve the needs of all – they were actually identified as the servants of the few. In this situation, public service ideals were a vacuous self-justification, conferring a false sheen of legitimacy on their privileged position.

In this vein, Sommerlad (1996: 295) identifies a 'classical paradigm' of legal professionalism – tied in with the public service model – while also locating a flaw between the ideal and a more tarnished reality. This reflected the difference between ideology and actuality. However, Sommerlad (1996) does not believe that seeing the public service model as simply an ideological construct invalidates it, raising two arguments for its continued use. First, it presents a benchmark with which to monitor historical change in the legal profession; though practice may never have completely conformed to the ideal, it can be measured in relation to it. Secondly, she invokes Weberian social action theory, suggesting that ideologies possess material reality for those who profess them – no matter what the contradictions may be. This approach allows us to use the classical paradigm, of a legal profession premised upon public service ideals, while still aware of its tenuousness – that this was never necessarily a reality. As such, we can draw on the insight of Thompson (1977: 264–65) that, from such rhetoric, radical critique can flourish.

Criminal defence has historically been a small part of the legal profession. Defendants were unable to give evidence on their own behalf until the early years of the twentieth century. The appearance of lawyers in criminal cases is a relatively modern feature of the English criminal justice system. The half-century preceding the Second World War had witnessed the piecemeal, but limited, introduction of legally aided representation in the criminal courts. This lay the foundations for the reformist zeal which greeted the instigation of the Rushcliffe Committee. Along with Beveridge's famous five pillars of the post-war Welfare State, criminal legal aid was greatly extended; although it was not deemed a priority. It took until the end of the 1940s for those recommendations to be enacted in the Legal Aid and Advice Act 1949. However slowly it took root, though, legal aid had become definitively established in the criminal justice system. While an important development for those accused of crimes, this advance had a concomitantly large impact on lawyers. Near universal coverage presented fundamental challenge to the classical paradigm of legal professionalism. For one, it positioned the state as employer, clearly increasing the extent to which the profession served the elite. However, it also put the ideals of public service to the test; they were put under the microscope by the reality of practice.

The introduction of the mass legal aid scheme has been held by Morrell (2006) to be largely responsible for the decline in status of this branch of the profession: their becoming 'secondary professionals'. Ceding responsibility to the government impugned the notion of professional control (Sommerlad, 1996: 297–98). The wider service this demanded also had the effect of countering the homogeneity that Sommerlad (1996: 297–98) claims to have previously characterised both lawyer – drawn from the upper ranks of society – and their – largely well-off – clientele. However, Paterson (1996: 158) disputes that the introduction of legal aid undermined the lawyers' professional project, as 'when legal aid was introduced some of the wilder critics predicted the end of the independent profession . . . in reality it had a negligible effect on the concept of professionalism'. In similar vein, Spencer (2002: 268) argues that these developments did not make new demands of professionalism, but simply drew upon their commitment to public service. It emphasised what was already there. For Sommerlad (1995: 165), Rushcliffe enabled the public service ideal to be enacted, moving lawyers beyond ideology:

> The expanded notion of citizenship implicit in legal aid . . . to an extent made a reality of the related notions of vocation and universal service which were crucial aspects of the traditional professional ideology but which were of course originally belied by the impossibilities of the market.

So, while Rushcliffe diminished the classical paradigm by contesting professional autonomy, it presented fresh opportunity to realise the public service ideal. At this point, ideology and actuality were closer than they ever had been previously. With the rolling out of legal aid, lawyers had more grounds to their claims of providing a service benefiting both clients and wider society.

LEGAL AID

The history of the criminal legal aid scheme can be written as one of an ever-increasing budget. Though the rise of legally aided representation in the immediate post-war years was dramatic, the most significant change experienced by criminal defence lawyers can be said to have occurred in the early 1960s. Remuneration changed from fixed fees to hourly rates. Lawyers felt this system fairer, as they were rewarded for the actual services they claimed. As a result, representation rates increased significantly. This prompted the convening of the Widgery Committee, which commended the provision of legal aid in the higher courts but sought to restrict it to a minority in Magistrates' Courts. To regulate this, the merits test was duly established. This did not have the desired effect and the following two decades saw an even greater explosion of legally aid representation.

However, from the mid-1980s, the Lord Chancellor's Department took over the legal aid scheme from the Home Office. Its smaller budget meant that, from then on, the legal aid bill showed up far more prominently; it became a more salient political issue. Over the past quarter of a century, governments of all persuasions have been increasingly concerned to manage it. There have been various experiments with means testing, but these were to no avail in controlling costs. Conservative regimes bore witness to a 300 per cent increase in such spending over the decade from 1984 to 1994 (Lord Chancellor's Department, 1995: 115). Such a rise was deemed unacceptable and, in an attempt to understand why the bill increased, they hit upon the thesis of *supplier-induced demand* (see Bevan, 1996). It was suggested that under hourly rates of remuneration, lawyers were induced to spend longer on cases and so inflate their fees. To counter this, fixed fees were reintroduced in 1995, so that remuneration was thereafter paid case-by-case at a standardised rate.

However, this move did little to check the advancing criminal legal aid budget. Instead, the following 10 years saw it double to £1.2 billion (Cape and Moorhead, 2005: 2). By this time, such spending had become a predicament for the New Labour administration. It was one they enthusiastically set about resolving. Lord Chancellors, Justice Secretaries and Legal Aid ministers alike displayed great zeal in publicly lambasting legal aid lawyers, castigating them as 'fat cats' on the 'gravy train' (see Rose, 2009). The former two offices were held by Jack Straw (cited Gibb, 2009), who keenly discussed what he saw as the astonishing growth of legal aid funding by comparing lawyers' remuneration to the increasingly reviled bankers, stating that:

> There is certainly nothing ordained by the Almighty which says that of those paid for by the public purse, lawyers should be any higher than in other professions ... Lawyers and law firms who are dependent on state funding – and I emphasise dependent, as there are many whose existence relies exclusively on the public purse – would be wise to reconsider expectations of earnings.

Thereafter, Lord Bach (cited Hirsch, 2009), then Legal Aid minister, implied that the majority of the £23 million he sought to cut from the budget would come from lawyer remuneration, and he anticipated their defensiveness:

> Of course they're going to defend what they've got . . . that's what anybody would do when it comes to earning their living . . . But sometimes it's easy to forget what the whole point of legal aid is, which is to protect vulnerable people. I do think that sometimes the debate about legal aid gets clouded over with just concerns about pay.

The New Labour Government went beyond sound bites, though, and implemented policies that actively targeted lawyer remuneration as an important element in reducing the criminal legal aid budget. A notable example of this was the cost-cutting White Paper, *Modernising Justice* (Lord Chancellor's Department, 1998) which paved the way for the Access to Justice Act 1999 and the introduction thereunder of the new Criminal Defence Service. The Act also launched the Public Defender Service – salaried defence – pilot scheme as a supposedly more economical means to meet legal aid needs. Most prominent, though, was Lord Carter's review of procurement (Department for Constitutional Affairs, 2006a) which proposed a market-based system in which the headline recommendation was for Best Value Tendering in distributing legal aid contracts – a reverse auction, lowest bidder wins.

There was much protest and grandstanding, from profession and government alike (see Hynes and Robins, 2009: 112–14). Lawyers were hostile, claiming the proposals were 'ill-considered', 'unresearched' and 'likely to be a disaster' and would 'destroy the criminal justice system', while Lord Carter labelled them 'Luddites; whining and whinging' (cited Hynes and Robins, 2009: 122). In the end, the Law Society won a judicial review against tendering with regard to family law. The High Court deemed the process 'unfair' and 'irrational', suggesting that fewer lawyers would simply create 'advice deserts' – diametrically opposed to the high quality service the scheme professed to enshrine (cited Baksi, 2010d).

Shortly before this decision was confirmed, and a matter of months prior to the planned commencement of my research, the original Best Value Tendering proposals in crime were abandoned (Baksi, 2009b). However, not long after that announcement was welcomed by the profession, the Ministry of Justice (2010a) outlined the government's vision for further reform, along not dissimilar lines, in their report, *Restructuring the Delivery of Criminal Defence Services*. This proposed consolidating the market for criminal legal aid so that larger volumes of work were given to a smaller number of providers. It was suggested that up to 75 per cent of criminal legal aid firms would be purged in little over a year, as Lord Bach estimated that no more than 500 firms would receive contracts (Baksi, 2010b). This situation remains in the balance with the subsequent Coalition Government indicating their willingness to explore the option of introducing competition in the medium to long term (Ministry of Justice, 2010b: 101–15).

The bulk of this research, however, was conducted before the 2010 proposals, when Best Value Tendering was considered imminent. Even at this time, the Law

Society (2009a; 2009b) had labelled remuneration as 'thread-bare' and 'crumbling'. National Audit Office (2009: 15–17) research supported such sentiments. On average, it was suggested that some 60 per cent of criminal legal aid firms' turnover was derived from their criminal legal aid work. This was despite 79 per cent of these firms deeming it less profitable then private work and 14 per cent of firms making only 1–5 per cent profit; 16 per cent not making any profit at all. It was predicted that 28 per cent of firms were unlikely to be practising five years hence. However, a more striking estimate was provided by Keogh (2009), who forecast a 'massacre', with 85 per cent of firms leaving criminal legal aid work.

Those firms that remained would be left facing what Green and Mendell (2010: 2) labelled a metaphorical 'north–south divide'; while the criminal legal aid budget heads south, demands for representation continues to move north. In the House of Commons, the Solicitor-General detailed an increase in acts of legal assistance from 2.5mn in 2008 to 2.9mn in 2009.[2] However, the Legal Services Commission had specified that the legal aid budget was frozen at 2006 levels of £2.1 billion (House of Commons Committee of Public Accounts, 2010: 17). Tracking increased demand would have put the budget at some £2.7 billion meaning a decline, in real terms, of some £600 million. Lawyers are well aware that they work under governments frustrated by their cost and which, one way or another, seek to reduce the amount spent on remuneration. It is vital, then, to consider the consequences of such attempts to limit the funding of criminal casework.

THE IMPACT OF LEGAL AID REDUCTIONS

In chastened financial circumstances, the professional ideal of service must be problematised. This is a problem for lawyers as it is the whole legal system, as described by Mansfield (2012), who suggests that:

> If market forces are to be the determinative factor in the quest for truth then, just like most economies, we will be heading for irretrievable meltdown. Justice is not a business enterprise, still less a commodity. It is 'truth in action'.

As a result, there is a need to question whether lawyers allow any pressures they feel from remuneration to impact on their relationship with the clients. To these ends, a hypothetical *alter-ego* lawyer has been constructed by Johnson (1980–81), based entirely on meeting the public service ideal, working only in the interests of their client. His lawyer is premised upon the rule that they would use every resource they could until the maximum net benefit was reached for the client. This device can be used to predict how a lawyer might change their efforts and, thus, reshape the lawyer–client relationship contingent on external financial circumstances. Under hourly rates, this lawyer would invest greater resources than their clients demanded

[2] *Hansard* HC vol 501 col 669 (26 November 2009).

as the lawyer gets paid more for putting in greater effort. However, fixed fees would see the lawyer devote less time because they did receive any extra financial inducement; they would do the bare minimum deemed necessary. There seems to be a point at which benevolent good intentions meet less righteous hard reality. The implication is that lawyers should be considered motivated by self-interest as well as, or even instead of, the public service ideal. Considering this, lawyer motivations can be understood in economic terms using contract theory – the lawyer's various work tasks are to be conceptualised as inputs into a system (see Fenn et al, 2007). By this line, the move to fixed fees means that lawyers will reduce their supply of inputs when the fee (the output with which the lawyer is primarily concerned) no longer rewards it. Attendance, preparation and advocacy time will all fall if lawyers do not feel themselves to be adequately rewarded. Perhaps, the basics of client care will also disappear into the ether.

As a result of this (dis)incentivisation, clients receive 'a different product' (Fenn et al, 2007: 17). This is likely to be an inferior one. The service will deteriorate further as the value of the fee paid declines. In a study comparing the decisions made by public defenders and private practice solicitors, Tata (2007) invokes the concept of ethical indeterminacy. For situations in which lawyers are faced with two courses of action – both carrying advantages and disadvantages – they might compromise their professional ideals and the good of clients or society. As such, Goriely et al (2001: 68–69) explain a fundamental problem resulting from making some approaches more attractive than others:

> In making difficult and evenly balanced judgements, greater weight is placed on advantages that flow from one course of action that is in one's own interests. Less weight is placed on those that flow from actions that run contrary to one's interests.

In this way, lawyers are able to justify (to themselves and others) taking the course of action that is in their own commercial interests. It becomes the most sensible decision to act in a rational, economically prudent manner – anything else would surely be frivolous and unsustainable. As lawyers face harsher economic circumstances, the concept of ethical indeterminacy can be used to show that corners are being cut, meaning clients could lose out (Tata and Stephen, 2006: 740–41). This theme has been highlighted in a fraud trial reported while this research was ongoing.[3] In a judgment, which he hoped would be widely distributed throughout the criminal legal profession, Judge Gledhill QC was highly critical of the quality of service provided by one lawyer towards her client. He was scathing that the firm had chosen to appoint a solicitor with Higher Rights to appear in the Crown Court, from within, to conduct the trial, rather than a barrister from a chambers. He recognised that, in so doing, the firm would receive both preparation and litigator's fee. However, he deemed her knowledge of the law, procedure and advocacy skills to fall below the acceptable level. This was considered a purely financial decision.

[3] *R v Qiu Yeu, Khi-San Voong, Qiang Xue and Dau Yee Cheng* [2009] Unreported Southwark Crown Court.

While Gledhill professed sympathy for the reasoning, he expressed his concern at the implications:

> I am well aware that recent reductions in the rates of legal aid have hit solicitors particularly hard. On a practical financial level, it must be sorely tempting to keep the trial within the company. I understand that. However, if the consequence is that an accused person is not adequately represented, it is simply not acceptable – not acceptable to the defendant, and not acceptable to the public as it is not in the interests of a fair trial and therefore not in the interests of justice.

The firm involved refuted Gledhill's claims as the prejudice of a judge with distaste for solicitors with Higher Rights (Baksi, 2009a). However, the pertinent point to take from this dispute is that it highlights Cape's (cited in House of Commons Constitutional Affairs Committee, 2007: 22) fears that the reformulation of legal aid remuneration might result in 'irreversible' changes. The legal profession, as it once was, might be reshaped under the pressures of market forces.

Such concerns are pertinent in light of the concern expressed by Lodziak (2000) who has castigated the rise of a neo-liberal ideology of consumerism in government – viewing it as subjecting welfare to the vagaries of the profit motive. Drawing on Gorz (1999) and his notion of the commodification of state provision, public services are rendered essentially meaningless when reduced to the status of products to be bought and sold. By this line, the obligations of state to citizen are those that require it to care for the common good, but the veracity of this care is challenged as they are exposed to the full force of capitalism and the drive to reduce prices by delivering standardised products that can be quickly, cheaply and routinely dispensed to a mass of consumers. State services become embroiled in the climate of consumption. For Lodziak (2000: 131), the 'standardisation of caring means that the latter is not tailored to the specific needs of particular individuals . . . When the "care" misses needs are left unsatisfied'. He suggests that we consider the impact of cost-cutting measure of the provision of health care, whereby the need to meet targets and drive for efficiency means that patients are offered standardised care – standard diagnoses within a standard consultation time all designed for a standard, model, patient. For a more personalised, tailored service, patients are driven to self-provision or more expensive private health care. In a similar way, I believe that this principle can be applied to legally aid criminal defence – another arm of the welfare state subject to the pressures of reduced funding and harsh economic circumstances.

Accordingly, this is an important time to study the lawyer–client relationship. There appears to be the very real prospect that business decisions might come to trump social welfare concerns; standardised, rational choices based on the value contained in a case for a lawyer supersedes how they can best meet the subjective desires of their clients. If, unlike an area like commercial law, this branch of the legal profession was premised upon a public service remit, such an understanding may look increasingly quaint and old fashioned as we glimpse a corporate mindset at play even in legal aid work. At the moment, we cannot be sure whether – like so much of the noblest idealism throughout human history – it gave way to the pervasive creep of greed; this is speculation based on some empirical research and a consideration of surrounding events. If there ever was a public service lawyer, they may have vanished already and we are too late to do anything about it or, alternatively, they might be stronger than ever, contrarily resisting the pressures against them and waiting for support. What we can be certain of is that the profession is evidently in flux, as lawyers will have to cope with the changes that come their way. This book will go on to explore whether and to what extent lawyers alter or modify their practices and, thereon, how this impacts on their clients. Will the pressures felt by such lawyers put a *strain* on the lawyer–client relationship?

By everyday usage, strain can involve stretching an object so tightly that it becomes taut or tense. These excessive demands cause the object to be subjected to great stress as it is exerted to the utmost. Being pressed to such extremes ensures it distorts from, and acts in violation of, its true intention or meaning. Think of an elastic band, which is supposed to have some give but, if pulled too aggressively, it can no longer cope with the pressure and breaks. The snapped elastic band can no longer be used properly as, devoid of its previous strength, it does not serve its original purpose. This study seeks to ascertain whether any such strain existed here in the lawyer–client relationship and, if it did, its nature and extent. It addresses whether clients still get the benefit they should and, presumably, used to, from lawyers. However, it moves beyond that, and attempts to describe how this strain manifested itself; the effect this had on the service offered and the manner in which lawyers dealt with the resulting state of affairs. Finally, it allows us to consider whether the strain had gone so far as to bend the lawyer–client relationship so out of shape that it was beyond repair, or if it could be patched up and reused in any meaningful manner.

However, before considering these results, I must first outline the way in which this research was conducted: the methods and methodology that underpin it. These are addressed in the following chapter.

2

Investigating the Reality of Legally Aided Criminal Defence

In this book, the lawyer–client relationship is explored by means of ethnographic research. This scholarly approach represents more than a single tactic and, rather, what Denzin (2009: 185) has described as 'a curious blending of techniques'. It is perhaps McCall and Simmons (1969: 1) who best sum up the wide scope of the method, which involves:

> Some amount of genuinely social interaction in the field with the subjects of the study, some direct observation of relevant events, some formal and a great deal of informal interviewing, some systematic counting, some collection of documents and artifacts; and open-endedness in the direction the study takes.

The sheer range of tools on offer suggests that this schema presents the ability to access information others might not. Accordingly, Flood (2005: 33) promotes its particular use in socio-legal studies as, while 'research methods have been devised to cope with the problems of social research – social surveys, observation, interviewing, social experiments . . . only one gives us insight into the richness of social life'. Ethnography allows for genuine engagement with local legal communities and their situated knowledge, an important development considering Hillyard (2002: 647) and his rejoinder that 'lawyers are Johnny-come-latelys to social inquiry . . . most are neophytes in research'. Accordingly, to date, work in the field of socio-legal studies has tended to function with a tacit emphasis on the legal portion of its moniker. In order to understand the reality of law in action, there is a need to bolster the social component of socio-legal studies. The law would only benefit from gaining the input of more sociologists – though they do not have to be assumed to be right. The nature of good sociology is that scholars raise matters for discussion – they could be wrong in their interpretation, but the important thing is that evidence is provided for a thorough and robust debate. The social research training of the scholar allows them to collect and deliver such data to ignite and inform the deliberation. That is what I am attempting to do in this book, using my experience as a sociologist to conduct ethnography and gain genuine insight. Though it can be an unwieldy and complicated research method, I was confident in using its constituent parts to contribute to improving the value of socio-legal studies by elucidating the activity of this branch of the legal profession.

Within ethnography, participant observation is the most prominent and, perhaps, key component. Participant observation involves an outsider entering the natural environment of a specific group such as criminal legal aid lawyers, accompanying individuals within as they go about their business – without ever attempting to become actively involved in casework. In this case, the researcher effectively shadows the lawyer. By spending an extended time period in the company of the community in this way, the researcher gradually gains acceptance and will be provided ever-greater levels of access. This is an ongoing and constantly evolving process. Once fully embedded, the academic is able to witness the reality of what the actors do first hand – a benefit Becker and Greer (1957: 28) duly commend as:

> The most complete form of the sociological datum, after all, is the form in which the participant observer gathers it: an observation of some social event, the events which precede and follow it, and explanations of its meaning by participants and spectators, before, during, and after its occurrence. Such a datum gives us more information about the event under study than data gathered by any other sociological method. Participant observation can thus provide us with a yardstick against which to measure the completeness of data gathered in other ways, a model which can serve to let us know what orders of information escape us when we use other methods.

Despite being a sociologist, then, I got to glimpse the world that the lawyer sees, providing me with an experience as close as possible to that of an insider without actually gaining a legal qualification myself. The privileged viewpoint duly provided by participant observation requires that it should take precedence over other research methods that, in comparison, only provide limited and partial results. Among those alternatives, the most frequently used is, perhaps, the formal interview. In the shadow of participant observation, Becker and Greer (1957: 29–32) criticise the interview on four grounds. First, the question of learning the native language, which isolated interviews are unlikely to allow. Secondly, there may be matters that interviewees are unable or unwilling to talk about so certain issues cannot be gleaned by the interviewer. Thirdly, the suggestion that people see through distorting lenses, which cannot be explored in an interview setting that precludes the checking of description against fact. Finally, matters of inference, process and context. This last difference does not highlight an error of interviewing as much as it emphasises the benefits of ethnography.

These are, though, problems of the stand-alone interview. Of course, interviews would be extremely limited in and of themselves and research seeking to explore the lawyer–client relationship solely through this method would be open to criticism. On the other hand, conducting interviews alongside and, in particular, *after* participant observation, as in this study, offers the opportunity to neutralise these concerns. In this situation, the researcher is more attuned to the participants in the study, knowing what questions to ask and how to frame them to get meaningful responses. Such interviews enabled the understandings I developed through participant observation to be tested against the claims of lawyers who had experienced the same events, highlighting possible alternative comprehensions. The interviews provided a means to appreciate the ways in which lawyers responded to their activity and explore issues that rarely came up in the participant observation. Most significantly, the timing of the interviews reduced the likelihood of interviewees seeking to pull the wool over my eyes, as they were fully aware that I had seen the reality of their practice.

When combined, participant observation and formal interviews allow for a finely grained investigation into a social space such as that occupied by lawyers and their clients within the criminal justice system. It is such an approach that holds the most potential to actually understand the reality of the situation. Recognising this value, it seems apt to consider past research that has taken such an approach.

STANDING ACCUSED AND THE REALITY OF LAW

Despite the merits of applying ethnography to the lawyer–client relationship, there has been a relative dearth of such research in the criminal justice system. This absence has been lamented by Abel (1988: 1), bemoaning the sparse banality of a literature in which 'we know little more about what lawyers do than how they allocate their time among different subject matters'. To redress this problematic situation, he issued a plea for ethnography to probe the daily activities of lawyers. Like buses, having waited an age for one such study, two came at once, as a pair of contemporaneous ethnographies emerged. These important, groundbreaking works were *Standing Accused* by McConville et al (1994) and *The Reality of Law* by Travers (1997b). Both studies tasked themselves with filling the gap in existing knowledge by capturing the practical content of what criminal legal aid lawyers actually did. As a result of their deploying the ethnographic method, these studies moved beyond the existing literature. Much previous research had relied on courtroom observation (Carlen, 1976; McBarnet, 1981), interviews (Thomas and Mungham, 1983; Heumann, 1978), document collection (Fennell, 1980; Flood, 1994) or conversation analysis (Maynard, 1990; Bogoch and Danet, 1984) – all using techniques with built-in limitations. In contrast, the research of both McConville et al (1994) and Travers (1997b) gained deeper access, and was able to collect data that would prove far more illuminating than other single methods would allow. To date, these remain key studies in this field meaning that any new research, such as my own, must acknowledge their status. The sad situation for this area of socio-legal studies is that, until now, no one has properly followed on from where they left off. These studies are nearly two decades old, and much has changed in legal aid and criminal procedure in the intervening period.

The situation is sadder still when it is noted that, for all the value of these studies, they also pose serious problems with regard to understanding the lawyer–client relationship. They produced two very different findings, presenting oppositional images of the lawyer–client-relationship. On the one hand, McConville et al (1994) have published a scathing judgement on the state of legally aided criminal defence. Law firms are generally neither committed to clients nor organised in a manner conducive to serving them. Lawyers are shown to hold low opinions of their clients and believe them undeserving of good treatment. The picture emerges of a deficient profession offering inadequate representation. In contrast, Travers (1997b) presents a quite dissimilar situation, in which highly knowledgeable and competent lawyers dedicate themselves to their clients. This is a glowing account, suggesting deeply satisfied clients receiving a high standard of care. It concludes that researchers need to give lawyers more credit and respect. Relying on these studies alone, it would be hard to know what to think – as the foremost accounts of the lawyer–client relationship, their divergence provides as much confusion as it does illumination.

It so happened that McConville et al's (1994) work was highly influential and become something of the received view of this branch of the legal profession in socio-legal circles. Meanwhile, Travers' (1997b) did not find a particularly wide audience. However, following publication, Travers (1997a) chose to attack McConville et al's (1994) findings and a heated debate (in academic terms, at least) played out in a prominent legal journal. He takes issue with the methodological approach of their research. While research methods refer to the practical business of actually doing research (collecting data), the research methodology pertains to the epistemological framework surrounding the research (analysing data). Methodological difference is credited with causing the bulk of the variance between the accounts and is also used as a means by which Travers (1997a: 370–71) attempts to assert the authority of his own. By this line, Travers (1997a: 370) claims that McConville et al (1994) marginalise the voices of those they researched and, rather, imported their own prejudices into the events they report, suggesting that, 'what this study has produced is an idealised, negative version of criminal lawyers . . . The reality of legal practice may be rather more complex'.

For Travers (1997a: 370), McConville et al (1994) have produced research that simply reflects their own understanding and values, meaning that it has not successfully conveyed the lawyers' point of view:

> This results from the methodological basis of these studies which seek to make a general case by presenting decontextualized examples of practices they disagree with, rather than attempting to explicate or address how . . . defence lawyers understand the particular people and situations they encounter in the course of their day-to-day activities.

However, the authors of McConville et al (1994), reconstituted as Bridges et al (1997: 379), counter Travers' (1997a) criticism, and dismiss his own methodological stance, for the manner in which it carries:

> The risk of an extreme relativism and individualization of findings, in which the researcher is left with no source of evaluation or criticism other than that derived from the 'actor's point of view' and value systems. Such research can easily end up accepting at face values practitioners' own rationalizations for their (mal)practices.

These authors explain that they do not believe that the type of research Travers (1997a) advocates is able to produce worthwhile socio-legal scholarship (Bridges et al, 1997: 380–81). Indeed, for Bridges et al (1997: 379), research should influence policy and enact social change that, they insist, can only be achieved by taking a more critical slant by means of a 'strategy that seeks to challenge the particular research subject's "taken-for-granted moral assumptions" '.

Both sides display strongly held ideological positions. This means that those designing research that follows in their footsteps need to be aware of the methodological differences. As such, I offer this research following a full consideration of their differences, which I believe can be best understood to represent the variance between the structuralism of McConville et al (1994) and the interpretivism of Travers (1997b).

STRUCTURALISM AND INTERPRETIVISM

Both structuralism and interpretivism are labels, and represent numerous divergent schools of thought, from Marxism and functionalism on the one hand, to post-structuralism and interactionism on the other. Any attempt to impose order on such variance will inevitably involve some level of caricature. However, there are threads which unite approaches on either side and, as such, several schema have become commonplace (see Archer, 1982). These have conceptualised the divide in various fashions, most prominently as the distinction between 'structure' and 'action' or the discrepancy of 'macro' and 'micro' sociology (Mouzelis, 1995: 22–23). There follows two particular amalgamations of structuralism and interpretivism offered in order to aid understanding of the differences between McConville et al (1994) and Travers (1997b) and the theoretical ground occupied by the present research.

In this dispute, the structuralist outlook is premised upon the development of largely politically motivated, theoretical frameworks that allow the attainment of privileged understanding (Glucksmann, 1974: 1–14). This approach can be best understood to represent a particular epistemological position called the 'correspondence theory of truth' (Travers, 1997a: 366). Under this, the reality being observed exists independently of the observer and, as such, a researcher is able to capture and disseminate it accordingly. This is the dominant, mainstream approach in socio-legal studies. It can be found in work influenced – in however roundabout a way – by two of the three most commonly cited 'founding fathers' of sociology, Marx and/or Durkheim; scholarship that seeks to uncover the rules governing society (Turner, 1977: 1–2). The academic is able to use their skills to uncover some manner of objective truth.

Structuralist approaches address society as a whole, over and above the individuals within it. As such, the constitutive elements of a system are little considered in isolation from each other or from the totality of that system. The overall objective is to reveal hidden laws or structures that operate beneath the surface and which explain the functioning of the totality. In this understanding, perhaps it can be best associated with Marxian theory. The fundamental aspect of this is the quest to uncover 'false consciousness'; a concept developed by Lukacs (1971: 46–55) and the Frankfurt School (Marcuse, 1964: 8–13). This requires analysis in order to discover the 'real motives' that underpin the functioning of social institutions and the actors within them, but which supposedly remain unknown to the 'layperson' (Torrance, 1995: 3–11). This tasks socio-legal studies with the objective of usurping practical and assumed everyday knowledge, and so imparting enlightenment from the privileged location the academic occupies.

In contrast, the interpretivist stance is 'post-foundational', an approach which abandons the notion that there is a position from which to make objective findings (Crook, 1991: 192–219). By this outlook, structuralist attempts to do just that are dismissed for providing an 'ironic' account of society, competing with the knowledge of actors themselves (Anderson and Sharrock, 1983: 565–69). The researcher cannot make definitive judgements on what they see in society, pertaining to an alternate epistemological position known as the 'congruence theory of truth' (Travers, 1997a: 366). This perspective is less common within socio-legal studies, so can be considered epistemologically radical. It is a position most often taken up by academics following the other founding father of sociology, Weber – and subsequently built on by figures such as Blumer, Garfinkel and Goffman (Turner, 1977: 4–7). By this perspective, society represents the shared understanding of a collection of individuals, and this renders it impossible to study the myriad meanings held therein with the precision of the hard sciences.

Interpretive approaches are premised upon the principle that social actors, themselves, need be treated with respect by seeking to uncover how they conceive their situation. Truth is, then, a product of the way the observer describes it and, under this more subjective comprehension, there will only ever be multiple realities. The task of the social scientist is simply to study how these are formed and reproduced in everyday situations. From this perspective, socio-legal studies should investigate social action through the meaning it holds for individuals, rendering its purpose as seeking to understand social reality in its 'concrete individuality' (Weber, 1949: 80–81). As such, social scientific understanding cannot take the form of generality and should, instead, set its goals as comprehending but limited segments of the infinite reality (Weber, 1949: 50–112).

The difference between these two approaches has been said to 'stalk through the history of sociological theory' (Archer, 1982: 455). Indeed, Archer (1982: 455) believes that 'theoretical developments, have tilted either towards structure or towards action, a slippage which has gathered momentum over time'. Accordingly, it is possible to identify socio-legal research that pertains to one side or the other. For example, McBarnet (1981: 1) criticises interactionists for their focus on what lawyers do and, instead, centres her analysis in *Conviction* on understanding how the state ruled through law. This is premised upon the Marxian notion that law benefits dominant groups and a desire to uncover the manner in which ideology works to keep the masses subservient. She seeks to impose her theoretical perspective on those she researched, thus to translate what she saw. Numerous other socio-legal researches can be identified with similar bents (see McConville et al, 1991;

Baldwin and McConville, 1977). An oppositional example can be found in Cicourel (1995) and his work *The Social Organization of Juvenile Justice.* Here he seeks to understand how juvenile offenders are categorised as problems, rather than taking them to be problems a priori. He presents verbatim accounts and reports of courts and police, with the background expectations that influenced them sketched in. In this manner, he attempts to draw the knowledge from those he researched and simply convey it. Again, other socio-legal literature can be found adopting comparable approaches, though they are not as widespread as those of the former variety (see Sudnow, 1965; Lynch, 1982). There is, then, a range of studies that can be recognised to have represented one side or the other in this structuralist–interpretivist divide.

It would have been straightforward to conduct my research under the influence of one of these positions; this was an area in which there are obvious structural influences – government, legal aid and inbuilt power relations – but it is also a community largely closed off to outsiders and imbued with specialist insider knowledge, making sense only to the lawyers themselves. A concentration on either aspect could have been justified and produced a satisfactory piece of work. However, I did not consider such an exclusionary approach conducive to making the most of the opportunity presented and sought to progress beyond the dualism.

INTEGRATED METHODOLOGY

While both structuralism and interpretivism have their strengths, in isolation there is the danger that each might lead to the neglect of significant areas of knowledge. In the structuralist approach, the actors' agency and self-understanding are downplayed because the author wants to give equal, if not greater, attention to the bigger picture. Under interpretivism, the opposite is true; those broader issues can be ignored in attempts to address the particular individuals involved. This variation in focus means that different studies may identify disparate aspects of the field they address. To proceed similarly would have meant acting as though the debate between the authors of the previous studies had never occurred, and to therefore purposively restrict the level of understanding that could be obtained in my own research. This highlighted the need to consider both methodological positions.

Structuration theory represents the attempt by Giddens (1986) to synthesise the two sides of the methodological partition, presenting a process in which social structure is actively made and remade. By this, groups only have social structure to the extent that individuals act in regular and fairly predictable ways, while action is only possible because each individual has a certain amount of socially structured knowledge. The duality of structuration theory means that all social action presumes the existence of social structure and vice versa. The contrasting foci of the structuralist and interpretivist lens do not exist independently of one another. In the sociological discipline he sought to promote, work would be conducted that was open to each sphere of knowledge as a fundamental organisational concern.

This research, then, was premised upon the notion that both McConville et al (1994) and Travers (1997b) offer alternative contributions to understanding the lawyer–client relationship. While the former allows generalisations to be made, the latter provides *thick description* of particular circumstances. Each piece presents what the other lacks. A richer account could have been given in McConville et al (1994) had they secured greater insights *from below*. There was a selectivity in what they showed which seemed to work against the lawyers in their study. As a result, there was little attempt to offer any defence on the part of the lawyers; they had no right to reply. This all adds up to McConville et al (1994) effectively talking over lawyers, thus reducing their voice and forcing the reader to take the authors' word for what this situation signified. The reader was expected to trust the authors to tell them what the lawyers were doing – and, in particular, what they were doing wrong. This situation is reversed in Travers (1997b) and his work is restricted by treating lawyers' perspectives unquestioningly. The reader was left to trust the lawyers as he, apparently, acted as something of an impartial intermediary. It is often unclear how far his own sympathies extend and the reader is left confused as to where his voice begins and the lawyers' end. Thereafter, the wider applicability of his results is ambiguous as the work only deals in the here and now that lawyers found themselves in. Most pertinently, he always put a positive shine on the few examples of legal practice that he choose to display – refusing to countenance alternative, negative readings, which were rejected on principle of belonging to another methodological position. This makes his account little different from that which he so despaired of in McConville et al (1994). While McConville et al (1994) at least proceed with their values open and acknowledged, Travers (1997b) fails to note his own epistemological, or professional, biases.

There are, then, areas where McConville et al (1994) and Travers (1997b) each offer a great deal but others in which their methodological standpoints hold them back. In order to provide a rounded picture of this social world, they really need to be read together. However, this is patently not a viable situation, and it has already been noted that one of their books has been far greater consumed than the other. Against this background, I set about designing my research with a view to resolving this problem. To do this, I sought to explore the lawyer–client relationship paying heed to both structuralist and interpretivist concerns. This work followed Hekman (1983: 193) and her plea for socio-legal research to 'bridge the gap' between structuralism and interpretivism. It is in this spirit that Lacey (1994: 34) declares:

> We need to avoid the twin extremes of being drowned in the quagmire of chaotic (if fascinating) detail and of being committed to a rigid theoretical model which blinds us to whole tracts of significant social practice. We can do no better than to embrace a self-consciously eclectic approach which entails moving back and forth between general conceptions and hypotheses, on the one hand, and the specificity of social practices, on the other.

This suggests the need to develop an integrated approach, akin to that which Henry (1983: 32–69) offers in *Private Justice.* When planning his research, he had possessed an avowedly structuralist bent, and he duly set about examining the external influence exerted by official regulations in the workplace. However, while engaged in fieldwork, he felt compelled to reassess his position. To his surprise, he had been confronted with particular, informal, means of order; these were specific to the local circumstances. He saw that his research could only continue if he recognised this; indeed, Henry's (1983) work can be seen as an attempt to persuade himself of the need for such transition (Nelken, 1986: 331). This resulted in his importing interpretivist theory to understand the meaning practices held for those he encountered. His work makes use of both methodological positions, arguing for 'a genuine pluralism' (Henry, 1983: 30).

Learning the lesson early, this research project was explicitly set up to recognise structuralism and interpretivism from the start. The sample was designed to allow for this. From the outset, I was aware that a year was deemed a substantive period of ethnography, one from which useful and authentic data could be drawn. This left the issue of how best to divide that time among firms. One approach was offered by McConville et al (1994: 13–16) who undertook research totalling some 198 weeks, conducted by several individuals and at an array of firms. The amount spent at individual firms ranged from a few weeks to several months. In contrast, Travers (1997a: 371) focused exclusively on a single firm, which he stayed with for a period of four months. It is likely that their varying methodological positions influenced their research methods, thus driving their research design. In these circumstances, McConville et al (1994) seem to have sought a large sample that allowed them to generalise, look at different types of firm and produce enough data to justify critique. On the other hand, Travers (1997b) considered it justifiable to study one firm and present a lengthy, nuanced, appreciative account of it. In setting themselves up in these ways, each project closed itself off from the type of insight sought by the other. There would likely have been less data collected for each firm in McConville et al (1994) which, alongside the space they had to report, rendered them unable to produce a thick description. Meanwhile, Travers (1997b) would not have considered it necessary to move beyond one firm, so did not allow for the opportunity to generalise.

I attempted to find some middle ground between the two, and sought several months at a small number of firms – spending the same the amount of time that Travers (1997b) spent at one firm at each one of three different firms. This allowed me to become immersed in each firm, see significant progression in cases and provided the chances of generalising to some level on the routine work undertaken and the results this produced. It also enabled comparisons and contrasts to be drawn through a process of data triangulation (Denzin, 2009). Accordingly, three months of participant observation was taken across three firms, followed by a month of formal interviews at each.

This approach enables the book to offer both the local and specific knowledge lawyers themselves would recognise and a more general critique that engages in wider debates. This offers a novel approach to the field that does not appear to have been considered in the studies to which this book makes reference. With research techniques established, it is time to move on to the way in which they are applied and, in particular, the firms that were studied.

THE FIRMS IN THIS RESEARCH

These firms were chosen through the snowball method of sampling. This is a respondent-driven means of selecting appropriate candidates; a search that gains momentum as the researcher ingratiates himself within the social network and, essentially, gets to know people. To these ends, the firms are all drawn from the same local legal jurisdiction: a large city in England.

As to the selection of the firms, these were premised upon a conceptual apparatus closely tied to meeting the objectives of this research, designed to draw out the best and worst of legal practice. I used a heuristic device whereby firms were classified as particular types, premised upon the extreme approaches to practice that they were supposed to present. As such the research is founded upon a hypothesised distinction between 'Radical' firms – a dying breed of lawyers who devote themselves to their clients – and 'Sausage Factory' firms – an emergent trend that put themselves, and their profitability, before their clients. I attached myself to firms that were adjudged as belonging to either side of this divide in the hope of capturing the full public service potential of the profession: the Radical; and its antithesis: the Sausage Factory. Accordingly, the three main firms in this research – and several others encountered along the way – come from one side or the other and are attributed illustrative names to aid those you reading the accounts to identify that to which they belong: *Radford Hope* and *Radcliffe and Musk* on the one hand; *Swining MacSage* on the other.[1] Although these firms were real, it should be recognised that their types constitute academic constructions and, as such, need to be properly defined.

The Radical firm follows similar scholarly constructions, designed to capture client-centred practice. The term *radical* itself is used by Travers (1997b). A similar conception is posited by Sarat and Schiengold (1998) under the notion of the *cause lawyer*, while Thomson (1992) labels it *critical*. This is closely allied to McConville et al (1994: 20) with their *political* model, 'a positive rejection of many of the principles underpinning the other kinds of firm . . . anything associated with the business ethic may be inimical to a client-centred practice'. Emergent across the authors' various definitions is a common series of features, encompassing a set of values as much as an approach to business. Premised upon private practice and being legally aided, these firms contain a high ratio of solicitors to clerks, establish links to reform groups and develop an association with the poor and disadvantaged. They eschew

[1] The names of firms, lawyers, clients and anyone else that I encountered in this research are all anonymised to protect their privacy.

the profit-orientated mindset of those just in it for the money and are, rather, more romantic and naïve in their organisation. These firms claim to care about their clients, as human beings in need of help and support.

These lawyers can be considered as creating a discourse of empowerment for their clients. As such, the Radical firm represents the practice of active defence: epitomised by the proactive approach outlined by Ede and Edwards (2008), on criminal litigation generally, and Cape (2006b) on police station work specifically. They profess an intention to provide quality service to those they represent, an ideology that overrides any notion of seeking to increase profits by maximising the volume of cases handled. This is a firm that will fight a client's case to the utmost, vigorously opposing police and prosecution. They allow due process values to be operationalised as they reveal and exploit the potential of the adversarial system. In short, they provide a combative defence that upholds the rights of the accused. However, the Radical firm might be increasingly superseded by the Sausage Factory firm.

The Sausage Factory firm can be seen as a somewhat oppositional entity to the Radical firm. It is roughly equivalent to McConville et al's (1994: 19) *managerial* firm, which rejects the 'altruistic professionalism' of the radical approach as somewhat amateurish and antithetical with regard to their, more pressing, business imperatives. So it is that, in the existing literature, these profit-centred firms are generally posited through contrast with client-centred firms of the Radical ilk. They are rarely categorised in and of themselves. However, parallels can be found in Sommerlad's (1999: 315) account of 'the factory model of practice' and Goriely's (1996: 49) 'sausage machines' – firms which churned out a mass of clients. While it is little used by academics, the notion of the legal aid factory has been coined by lawyers themselves (Lewis, 2003; Mason, 2006; O'Hagan, 2008), as visible from the research carried out by Sommerlad (2001: 345, 350, 357; 2003: 214). The key notion typifying this firm is a focus on efficiency. However, the term Sausage Factory should not be seen as necessarily representing any and every efficient firm. It is a mistake to assume that firms cannot combine being run well (in the interests of clients) with being run properly (efficiently). Moreover, this typology does not deny that a by-product of an efficiently run firm might be a satisfied client, who received better quality representation than at a more ramshackle Radical firm. Rather, it concerns a matter of the ideology underpinning the Sausage Factory – they are defined by the motive of increasing efficiency to ensure profitability, over and above a sense of duty to clients. This echoes Black (1988) and his fear that, 'developments in legal aid and criminal work have forced practitioners to consider cost effectiveness as a priority over services to the client'.

As a result, the Sausage Factory is associated with the notion of passive defence. Within the food industry, sausage factories are presumed to reduce their diverse raw materials into uniform, easy to manage, and essentially cheap, products, thus rendering them suitable for standard packing, storage and display in the marketplace. Within a Sausage Factory firm, defendants become similarly homogenised. The firms favour high turnover and swift throughput of clients, with little individual contact, much discontinuous representation and a large proportion of the work undertaken by unqualified clerks. The contention is that clients are reduced to offal, the bits that nobody really wants – at least not in non-standard, awkward shapes and sizes. They assume the status of a product. In this manner, the Sausage Factory reflects a wider trend in the criminal justice system, pressuring defendants to admit offences and pass through as quickly as possible. The focus on brevity has been nicely encapsulated in Rhode's (2004: 12) phrase, 'meet 'em, great 'em and plead 'em'. As such, McConville and Baldwin (1981: 211–22) note the 'pressures placed upon defendants and lawyers', which, far from being accidental, represent the widespread encroachment of a 'denial or emasculation of rights'. In these circumstances, Cape (2004a: 415–16) identifies a 'growing antipathy toward adversarial principles and the adversarial role of lawyers'.

The rights of the accused are minimised; they become a background consideration in a criminal process that places more emphasis on the rights of the accuser. The role of the Sausage Factory lawyer becomes that of transmitting crime control messages to the client – centrally, the advantages of pleading guilty – in order that victims are spared the ordeal of a contested trial and the efficient repression of crime can be secured. They operate within a criminal process said to involve the 'mass production of guilty pleas' (Sanders et al, 2010: 438–98).

These two types of firm are not offered to map reality precisely; rather, they provide a useful conceptual lens through which to view access to justice in the functioning of the lawyer–client relationship. This heuristic device allows the contrast between a public service ideal that works for the client and a business-minded approach that sees lawyers work largely for the money they can earn. In this way, the research has a similar impetus to Banton (1964: vii) and his ethnography of British policing in the 1960s seeking to champion research into institutions 'working well'. The difference, though, is that this study was undertaken aware that the Radical firm might be in decline, wanting to learn the lessons while there might be still be a chance to do so.

In applying these theoretical criteria to the real world of criminal defence, there was an obvious first port of call: *Radford Hope*, whom I had already reasoned a Radical firm following a month-long pilot study conducted one year prior to this fieldwork. This was a firm that characterised itself as Radical, as evident from their mission statement and claims to practice active defence. The senior partner, James, was heavily involved in political agitation for the rights of those suspected and accused of crime and he intended that the firm be led by such righteous principles. A key aspect of this could be found in their engaging in various pro bono and campaigning groups and it was from my membership of one such organisation, working on miscarriages of justice, that I became acquainted with them. In particular, Gordon, a solicitor on that project, convinced me of their suitability and set up my placement in the firm.

Once embedded in this Radical firm, the remaining firms were selected by making use of the new contacts I accrued. I combined my own tentative perceptions, from regularly attending the courts, with overheard gossip and, crucially, advice from the lawyers themselves. From those in *Radford Hope*, I was presented with two names for Radical firms, *Raddled and Left* and *Radcliffe and Musk*. The former proved elusive so it was the latter on which I focused. Their senior partner, Leo, was every bit as passionate about access to justice as James at *Radford Hope*. Also seeking to manage the firm in his own image, he assured me that they saw themselves as Radical, seeking to give their all for clients over and above any thought of profits. In addition, I was aware of their reputation for engaging in pro bono work within their local area and helping to organise various community schemes. In this regard, they were a prominent presence. These features made them seem a suitable choice as my second Radical firm.

With regard to the Sausage Factory, it was quite difficult to categorise this type of firm from the outside; essential qualities such as efficiency, profitability and standardisation of clients cannot be judged without exposure to internal mechanisms. In addition, it did not seem wise to ask *Swining MacSage* lawyers whether they identified with a term carrying such pejorative overtones from the outset. As such, any selection need be based largely on reputation. Luckily this resulted in a simple choice, as solicitors at *Radford Hope* and *Radcliffe and Musk* alike repeatedly labelled the firm *Swining MacSage* as a Sausage Factory. They were derided for the mechanical way they churned out clients. Time and again, I was told that they would provide a great point of contrast, such that:

> There are such differences in terms of attitude; they just get through so many clients. I wouldn't want to work in that way, personally. Yes, I think *Swining MacSage* will be very different [laughs].
>
> (Leo, senior partner, *Radcliffe and Musk*, IC)[2]

Though some were wary about criticising them, restricting themselves to knowing smiles and laughter (very much, *nudge-nudge, wink-wink*), a *Radcliffe and Musk* solicitor, Shelly, referred to their having a 'dodgy' reputation. Another signalled their view that *Swining MacSage* had much that they would wish to hide:

> Good luck [laughs]! I don't reckon Tommy [police station clerk, *Swining MacSage*] will want you following him around – there are things he definitely won't want you seeing. What they get up to with their clients. It can never be proved though because they're in four walls aren't they?
>
> (Maddie, clerk, *Radcliffe and Musk*, IC)

On the whole then, the overall process of selection can be justified as a suitably organic one; it was borne from perceptions within the social environment itself.

While the choice of firms was straightforward, gaining access was a slightly more daunting prospect, often described as being fraught with difficulties (Bryman, 2001: 296). The process is summarised by Van Maanen and Kolb (1983: 11) who caution that, 'gaining access to most organisations is not a matter to be taken lightly

[2] Quotes are coded in order to communicate the method of data collection. The glossary of this code is: **IC** – Informal Conversation with Daniel Newman; **OR** – Overheard Remark; **INT** – Formal Interview, and; **EM** – Email Correspondence.

but one that involves some combination of strategic planning, hard work and dumb luck'. This research proceeded with a combination of all three qualities. It was a matter of strategic planning that I would make use of my sole contact, *Radford Hope*, as a starting point for this research. Although almost all the lawyers I had previously spent time with had since left the firm, I was still able to contact Gordon, who had himself moved on. I asked his advice on how to approach them. Gordon recommended the solicitor, Norma, whom he believed cared deeply about access to justice, and thereon suggested how I might best pitch my proposition to pique her interest. I did as he said and duly found myself accepted back at *Radford Hope*. This was initially for a trial period, but gradually stretched to cover the full three months, with little question.

At *Radford Hope*, both hard work and luck played their parts. While the senior partner at *Raddled and Left* did not follow up the initial interest he showed, Denise, a solicitor from *Radcliffe and Musk*, accepted me on the basis of a phone call and an email. She was impressed by having seen me regularly at the courts with Windom, a *Radford Hope* solicitor, with whom she was friendly. Initially this placement was for six weeks, Denise suggesting that she could get me in to *Raddled and Left* for the other six weeks. In practice, this transfer did not materialise. Instead, at court one day the senior partner, Leo, followed my hinting by suggesting I serve the full three months at *Radcliffe and Musk*. *Swining MacSage* seemed to be just as simple, at first. The senior partner, Ed, agreed to provide access five months in advance on the basis of a phone call, a letter outlining my position and a personal reference from Windom, who had previously been at the firm. However, when I tried to reinvigorate contact shortly before attending, I found Ed difficult to pin down. On hearing of my problems, both Leo and Denise took it upon themselves to harangue Ed at court, taking him aside from a hearing he was engaged in to tell him he should accept me. He did and – after sending an email of my intentions, to be distributed among the staff – I was promptly granted the full three months.

The second phase of the research proved an even smoother process of gaining access, with all three firms readily agreeing to my returning for formal interviews later in the year. In addition, I augmented the results of the main firms by conducting a handful of interviews with lawyers from other local firms. These were lawyers with close ties to my main sample and who had been recommended or volunteered themselves after I had spent significant periods of time with them over the course of the research.

The period covered by the research is presented in table 1 opposite.

From the previous timeline, it should be clear that the fieldwork was a lengthy, ongoing process, meaning that careful consideration needs to be given to the role adopted by the researcher. In the research literature on the ethnographic method, it has been suggested that taking on the position of the 'acceptable incompetent' may prove most conducive to gaining acceptance (Lofland and Lofland, 1995: 56–57). This status ensures that the researcher gives off an impression of naïvety and humility (Fielding, 2001: 149). Following this line, they can take on the mantle of new recruit. A logical extension from becoming this new recruit seems to be that

it minimises the perception of being the outsider, and all related conceptions such as interloper or intruder. Rather, it suggests that while new, this individual is *one of us*, at least in the making, and as such it can lead to a greater deal of acceptance. This will be especially the case the longer that individual spends time in a setting so that they might even progress from being the new recruit to a junior member of that society. This is the position I took up on conducting this research, and it was in this manner that I was quickly accepted.

Table 1

Year	Dates	Firm	Activity
2007	May–June	*Radford Hope*	Pilot Study
2008	January–April	*Radford Hope*	Participant Observation
2008	May–August	*Radcliffe and Musk*	Participant Observation
2008	September–December	*Swining MacSage*	Participant Observation
2009	May–June	*Radcliffe and Musk*	Formal Interviews
2009	June–July	*Swining MacSage*	Formal Interviews
2009	July–August	*Radford Hope*	Formal Interviews

At each firm, I speedily fell into routine and was allowed the freedom to drift in and out of the offices and accompany almost any lawyer on a particular day. It is unlikely that an overt observer could conduct research without exerting any impact on those they studied and it is worth noting that I was very occasionally steered away from certain situations; however, it was extremely rare that I was denied access in this manner. I was soon treated as a confidant at each firm, accepted into the inner circle and told all manner of confidences. I became regarded as part of each firm, being taken to lunch, going to drinks and attending staff parties. I would even suggest that friendships developed, with contact remaining to this day (though, portentously I fear that things may be a little different by the time they finish reading the book).

As such, my research position swiftly and organically developed into that of an 'insider', a situation Strauss et al (1964: 27) would champion for the manner in which the fieldworker had become 'part of the natural flow of events, without necessarily determining the course'. Considering this status it can be understood that I was provided with access to the full range of lawyers' daily routines, at the offices, police stations, Magistrates' Court and Crown Court. This encompassed all manner of activities, from consultations with clients to negotiations with prosecutors, police station interviews to court hearings. Perhaps most significantly, I was present before, during and after all the official areas of their engagement in the criminal justice system, exposed to the reality of the situations away from the formal process.

The extent of this access can be appreciated from table 2 below, offering 'guestimate' averages derived from my fieldwork diaries.

Table 2

	Radford Hope	*Radcliffe and Musk*	*Swining MacSage*	**Total**
Number of lawyers formally interviewed	10	9	10	29
Number of lawyers accompanied for at least one day	9	9	11	29
Number of hours' observation conducted in police station	20	25	25	70
Number of hours' observation conducted in Magistrates' Court	204	219	111	534
Number of hours' observation conducted in Crown Court	35	40	40	115
Number of hours' observation conducted in office	69	73	71	213
Number of hours' observation conducted elsewhere (cafes, travelling, etc.)	20	45	40	105

Overall then, I spent a little over 1000 hours attending with 29 lawyers from the three firms in this study.

Within those firms, the range of my experiences can be captured in tables 3, 4 and 5 below which document my participant observation of the lawyers across the three main sites in which they operated.

Table 3

	Radford Hope	*Radcliffe and Musk*	*Swining MacSage*	**Total**
Number of client consultations	7	7	7	21
Number of informal conversations with clients	4	9	7	20
Number of conversations with officers	7	10	8	25
Number of formal interviews	7	6	6	19

Considering the numbers of this research, it can thus be appreciated that the majority of my time was spent with lawyers in and around the Magistrates' Court. The business they conducted in this realm provided the daily routine for most lawyers; it was the bread and butter of their practice. The lawyers' professional lives tended to revolve around the Magistrates' Court – it provided a central hub, not only for representing clients, but for meeting clients, working on files and engaging with fellow lawyers, prosecutors and other court staff. I judged it sensible that this site should also form my main base of activities.

Table 4

	Radford Hope	*Radcliffe and Musk*	*Swining MacSage*	**Total**
Number of client consultations	200	220	195	615
Number of informal conversations with clients	140	186	162	488
Number of conversations with other lawyers	260	432	386	1,078
Number of conversations with prosecutors	248	262	175	685
Number of conversations with other court staff	343	373	360	1,076
Number of court room hearings	204	216	212	632

Table 5

	Radford Hope	*Radcliffe and Musk*	*Swining MacSage*	**Total**
Number of client consultations	6	8	12	26
Number of informal conversations with clients	10	14	8	32
Number of conversations with other lawyers	14	20	7	43
Number of conversations with prosecutors	6	8	8	24
Number of conversations with other court staff	10	12	8	30
Number of court room hearings	8	10	11	29

By obtaining this direct experience of the social world, the research captured some of the meaning that the actors placed on their activities. It was able to reach behind the scenes, and onto the informal level. This point can be best comprehended with regard to the 'dramaturgical' metaphor, which Goffman (1990: 83–140) developed for categorising the performance of social actors: 'front-stage', 'back-stage' and 'off-stage'. This research has been able to cover that range of settings. The differences they present, in both formality and audience, enable a more truthful appreciation of the performance of criminal defence lawyers. As such, the research was able to go considerably beyond the official stance. This will be seen in the coming chapters, as the richness of the data reveals itself.

THE ORGANISATION OF THIS BOOK

In collecting the data, three dominant themes emerged and the results of this study are subsequently organised to reflect these, presenting substantive chapters on the attitudes lawyers held towards their clients, the manner in which lawyers behaved with their clients and the outcomes lawyers obtained for their clients.

Each of these chapters is thereon divided into three sections. In the first two sections, representative data from the research is presented in order to convey the lawyer–client relationship as I encountered it. The interviews are offered first and, then, the participant observation. Owing to the nature of collecting these different types of information, the former is more readily quantifiable than the latter. This means that while statistics can be offered to contextualise the interview quotes, the dialogues drawn from the participant observation are merely offered as the dominant, mainstream view – expressing characteristics regularly displayed by lawyers in each firm. These accounts are offered relatively free of critical engagement though they are selectively arranged to facilitate understanding of the actors and their experiences. These two sections set out the majority positions. As such, the approach can be characterised as thematic analysis: a method for identifying, analysing and reporting patterns across a data set that, thereon, minimally organises this information in rich detail. Accordingly, the first two sections of each chapter meet the valuable guidelines for conducting good thematic analysis set out by Braun and Clarke (2006: 96) to ensure that any themes identified match the original data. In the opening sections, lawyers tell their own stories through the formal interviews, while these are followed up by my reporting of what I saw in the participant observation. It is only in the third section of each chapter that I critique, and thus move beyond, this data. In these sections, the data is evaluated in the round with extensive reference to existing academic literature and previous research.

This organisational structure was developed to aid an analysis that pays heed to both the structuralist and interpretive traditions. It provides spaces in which the lawyers' voices can be heard – separate from that of the researcher. You, as the reader, have the opportunity to make your own judgements based on what you see before I influence it unduly with my own standpoint. I believe that, by taking this approach, the book can be used to reach defensible conclusions upon the data it presents – open yet authoritative.

Originally, I intended to allow the lawyers even greater freedom to speak for themselves. That perspective was inspired by recognition of Travers' (1997a) interpretivist concerns that studies such as that of McConville et al (1994) silence lawyers, thus acting to misrepresent their position. I was worried that lawyers had suffered a raw deal previously and were being unfairly castigated by structuralist research. I set about this research, then, aware of the (social) scientific method, keen to disprove (Popper, 2000: 66–67). By being faithful to the data, as Travers (1997a) required, I believed that it would work to contradict the prevailing understanding offered by McConville et al (1994). To these ends, I planned lengthy passages of dialogue and extensive chunks of quotation – free from comment or interpretation. However, as writing up the data played out, it soon became clear that there was little need for this and a more constrained presentation had the same effect. It did not matter how much room I gave the lawyers, this became merely rope on which they would hang themselves.

Lawyers did talk encouragingly about the lawyer–client relationship in their interviews and disseminating this provides a contrast to the negative structuralist accounts. However, the participant observation data showed the lawyers in a very poor light, in accordance with the structuralist critique. The following chapters, then, are characterised by a striking divergence between the formal interviews and the participant observation. The data in the former tallies with the healthy relationship depicted by Travers (1997b), and the lawyers emerge as holding a strong public service orientation – relatively Radical. My participant observation data, though, is reminiscent of that presented by McConville et al (1994) which led to them adopting a condemnatory tone when discussing the strained lawyer–client relationship they saw. They came out as Sausage Factories. This negative portrayal emerged despite my research being conducted two decades later, following the various steps taken to improve the quality of legally aided criminal defence in the intervening period, measures such as introducing the duty solicitor accreditation scheme.

Overall, I feel the need to give more weight to what was seen than what was said – after all, seeing is believing. As such, even though I explicitly designed a research project informed by both interpretivist and structuralist methodologies alike, trying so hard to give the lawyers the benefit of the doubt, I ultimately produced a piece of work that made the structuralist account seem more plausible. It is for this reason that the data is organised in the manner in which it is: lawyers' accounts; my accounts; and critique. In each substantive chapter, I fully consider the lawyers' perspectives before moving on to dismantle them, more or less comprehensively. If, in the following chapters, then, it should seem that I am being overly critical, it is important to remember that this was expressly not my aim. It was the data that led me to this situation and not me who led the data. The critical findings of this research cannot be dismissed or downplayed as simply reflecting my own biases. This research purposively targeted firms that it was supposed would show lawyers in a good light, and this inevitably affected my pre-suppositions. Initially, if anything, I was inclined to put a positive spin on all I saw and heard as that was what I had wanted to believe. Over time, though, the flood of negative data made it necessary to take a far more sceptical approach.

The necessity of this critical stance should become clear as I begin presenting my findings in the following chapter, starting with the attitudes of lawyers.

3

Attitudes

This chapter focuses on the attitudes that lawyers held towards their clients in this study. Attitudes are fundamental to the topic of access to criminal justice; they underpin the entire lawyer–client relationship. At root, the relationship is a social interaction, an interpersonal encounter premised upon a fundamental 'exchange of knowledge' (Suseno et al, 2006: 278–80). Understanding the manner in which lawyers relate to their clients offers a means of comprehending the lawyer's practice as a whole, assessing the foundations so as to pass judgement on the stability of the overall structure. The issue of attitudes, then, represents a sensible point from which to begin engaging with the ethnographic data obtained through this research.

This ethnographic data, though, has not produced a simple, unified picture of the issue of attitudes in the lawyer–client relationship. Instead, two apparently contradictory narratives arose. In the formal interviews, lawyers presented *positive* attitudes when talking about their clients. This pointed towards a healthy relationship. However, the participant observation showed lawyers displaying *negative* attitudes when discussing clients. This was, rather, indicative of a strained relationship.

In this chapter, both accounts are offered individually and only thereafter brought together. In the first two sections, I do not engage with either the comments of lawyers or arguments from the wider academic literature to any great degree. Rather, material is presented to allow an appreciation of typical statements made by lawyers, first, in interview, and then at work. It is in the third section that these are drawn together into a critical debate reflecting on why there was such divergence and considering what impact this may have had on the lawyer–client relationship. I conclude that the issue of attitudes reveals a strained lawyer–client relationship. To begin, I consider the formal interviews.

* * *

SECTION 1 – WHAT LAWYERS SAID ABOUT ATTITUDES

The formal interviews I conducted allowed the lawyers to have their say on topics salient to the issue of attitudes. The resultant data depicts positive attitudes and a healthy lawyer–client relationship.

In this first section, my results are presented free from critique, so as to give maximum voice to the lawyers. However, I have chosen to organise the quotes in order to highlight the dominant themes that emerged, dividing the responses under three headings:

1. *Social Agenda* – the lawyers' reasons for being engaged in this area.
2. *Professionals* – the role the lawyers saw themselves fulfilling.
3. *Healthy Relationship* – the manner in which the lawyers conceptualised the relationship with their clients.

Social Agenda

I judged that a natural place to commence these interviews was by establishing why the lawyers entered legally aided criminal defence in the first place. It seemed likely that this factor would underlie both how the lawyers understood their own role and their relationship with clients; these topics might be interlinked.

There was no discernable pattern differentiating Radical and Sausage Factory firms. Instead, the mass of lawyers fell broadly into two categories, as identified by one particular interviewee:

> I think some people do criminal defence because they're fairly altruistic and they think it's a worthwhile thing to do to help and support the most vulnerable people in society: people who find themselves in custody for whatever reason. I think there are also criminal defence solicitors who've almost felt that they've fallen into it. I mean I thought I was coming to do matrimonial law. So people come into crime for lots of different reasons. So I think it's something that people do tend to either do deliberately because they feel that is something important or come into by accident like I did.
>
> (Evelyn, police station clerk, *Swining MacSage*, INT)

It was a minority of the lawyers from across the firms, 14 out of the 35 interviewed, who could be described as having 'fallen into it'. These lawyers had possessed no tangible plan or ambition. An example of these was provided by Dale, a senior partner at *Swining MacSage*:

> When I was in school, I wasn't quite sure what I wanted to do. I was fifteen years of age and, to be perfectly frank, a friend of mine whose father was a solicitor – he wrote quite a famous legal text book – he said I should go to university and study. And, not to put too fine a point on it, I used to do a lot of [a particular sport] at the time and I thought that possibly going to [a particular university] would be fun, because I could [do that sport] out there. I didn't have any particular dilemma, people said: 'Well, a law degree is something you could use for lots of different disciplines'. And, I do remember seeing about that time a film – you're probably too young – *Twelve Angry Men*. And I thought it was quite good. And I liked the analysis and the twists and turns of it. You know, it gave me a bit of an idea. So, it was a combination of factors really. And one of them, of course, at university doing law, as an Honours, you only had to do eight hours lectures a week. So, all the right reasons! And, if I'm honest it was all that was in my mind. And then, once I got my degree, I went to do the Part Twos, very intensive, six months. I did that, and then,

> you know, you've gone that far and you just get on board, as it were, you know, the train's running.
>
> (Dale, senior partner, *Swining MacSage*, INT)

The majority of lawyers, from all three firms, represented the other category; they claimed to have thought the profession worthwhile, entering for more altruistic reasons. A little over two-thirds – 24 from 35 – of the lawyers professed these motivations. They spoke of a calling for law and, in particular, the ability to help those less fortunate than themselves offered by legally aided criminal work:

> When I was a teenager, it was the thrill and excitement of supporting the underdog. It's always attractive to support the underdog rather than backing the person who's got the upper hand. And so it suited my philosophy and politics I had at the time.
>
> (Windom, solicitor, *Swining MacSage*, INT)

> I wanted to go into legally aided work – I had idealistic views on helping people: the less advantaged, etc. So I was looking at crime, justice, human rights aspects. I had spent a year working for a charity before that. It was all about helping people for me.
>
> (Catherine, solicitor, *Radford Hope*, INT)

While three of the four clerks stated that they fell into this line of work, among the solicitors and barristers there was no apparent distinction between rank or the type of firm in which they practised. The bulk of these lawyers expressed values that could be best described as representing a 'social agenda'. These lawyers' central claims were that they cared about their clients and felt a vocational calling to help those in need. These standards were tied into the conception they held of their role and so considered intrinsic to their being professionals.

Professionals

According with many lawyers' social agenda motivations, the majority, from all firms, espoused a belief in the value of the principle of access to justice, with 32 out of the 35 echoing views to the effect that:

> I'm very passionate about justice. I wouldn't even consider doing anything else. I mean, I know logically, if I did another type of law, I might earn twice what I'm being paid. But that wouldn't interest me. It's access to justice I believe in.
>
> (Maddy, barrister, *Radford Hope*, INT)

Lawyers seemed particularly keen to tie this principle in with their own roles as professionals. As such, 33 out of the 35 talked of the importance of their position, many identifying the manner in which they both enabled and upheld access to justice, as in the following quotes:

> My role is for access to justice. There are times where you really feel that your being there makes a difference to somebody. I think the role of the defence solicitor is very important

> in protecting defendants against the state because there are an awful lot of people who are against them.
>
> (Ronette, solicitor, *Radcliffe and Musk*, INT)

> Access to justice is very important. Without that, you wouldn't have a fair society. There's got to be punishment for people who do wrong so you've got to make sure that the people who do wrong are brought to justice. But then, you know, other people, you've also got to treat their case justly, so that you ensure that, if they haven't done wrong, they're acquitted. I always try and remember that, for a client, it's their life.
>
> (Josie, barrister, *Swining MacSage*, INT)

It was the more experienced lawyers, though, who most expansively highlighted the responsibility they saw themselves holding:

> I go back to a quote that, 'a properly funded legal aid service is the very hallmark of a civilised society'. And it is. If people are thrust into the criminal justice system and have the weight of the state pushed against them – for example, if someone is facing a serious legal charge, then they have 50 police office working amassing evidence and they have a vast array of forensic scientists putting evidence together. Then it must feel like the whole world and the state is against you and the only person you've got on your side is your solicitor. That's a pretty daunting prospect.
>
> (James, senior partner, *Radford Hope*, INT)

> It's that sense of standing up for the individual. Because they can't do it for themselves; they don't have the expertise and they don't have the knowledge. And that's all we're doing. We're providing expertise and knowledge for a citizen who can't do it themselves and would be disadvantaged if they were not represented . . . that's one of the essential safeguards and therefore it's essential that there is always maintained a robust, independent profession that deals with criminal defence.
>
> (Bobby, senior partner, *Sosig and Sage*, INT)

The self-importance contained in their professional position was disseminated regardless of whether the lawyer had presented such principles as an initial driving force behind their entry. All stressed it to the extent of presenting a united front. For lawyers, their apparent determination to do their best to uphold their clients' rights signified a healthy lawyer–client relationship.

Healthy Relationship

The interviews indicated a strong consensus that legal professionals should have a healthy relationship with their client, and that this meant firms had to be client-centred. This contradicted the supposed Radical/Sausage Factory distinction, as lawyers from both sides of the spectrum espoused views such as the following:

> A client-centred firm is what anybody should be. You're not doing it properly if you're not client-centred because that's the whole idea of the job.
>
> (Shelly, solicitor, *Radcliffe and Musk*, INT)

> I think our relationship [with clients] has always been very good; the strength of this practice is that we do a lot for the client, sometimes more than we should do, offering them mints and ringing them. I think it's an approach that filters down from the partners. It's the way I've always worked and I would always teach people to do it that way as well. You don't get any extra funding, you do it because you want to.
>
> (Nadine, partner, *Swining MacSage*, INT)

However, the lawyers' sentiments went beyond this professional duty and towards some degree of amity. Lawyers appeared to collapse the hierarchies that might be expected between such professionals and their criminal clientele, as in these examples:

> You meet, or at least I have met, over the years I've been practising, a lot of very interesting people. From both sides of the fence, both criminals and other lawyers. They are characters that I would not have met had I been in any other profession.
>
> (Harold, partner, *Radford Hope*, INT)

> What do I enjoy most about the job? I enjoy, at the moment, the contact with people . . . I like the unpredictability of the job: the fact that I'm dealing with people on a day-to-day basis and that these people are from all walks of life.
>
> (Leo, senior partner, *Radcliffe and Musk*, INT)

The lawyers experienced their clients as rounded individuals and, resultantly, several eulogised the long-term relationships that had developed. This was particularly prominent among the police station clerks, who described the greater bonds that could arise:

> I think there is a difference in the relationship you build up between the police station and Magistrates' Court, which is literally a time thing. At the Magistrates' Court, you simply don't have that time because of the demands upon you whereas at the police station you don't have the time constraints. With what I do now, you get to know the clients, there's a certain amount of time that you have to have around the police stations and make chit-chat. With 75 per cent of my clients, I know what they're about; I know how they grew up and how many kids they've got, I have that relationship with them.
>
> (Maddie, police station clerk, *Radcliffe and Musk*, INT)

Though solicitors had more disparate and transient contact with clients, lawyers of all rank described the satisfaction derived from leaving a client happy. Accordingly, 29 out of the 35, from Radical and Sausage Factory alike, identified this to be important, as in the following:

> It can be a very satisfying job – to see the gratitude of a client when you've done well for them. Some of these clients, you get to know them, long-term thing, and it feels good to do right by them. You're happy that they're happy.
>
> (Thomas, partner, *Swining MacSage*, INT)

> It is satisfying to have a positive effect on the client, to leave them pleased with a good result. I mean, compared to my previous job [Magistrates' Court legal adviser], this is more satisfying. It feels like you're helping people. You feel like you are actually making a

> difference in terms of applying law; you can actually apply it and try to get the best for the client in the situation.
>
> (Leland, solicitor, *Radford Hope*, INT)

Lawyers from all firms, then, presented an image of a healthy lawyer–client relationship. This appeared to be a relationship constructed upon the positive attitudes that lawyers held towards their clients; clients were important, deserving and even became their friends. However, the following section documents data from the participant observation that puts a quite different slant on the issue of attitudes in the lawyer–client relationship.

* * *

SECTION 2 – WHAT I SAW ON ATTITUDES

In this section, I augment the interview data presented above with extracts from the participant observation. The opinions lawyers expressed while going about their work suggest negative attitudes and a strained lawyer–client relationship.

As with the formal interviews, data from the participant observation is offered with minimal assessment so as to allow for a greater appreciation of the state of affairs encountered. However, to aid comprehension, this data is disseminated under three titles, namely:

1. *Intelligence* – clients were believed to be stupid.
2. *Moral Culpability* – clients were also considered to be of questionable character.
3. *Factual Guilt* – finally, clients were assumed to have committed a crime.

Intelligence

The lawyers, regardless of firm, seemed to share the opinion that the fundamental character trait of their clients was that they were mentally lacking. Indeed, lawyers seemed at pains to emphasise this supposed stupidity as frequently as possible, as shown below:

> I wouldn't waste my time listening to that client. She doesn't know what she's saying. I know how to talk to her – you have to tell her things. You see, she's not worth listening to. Total brain dead. You know the sort?
>
> (Jerry, Crown Court clerk, *Swining MacSage*, IC)

> This one is a complete and utter idiot. I hate having to deal with him; he must be one of the stupidest criminals in the city. You'll see what I mean, he really is thick.
>
> (Maddie, police station clerk, *Radcliffe and Musk*, IC)

Lawyers, though, were not simply offering an analytic judgement of their clients; they were using this device to make fun of the clients. The clients' intelligence had great value as comedic material, presenting something of a currency between lawyers as they sought to outdo one another with their tales, as follows:

> I'm going down to see Mr Pattinson [client]. Oh! He's such an idiot [laughs]!
>
> (Laura, solicitor, *Swining MacSage,* OR – to a colleague)

> It's an offence to real criminals to call this a fraud [laughs]. It's a joke. How stupid must this man be? Oh Gosh! I can't believe it, says he's 30. It's just so childish, only a child would think he could get away with that. I mean, he seemed intelligent, he was articulate. But he's a fool! We have to tell Catherine [solicitor] about this one! She'll love it.
>
> (Leland, solicitor, *Radford Hope,* IC)

> [Lawyer One] Bit thick is he?
>
> [Lawyer Two] Like you wouldn't believe [laughs].
>
> [Lawyer One] Well, I had one the other day . . .
>
> (Dale and Ed, senior partners, *Swining MacSage,* OR)

Lack of intelligence did not stand in isolation as an identifying trait; rather, it seemed to underpin an assessment of the moral culpability of clients.

Moral Culpability

The lawyers acted as if clients were a different breed and duly set about categorising them. To some extent, this was apparent from the numerous sneering asides regarding clients being of a lower social class than the lawyers, as in these examples:

> [Lawyer One] Having TV screens will be good for placating them.
>
> [Lawyer Two] Of course it will. After all, that's what this sort spend their days doing.
>
> (Derek, solicitor, *Sosig and Fest* and Bob, solicitor, *Radford Hope,* OR – discussing the imminent installation of television screens in the court waiting area)

> He came in here looking all smart. It's just a pity his trainers didn't match his suit [laughs]!
>
> (Leland, solicitor, *Radford Hope,* IC)

> I did not expect someone with such a posh name to look like that. Typical inbred.
>
> (Shelly, solicitor, *Radcliffe and Musk,* IC)

However, there appeared to be a more significant division drawn than simply that separating middle and working-class. The division was encapsulated by Bob from *Radford Hope.* On first meeting this solicitor, at the beginning of my research, he went out of his way to define the 'type' of client they dealt with as an 'underclass'. All lawyers, albeit often less explicitly, articulated a distinction between *us and them* at some point, as in the following:

> This is just what they're like. They won't accept reality. They think they can live their lives like that [committing crime]. It's a total lack of responsibility. They don't deserve help.
>
> (Bob, solicitor, *Radford Hope*, IC)

> These are regular clients. They come from one of our crime families. Crime's a way of life for that kind.
>
> (Ed, senior partner, *Swining MacSage*, IC)

> She'll be back. As soon as she needs something, she'll just steal it. It's a way of life. She's bound to activate that suspended sentence. They're all the same.
>
> (Leland, solicitor, *Radford Hope*, IC)

The lawyers clearly thought very little of their clients' characters. This was a perspective carried through into the most significant trait of all: lawyers' working assumptions that clients were factually guilty.

Factual Guilt

Lawyers from all firms routinely discussed and approached clients as if they were guilty, whether or not they had talked to them or read their file. Sometimes this was based on what the prosecutor told them, others on past experience of that client; it could even be premised on the area in which they lived. Regardless of the reasons, I witnessed each lawyer treat a client as if they were guilty before they had heard their story, as reflected in these examples whereby lawyers had received instructions to proceed to trial:

> Believe her? Look at the colour of this file. Never believe a client from there. Did I just say that? Whoops!
>
> (Teresa, solicitor, *Radcliffe and Musk*, IC – at this firm, files were colour-coded for different areas of the city. This one came from a notoriously run-down, working-class, estate)

> If there's one person you shouldn't lie to it's your solicitor. But they all do. They all lie! Just lie after lie, like I don't know they did it.
>
> (Leland, solicitor, *Radford Hope*, IC)

Further, though, oftentimes clients would tell the lawyers they were not guilty but the lawyer refused to believe them. The following statements, made by lawyers following meetings with clients, facing charges of theft, fraud and indecent assault respectively, highlight something of the pervading cynicism:

> No, I didn't believe her. Not at all. Why, did I do a good impression of making it seem like I believed her?!
>
> (Eileen, solicitor, *Radcliffe and Musk*, IC)

> He doesn't know lies from truths any more. People like that get to a point where they start believing their own lies and no longer know the truth.
>
> (Bob, solicitor, *Radford Hope*, IC)

> He isn't pleasant at all is he? Clearly guilty, he's a sexual predator. I wish I didn't have to take him to trial tomorrow. Maybe I'll get him to crack in the morning.
>
> (Thomas, solicitor, *Swining MacSage*, IC)

The lawyers appeared to take on the role of arbiters of truth, and in so doing, were unsympathetic to the stories of their clients.

All three strands were reflected in the following exchange between a barrister, Andy, and the *Radcliffe and Musk* solicitor, Shelly, immediately following a conference with a client. This young man denied a very serious assault charge for stabbing another in a fight and scheduled to go to trial the following month. While the lawyers were polite and accepted his story during the meeting, after the client left they began mocking him:

> [Lawyer One] Well, do you agree or do you think I was being terribly pessimistic and he should have a trial?
>
> [Lawyer Two] [laughs] Well if you win a trial like that then you're winning it on the basis of something you've said and not something he's said.
>
> [Lawyer One] He's as thick as pig shit. I mean he's a nice lad but, you know.
>
> [Lawyer Two] I don't know how you said 'an intelligent man like you' without pissing yourself. Really, because he's such an idiot [laughs]!
>
> [Lawyer One] Well [laughs]. Put a suit on him and he's almost presentable.
>
> [Lawyer Two] Yeah, but have you seen that tattoo? That's boxing gloves. I was sitting there working it out. He smacked somebody else that's how he broke his wrist but he said that he just banged it. Such a liar. Oh well, he said nothing was going to come of it so, well, I mean if something comes up then it serves him right.
>
> [Lawyer One] Yeah.
>
> [Lawyer Two] No, I think he's in big, big, big trouble.
>
> [Lawyer One] Yeah.
>
> (Andy, barrister, and Shelly, solicitor, *Radcliffe and Musk*, OR)

Exchanges such as this typified the manner in which lawyers talked of their clients throughout the participant observation.

Spending time with these lawyers revealed what appeared to be a strained lawyer–client relationship across the firms. The lawyers routinely displayed negative attitudes towards their clients; they thought little of them and were openly derogatory. This participant observation data has supplemented that of the formal interviews to cast a different light on the issue of attitudes in the lawyer–client relationship. The disparity between the two forms of data is explored in the following section.

* * *

SECTION 3 – ATTITUDES

At this point, it should be clear that this research uncovered two apparently contradictory accounts of the lawyers' attitudes towards their clients. Across Radical and Sausage Factory firms, lawyers claimed in interview that relations with clients were positive, despite the fact that the participant observation suggested that they were negative. This discussion is tasked with attempting to reconcile these positions and, in so doing, is offered as an evaluation on that which has gone before. As such, it seems crucial to pose the question; how can lawyers claim to hold positive attitudes yet actually display negative attitudes?

One approach – which might seem obvious to many – is that a party has lied. In a case of such divergent findings, this would offer an immediate means of understanding the schism. First and foremost, it could be suggested that I was lying. The lawyers' accounts in the formal interviews represented the truth of the situation; they had positive attitudes. What I disseminated from the participant observation was at best, distorted, or at worst, fraudulent. By this line, there was a healthy lawyer–client relationship; it was all sweetness and light. I have twisted things for my own ends, perhaps bent on some lawyer-bashing crusade; the idealised – negative – depiction of lawyers which Travers (1997a: 370) criticises McConville et al (1994) for constructing.

These would not be charges I could conceivably defend. I might offer my notebooks – the dozens of volumes collecting the events that I witnessed. However, that would prove little more than that I had at some point handwritten the words that appeared in this chapter. Instead, I must leave it to the judgement of those of you reading the book. All I can contribute are sentiments, the foremost of which is the assurance that I have sought to abide by the rigorous ethical code of the university law school from which the research was undertaken, as well as working within my own moral framework to be as honest as possible. In so doing, I worked tirelessly at collecting the data for this research – from 8.00 am to 5.00 pm each day accompanying the lawyers, then late into the night (frequently on into the early hours of the next morning) transcribing the accrued notes. However, this was not a task I complained about; rather, it was something I wanted to do successfully. The level of commitment I devoted to this fieldwork must be seen as a sign of my desire to produce research that was genuine and as close to the reality as I was able to capture. Frankly, I don't see the point of putting in all that effort when I could have just stayed at home with a nice cup of tea and made it up in a fraction of the time. More so, it should be recalled that I entered into this endeavour with a conviction in the importance of access to justice, to encourage more support, materially and philosophically, for legally aided representation. I set out hoping to find examples of noble and exemplary lawyering; that was one of the reasons I purposively sought Radical firms. As such, I write this book with the same fear that informed the work of McConville et al (1994); that it might be used against legally aided criminal defence despite authorial intention to the contrary (Bridges et al, 1997: 378). Ultimately, though, any external evaluation is out of my hands.

The others who might be accused of lying were the lawyers themselves. The negative attitudes that I reported from the participant observation were accurate; however, the lawyers' response in the formal interviews was an attempt at deception, subterfuge. This would run the common sense line that friends and colleagues typically comment on hearing of my data: *what else would they say?* It would be inevitable that lawyers would seek to justify what they did and protect themselves from criticism – the lawyers knew they had not met the standards demanded of them. These expectations can be gauged from the *Solicitors' Code of Conduct* (Solicitors Regulation Authority, 2007) which duly posits their central responsibility to clients. Although this document provides the lawyers' official regulatory document, it need be recognised as but a vague and general outline of practice. In contrast, the more effusive Public Defender Service *Code of Conduct* (Lord Chancellor's Department, 2001) captures the specifics of practice far more evocatively, providing a better insight into the presumptions made of these lawyers as professionals. Indeed, Cape (2006a: 62) shows the manner in which testimonial that ostensibly applies to that particular organisation can be appropriately applied to the wider Criminal Defence Service they work within. Hereafter, it is this latter publication that this book uses in discussions around professional obligations. Accordingly, this code can be used to discern the manner in which protecting client interests is the 'primary duty' of lawyers, as they are tasked with providing 'fearless, vigorous and effective defence to secure the best outcome for the client' (Lord Chancellor's Department, 2001: 4). Considering that lawyers were charged with such duties, it is likely they would be alert to the need to deflect any claim that they neglected their commitments.

There may be some validity in this position, and the preceding sections can conceivably be read in this manner. Lawyers were off-guard for much of the extended period of participant observation. They accepted me and largely acted naturally. The lawyers had little control over how or when – or even whether – what they said or did was documented in my field notes. They did not know what I was recording about them, but the formal interviews offered a chance for them to paint themselves in a positive light. These were audio recorded meaning that lawyers were to be captured for posterity speaking on tape and, as a result, could be played back to anyone who cared to listen; all that they said here clearly counted. In this artificial setting, they bore witness to this evidence collection so were highly attuned to my role and, thereon, what they should say. In these circumstances, they fed me lines to portray themselves as they wanted and so took control of managing the image I saw. In particular, they would expressly avoid disseminating negative attitudes towards their clients, aware of the bad light this would cast on them professionally. Accordingly, it was eminently foreseeable that I should be told something different from what I saw; lawyers would not knowingly contribute to their own mortification.

There are problems with this explanation, though. Its wholesale adoption would make me feel uncomfortable at a personal level. This may be evidence that I have gone native, or simply that I am hopelessly naïve, but I trust these lawyers with whom I spent so long and developed genuine friendships. I am not convinced that they were consciously deceiving me. More significantly, perhaps, is that, on an academic level, the *lying lawyer* strikes me as a rather hasty, knee-jerk attempt at an explanation anyway. Sometimes the simplest answers are the right ones, but that truism should not prevent more measured exploration, in the hope of a more nuanced and, ultimately, persuasive understanding of the data.

As such, in this section, I explore a proposition which can be either read alongside or in place of the suggestion that lawyers were deliberately lying. This discussion, then, entertains the possibility that lawyers were able to profess positive attitudes while concomitantly displaying negative attitudes. They could do this without being, necessarily, cognisant of the contradiction. This notion rests upon the lawyers learning to distinguish between *the* client – in general terms – and *a* client – as particular example.

In so doing, I describe attitudes in psychological terms, positing that lawyers learnt to adopt specific attitudes towards their clients. This is followed by a discussion of how the lawyers might have come to develop these attitudes, focusing on their self-image and the manner in which this was challenged by their position within the legal profession. Ultimately, I use this to suggest that positive and negative attitudes could co-exist but that this jeopardises the health of the lawyer–client relationship.

Attitudes in Psychology

Thus far, this chapter has implicitly used an everyday understanding of the term attitude, assuming the common sense meaning that takes it as a simple measure of whether an individual liked or disliked something. However, attitude is a psychological construct. As such, it should be noted that most technical definitions also tally with this notion of deducing fondness. The psychologists, Bohner and Wanke (2002: 5) define an attitude as 'a summary evaluation of an object or thought'. Under this conception, attitude relies on two components: an object, and a response to that object. The former appears straightforward and can refer to any number of stimuli, from the inanimate to the individual, the abstract to the concrete. It is the latter facet that requires a little more unpacking. A three-component model is presented by Rosenberg and Hovland (1960) whereby the evaluative aspect of the attitude consists of cognitive, affective and behavioural parts – which essentially amounts to beliefs, emotions and responses.

With attitude so defined, the question arises as to how these attitudes are determined. Persuasion is essential to the process of attitude formation and development, according to Bohner and Wanke (2002: 69–186). They identify a number of means of persuasion, categorised by the amount of mental effort required on the part of the individual. However, prominent among these – and necessitating little effort – is the process of classical conditioning; an evaluative response to an object is brought about, and changed, through repeated connection between object and a positive or negative stimuli. An individual gradually learns to take a particular attitude as a result of certain associations. So it is that Berkowitz and Knurek (1969) managed to elicit consistently positive or negative responses to individuals named *Ed* and *Ben* among a research group to whom the names had been variously paired with positive or negative adjectives.

This understanding could be applied to the lawyers in this research. Through years of practice, the lawyers had learnt to hold particular attitudes towards their clients. These, though, were conflicted, as explored later in this discussion. For now, it is necessary to comprehend the course by which these attitudes became conflicted. This process is posited to have arisen from a challenge to the self-image of these lawyers.

Lawyers' Self-image as Professionals

Self-image is a term, originating in psychology and later developed by psychoanalysis, referring to the representations that individuals have of themselves (Meffre, 2005: 1571–72). It entails a process of self-evaluation, across several fields: physical, physiological, psychological and sociological. It is, understandably, the latter that I am concerned with in addressing the lawyers in this research. In particular, I am interested in the psychoanalytic proposal that self-image is created through identification with others, be they real or imaginary. In so doing, this is not offered as some rigid application of psychoanalytic examination. Rather, the book loosely utilises insights appropriated from Freud's (1989c) exploration of the ego, with which to elucidate the situation in which these lawyers developed their attitudes towards their clients.

In so doing, the study offers an attempt at an embryonic explanatory framework revolving around self-image that is intended to open a dialogue and initiate debate. This usage is not to suggest that alternative theoretical positions lack validity as, for example, Hoyle's (1998) research on the use of language by police wherein disparaging statements are made as something of a stress reliever, without any necessary underlying feeling. As such, she sees no reason to search for pervasive or long-term influences. However, Shiner's (2010) more recent study on police activity uses self-image as a means by which move beyond Hoyle's (1998) work. Delving deeper into the psychological processes underlying what the police say allows their exploits to be conceptualised as organisational defence mechanisms, deeds privy to change as they are exposed to particular stimuli. This highlights the value of Freudian theory; it allows the prospect of a more multifaceted, profound analysis with which to augment existing knowledge. As with the police, such understandings have previously gone unheeded in work on the legal profession – and this is a problem long overdue a remedy.

When considering self-image, Freud represents the most notable authority (Carveth, 1996: 25–29). Indeed, it was Freud's work that really legitimised the seeking of the impact that subconscious processes exert on personality (Brym and Lie: 2007: 96–99). Freudian theory long ago permeated day-to-day life and popular culture, from common conversational recourse to concepts such as the Freudian slip, to attempts at looking for the meaning behind apparently irrational acts. However, Bocock (1981: 346–47) highlights the extent to which Freud's work has been much maligned in the British social sciences – in stark contrast to the engagement of scholars in France, Germany and the United States. Freud's work is highly theoretical, and makes claims to scientific validation, so presenting itself as a particularly dense *grand narrative*. As the twentieth century progressed, all-encompassing, positivistic, theories became increasingly unpopular, and Freud did not make the inroads that Marx's equally comprehensive oeuvre had previously. This has been attributed to a fundamental failure of sociologists to approach Freud as a social theorist, rather ghettoising him to the realm of 'the therapist' (Bocock, 1981: 357–58).

Freud focused largely on the unconscious; however, it would be a mistake to consider his work as shut off from the social (Craib, 1989: 2–7). Indeed, Freud (1989d: 794) saw sociology as a type of applied psychology – a means to watch his theories play out. In this manner, Golding (1982: 556–57) depicts Freudian theory as occupying a crossroads between society and individual, exploring the ways in which the social entered the individual and the effect that what happened within subsequently had on the social. So it is that Parsons (1964: 78–79) posits social theory lacking if it does not give due attention to such psychic mechanisms. The absence is understandable on Craib's (1989: 195–98) supposition that it has been easier for sociologists to avoid the complexity that engaging with the individual necessarily imported into their theory. The result, though, was a stunted social theory, which operated on the surface and failed to understand how individuals related to one another. In these circumstances, Craib (1998: 70) suggests that sociology is held back, in particular micro-theory and attempts at understanding personality; Freudian theory offers great, unrealised potential.

Any attempt to fulfil this, though, should be premised upon an acknowledgment of Freud's flaws. In particular, Freud was misplaced in positioning his psychoanalysis as a science. Popper (2006: 43–51) debunks such claims as failing to satisfy the 'falsifiability criterion' that separates 'genuine' from 'pseudo' science. Indeed, even an advocate like Craib (1998: 69–70) is duly alert to the manner in which Freudian theory has long been expressed in dogmatic, exclusive and bigoted terms by some of its advocates. This is an unpleasant – possibly dangerous – element, which does not allow criticism or deviation. However, this usage should not blind one to the insights held within, which even Popper (2005: 17) was want to recognise. Perhaps the most fruitful way to do this would be to pay heed to the *bricolage* style taken by Butler (1999) in her *Gender Trouble*. Despite initial feminist opposition to Freud, Butler (1999: 73–84) follows a host of post-structuralist scholars in engaging with Freud and, in so doing, she makes selective use of particular Freudian concepts.

Though Freud (1995b: 171) has shown himself appalled by such 'eclecticism', this approach allows insight to be drawn without chapter and verse adherence to the cannon. Being open to the possibility of alternative accounts allows many of the pitfalls of Freudian theory to be avoided. Freud's greatest legacy to social theory is the set of conceptual tools which can be drawn upon to reveal the otherwise hidden processes which might influence social actors (Young, 1940: 869). In this section, I recognise this while adopting an open approach, as particular Freudian concepts are loosely drawn upon for the explanatory potential they might provide.

For Freud (1989c: 630–31), self-image is tied into the ego. Ego sits alongside *id* and *super-ego* as the three parts of Freud's (1989c: 631–40) vision of the human mind. The id represents the base level of the mind. Entirely unconscious, the id is that uncoordinated and instinctual part of the mind constituting the basic drives which seek to follow the 'pleasure principle' of avoiding pain or discomfort (Freud, 1989a: 301–02). On the other hand, the super-ego works in contradiction to the id, at the top layer of the mind. Mainly unconscious, it strives for social acceptability, fulfilling the critical and moralising element of the mind as it seeks perfection. Mediating these can be found the ego, striking a balance between the primitive drives of the former and the idealistic assessments of the latter. It is this part of the mind which contains the consciousness.

The term ego derives from a Latin translation of Freud and it is, perhaps, more accurate to use direct translation of the original German, whence *das ich* can be understood as 'the I' (Bettelheim, 1983: 53). With this handle, the concept of ego seems rather more self-explanatory; though Freud later refined his conception, the ego can be understood to correspond with a 'sense of self' – the understanding most beneficial for this lay application (Levine, 2000: 107–08). As such, the ego is the part of the mind that allows individuals to deal with reality and go about their everyday lives, enabling the individual to satisfy their desires in socially appropriate ways. In this manner, the ego plays a central role in self-image. Self-image is constituted by various interrelations between the three parts of Freud's structural model of the psyche – ego, id and super-ego – notably involving the 'ego-ideal', a model of perfection that the ego attempts to achieve (Freud, 1989b: 556–60).

This ego-ideal begins in the super-ego, which Freud (1995a: 81) suggests provides 'the vehicle of the ego ideal by which the ego measures itself, which it emulates, and whose demand for ever greater perfection it strives to fulfil'. The ego-ideal replaces childhood narcissism; as belief in one's own perfection is lost, the ego-ideal offers the possibility of its realisation in the future. To achieve this, the individual sets rules and standards of good behaviour. When these are achieved, feelings of pride, value and accomplishment are duly experienced.

Select insights from Freudian theory can be adapted and applied when considering the lawyers in this research and their self-image. The interview data revealed the satisfaction with which they self-identified as professionals. The lawyers expressed those feelings of pride, value and accomplishment in this designation; it seemed to offer a sense of perfection for which they had strived. In occupying this role, lawyers were imbued with an awareness of their own importance, revelling in the responsibility placed in their hands. As such, 31 out of the 35 lawyers – from all firms – presented this position, as characterised by the following examples:

> I am proud to be in criminal defence. It's an ego thing, I suppose; I think it's hugely important. You have a member of the public who knows nothing and they have the might of the state against them and we are the knights in shining armour standing between the individual and the dragon of the state.
>
> (Mike, senior partner, *Radison and Muddle*, INT)

> Criminal defence work is important and I think societies are often judged on how they treat the sick, the mentally ill and their own criminal population. There is part of me that feels incredibly privileged to be a part of all of this, to have a perception of this and a knowledge and an understanding of our society that means, one, I am not scared of it, and, two, I'm trying in some small way to do something that contributes perhaps to improving it.
>
> (Eileen, solicitor, *Radcliffe and Musk*, INT)

It is understandable that the lawyers should revel in such a title. To be considered a professional in the United Kingdom is a rank permeated with the trappings of high social status: an association with the aristocracy and nobility that stretches back to the establishment of the three learned professions – law, medicine and the clergy – in Medieval England (Freidson, 1994: 16–19). Recognition as a professional was seen to confer 'gentlemanly' or 'gentry' status, and so was highly sought after (Freidson, 1994: 17–18). Accordingly, the legal profession is well characterised by Elliot (1972: 14) terming it a 'status profession', existing in some contrast to the lesser 'occupational professions' of more recent times.

The deference that so elevates the status of these professions in the United Kingdom has been characterised as 'the British disease' (Fores and Glover, 1978) and is well evinced in a cross-national study of first-year law students (Asimow et al, 2005). That research features students drawn from institutions in Argentina, Australia, Germany and the United States, but it was those in English and Scottish universities who provided the greatest conviction as to the exalted status that lawyers held. Over 80 per cent of British respondents believed that lawyers hold 'a lot of prestige', contrasting sharply with the 44 per cent in Buenos Aires (Asimow et al, 2005: 421). So it is that Francis and Sommerlad (2009: 73–78) are able to document some of the ways in which the legal profession has striven to maintain social closure for those hailing from backgrounds rich in social and cultural capital. This represents a profession at pains to preserve itself as a class apart. As such, it seems clear that, in seeing themselves as professionals, the self-satisfaction of the lawyers I interviewed was essentially founded upon the high status they felt it conferred.

However, such a claim was problematic in that such high status was not reflected when it came to the matter of how they were valued financially. This presented a challenge to the lawyers' self-image.

Lawyers' Self-image and Remuneration

Legally aided criminal defence lags behind many other professions in terms of remuneration. The *2009 Annual Survey of Hours and Earnings* (Office for National

Statistics, 2009) reveals that legal aid solicitors earn an average salary of around £25,000 pa, decidedly towards the bottom of the public sector pay list (see Rogers, 2009). Responding to this, the Law Society (2009a) and, in particular, their chief executive, Desmond Hudson, has been quick to show their chagrin that these figures mean legal aid solicitors earning are 'well below the average for professional salaries'. The report received a similarly disgruntled reaction from various media organs of the legal aid sector (see McPartland, 2009; Family Law Newswatch, 2009). These have been particularly eager to highlight the fact that legally aided solicitors earn less than sewage workers, or, as *Family Lore* most graphically illustrates it in its headline, 'Legal Aid: Worse than shovelling s*it [sic]' (Bloch, 2009).

This devaluation of the legal aid solicitor's status, though, was not a burden shared equally by brethren lawyers in other fields. Indeed, Moorhead (2004: 173–76) reports a survey commissioned by the Legal Aid Practitioners Group and the Law Society, which showed such lawyers have been quick to compare their position relative to other lawyers, and feel that they come out short. This view is substantiated by the final year of the Law Society cohort study (Duff et al, 2000: 43), which shows that solicitors in City firms receive twice the average wage of those in high street firms within a couple of years of qualifying. Reacting to the aforementioned public sector pay research, McPartland (2009), writing in *The Lawyer*, lambasts this situation, frustratedly citing the £25,000 pa figure in the light of trainee solicitors at City firms starting on £40,000 pa salaries.

The lawyers in my study were acutely aware of this financial situation. Throughout the research, I was privy to seemingly boundless levels of griping and grumbling concerning the lawyers' lesser levels of remuneration compared with their peers. During the participant observation, I often recorded in my notebooks that this was the main subject of conversation. Lawyers bemoaned these circumstances with such frequency to anyone who would listen – one another, prosecutors, other court staff, clients and especially, it felt, to me – that I eventually stopped recording it through a combination of saturation and tedium. This was duly reinforced by the formal interviews as the majority, 28 out of the 35, expressed concerns that their rates of remuneration were unfair when compared with other professionals. This viewpoint was to be found across the firms, and can be appreciated from the following quotes:

> I'm earning less money now than I was earning ten years ago. Less money! It's incredible. I don't really think many people would stay in a profession where they earn less money. Once upon a time you could afford to pay people a salary of, say, £25,000 a year, for a qualified solicitor with a couple of years of experience. Back then, that was favourable, compared with what teachers or nurses or policemen would earn. Now, I think somebody who had got all their qualifications, been through university, law school, with debts of £30,000 to £40,000 will still only be picking up about £25,000 a year. Whereas, if they decided to teach, to go into the National Health Service, if they went into social work, they're going to earn similar money without having to do, necessarily, the extra work. They'd also probably have a better career structure.
>
> (Windom, solicitor, *Swining MacSage*, INT)

> The financial rewards have been limited for some considerable time. It is not worth doing this job for the rewards that we get . . . In terms of doctors who [we used to enjoy] a reasonable parity with in the early 1990s, in particular; they are probably now partners in GP practices and they are probably earning double what we earn.
>
> (Garland, partner, *Sosford and Banger*, INT)

Many lawyers, though, were more sensitive still to the way in which they badly trailed other branches of the legal profession. This stark reality was one that they saw drummed into them early on in their careers, and reinforced by later experience of other lawyers, as in the following:

> When I did my LPC [Legal Practice Course], they always give the impression that if you're any good at law, you'll go into something commercial, something higher paid.
>
> (Annie, solicitor, *Radcliffe and Musk*, INT)

> The criminal profession is struggling to bring new blood on board. In part, that's because the law schools are advising the law students not to do crime, for financial reasons . . . and so many of the old criminal defence solicitors I used to know are leaving. There are lots of advocates who have moved onto other areas of law because they can't afford to be doing it.
>
> (Gordon, solicitor, *Radford Hope*, INT)

> People are just leaving because their contemporaries have gone into different areas of law, and they can see them earning a lot more money and not working as hard; the temptation is clear – especially if they want to start a family.
>
> (Norma, solicitor, *Radford Hope*, INT)

Considering their peers, the substance of their complaint appeared to revolve around the supposition that their remuneration did not match the high status they merited as professionals. Money does not simply provide the ability to buy things, it acts so as to confer respect – and these lawyers clearly had neither the requisite amount of stuff or deference that they supposed they should. This is reflected in the following quote:

> There's so much hype that the legal aid budget costs us £2 billion a year. I don't know what the total defence budget is, but it's a huge spend on just a couple of ships and submarines. That £2 billion wouldn't keep the NHS [National Health Service] going for five or six days! Yet it's considered too much for us? It makes the mind boggle. But let's be clear about this: in 1949, when legal aid came into being, at the same time we had Social Security and the NHS – those were the three [sic] pillars of the Welfare State. You are now getting to the stage where one of those pillars is being knocked down – the legal aid system. One hopes that somewhere there will be an enlightened, honest politician who recognises the importance of criminal defence and what it's worth, but there doesn't seem much sign of him.
>
> (James, senior partner, *Radford Hope*, INT)

Most of these lawyers understood that they were not valued as high status professionals in financial terms. Perhaps, they felt that their very designation as professionals was challenged. This is understandable on considering Larson (1977: 4–8) and his modelling of 'the professional project' that, in large part, is characterised by the ambition of establishing market primacy. As such, Larson (1977: xvii) suggests that, 'professionalization is thus an attempt to translate one order of scarce resources – special knowledge and skills – into another – social and economic rewards'. So can be seen the image of the profession which Collier (2005: 55–56) reveals to be disseminated by the more successful commercial firms to prospective trainees; to be a legal professional is fundamentally linked with all the achievement of high remuneration. In this manner, my lawyers represented something akin to failures in the professional project, certainly compared with their peers. This understandably elicited both pain and discomfort, as the economic value placed on the lawyers did not match that of their self-image, conceptualised as the ego-ideal. In order to reach towards that glimpse of perfection, it appears that the lawyers had to set themselves different rules and standards. Rather than attaining the high status that they saw professionals to possess through financial remuneration, lawyers elevated the prominence of their social agenda. It was through enacting this that they could meet their ego-ideal and achieve the feelings of pride, value and accomplishment while avoiding the pain and discomfort they would otherwise experience as economic failures.

Lawyers' Self-image and the Social Agenda

The social agenda, then, was located as central to their practice – the reason they entered and, thereon, that they stayed – and the formal interview data showed the prominence these lawyers attributed these values. Indeed, 29 out of the 35 lawyers from all firms suggested that fulfilling this role mitigated for the lesser remuneration they received compared with their peers, as shown in these quotes:

> Crime was never well paid and if that's what you were interested in you would never have gone into it in the first place . . . it's all about the vocational aspect of it.
>
> (Shelly, solicitor, *Radcliffe and Musk*, INT)

> It must be obvious to new solicitors that, 'there's no money in this, I'd rather go elsewhere, not go to an avenue that has no future'. The only people it is attracting are people who've got a real vocation; it is becoming a vocation. You've got to have a real passion for assisting people who need defending and need protecting from the police or the authorities. And, if you haven't got that passion for it, it's a no go really.
>
> (Gordon, solicitor, *Radford Hope*, INT)

> I don't think it is a viable career choice: you don't get paid very much and you have to do an awful lot – and that's why a lot of people turn away and move into prosecuting. I can see the attraction there. I can't see myself as a prosecutor though. I just couldn't do it! I defend people; that's what I do.
>
> (Nadine, partner, *Swining MacSage*, INT)

The majority of lawyers, from Radical and Sausage Factory alike, then, earnestly identified themselves engaged in a vocation, doing something essential and making a difference. This relied on a traditional professional evocation: that they could use their specialist knowledge to fulfil a socially important role (Eraut, 1994: 223–25), imbuing the assumption that public service and professional status were linked (Abbey and Boon, 1995: 263). In this situation, it was the social agenda and not financial remuneration that provided their rewards, and it was meeting those aspirations that earned the designation professional, with the high status that accompanied it. However, this claim to possess a social agenda is not something that should be accepted uncritically. The participant observation data demonstrates such a discrepancy from these values that it must cause us to question its substance. In particular, I believe that this trumpeting of the social agenda may be deemed an act of *rationalisation*, thus providing an alternative explanation for lawyers' engagement in legally aided criminal defence.

Rationalisation is one of Freud's (2009: 3–4) defence mechanisms: manipulations of perception designed to protect individuals from anxiety. These entailed means to deny or distort reality, and were originally organised by Sigmund's daughter, Anna (Freud, 1993: 42–50) and later classified by Vaillant (1992). One of their chief functions is to shield the ego from the pain or displeasure presented by an external threat – a situation with which an individual would struggle to cope. In this manner, some element of distortion of reality is utilised in order that the individual's self-image can be maintained. Rationalisation is a 'disavowal defence', whereby the ego logically justifies a past decision that was made in a different state of mind; it represents a fallacy of reasoning, of which the individual is typically unaware (Vaillant, 1992: 256). The individual avoids dealing with the true explanation behind their actions, devising reassuring or self-serving, though fundamentally incorrect, explanations.

In the case of these lawyers, the true explanation might be that they were engaged in legally aided defence because they were simply not good enough for other areas of law. The lesser remuneration available reflected this area's position on the lowest rung of the profession; as such, it was not one meriting high status. The lawyers could have been alerted to this by their relative financial position, and it would have provided a great blow to their egos, shattering the perfectionism of their ego-ideal. They would be failing to live up to the standards that associated professionalism with earnings. As a result, the lawyers needed another means to meet their ego-ideal, and professing the alternative explanation found in a commitment to the social agenda allowed their financial failure to be circumvented. These lawyers possessed extremely marketable skills: qualifications which would have been attained through hard work, over several years and at a considerable cost. Before they qualified, the lawyers were aware that there was less money in legally aided criminal defence than other areas of the profession. They claimed, though, that they were not money-orientated and that the social agenda over-rode financial concerns.

However, these lawyers frequently talked about money and in particular, what they did or did not earn. They decried their own remuneration, though the £25,000 pa matched that of the average wage in the United Kingdom (Office for National Statistics, 2009: 1). Even at this figure, they earned more than welders, carpenters, joiners, driving instructors or construction workers, all of whom had useful and necessary skills and trades that we all (lawyers included) rely on. They also trumped members of another of the original professional triumvirate, clergymen. More so, law students are said to earn an average of £245,000 more than non-graduates over the course of their careers, second only to those who study medicine (Faulkner, 2010). Even more significant than pure earnings, though, is the rate of return on a qualification – rather crudely reducing higher education to economic practice. While medical students earn more, they have to study for longer than those completing law degrees. This ensures that the latter offers the best 'investment', as they see a rate of return of 17.2 per cent compared with the average of 12.1 per cent (Faulkner, 2010). That the lawyers in this study were so dissatisfied could be considered somewhat greedy. The arrogance of such a stance was most pronounced in a common complaint, encountered on numerous occasions in the participant observation: that they worked for less on-call than would a plumber. One such quote to this effect griped that:

> I was out all night. The amount we get paid for it, pah – you wouldn't get a plumber out in the middle of the night for the kind of money they pay me. It's a disgrace.
>
> (Bob, solicitor, *Radford Hope*, IC)

This lament can also be seen in the following interview excerpt:

> I do enjoy doing crime, but not half as much as I used to. You've never made a lot of money doing crime. You would never go into crime for the money, but you used to be able to make a reasonable living and do a reasonable job for the client. But now you're not paid very much, and a lot of people – I don't go to police stations in the middle of the night – but people working crazy hours, 60-odd hours a week, for a very poor pay, earning less than their plumber or their electrician who hasn't studied, got a degree, and hasn't got people's liberty in their hands and that depresses me.
>
> (Norma, solicitor, *Radford Hope*, INT)

Clearly, then, financial remuneration was a prime concern. Accordingly, there appears to be ample reason to suppose that, contrary to the majority of sentiments expressed by lawyers in the interview data, financial considerations were a motivating factor in some lawyers entering the profession. Certainly, it presented a wage that most in society would gladly take. While the majority of the interviews saw the lawyers profess that they had always been interested in crime, it might be considered a significant minority that acknowledged that they simply entered the law in general, and only later came to specialise in crime. A senior partner, Dale, from *Swining MacSage* was one such lawyer:

> Was it crime from the start? Umm, no. I did have quite an interest in tax. And when I got my articles, when you did articles, you just did whatever you could. And the firm I did my articles with did a little bit of criminal work, but just as a duty solicitor, lip service. And, that was it. But, my first exposure to crime was when I joined *MacSage and Co* in the 1970s. I'd been away with my friends for the summer. And, anyway, I went back to see my mother, and she said, 'there's a job going in the city, I've got you an interview'. She said:

'I phoned up and got an interview for you, and I asked them to hold off until you came back'. So, I wasn't planning on getting back, but I did, I came back, I thought I'd see my family and then go off again. Fortunately, I got the job. It wasn't in those days a high-street practice, it was broad based. So I was doing personal injury cases, some divorce and some crime. But, for some reason or other, I seemed to get a big following in criminal work. So that was it really, I just ended up having to do that.

(Dale, senior partner, *Swining MacSage*, INT)

Those with stories akin to Dale appeared reflective of the aforementioned Law Society cohort study (Duff et al, 2000). Earlier research, by McDonald (1982: 270–71) and Sherr and Webb (1989: 232–33) suggests that social agenda is not a major pull-factor in terms of law student motivation compared with financial considerations. This prompts Boon et al (2001: 591–94) to conclude their assessment of the six-year longitudinal cohort study by questioning the very viability of this social agenda in the face of economics. Reflecting on these sources, Boon (2005: 236–38) directly juxtaposes these altruistic claims with more selfish motivations. In so doing, Boon (2005: 236) considers that, 'practical and selfish aspirations came far above altruistic aspirations'.

These surveys showed that legal qualifications were most likely to be sought with an eye towards employment concerns. Public service desires lag behind both individual and vocational priorities as relevant variables. This position could clearly be attributed to some of my lawyers, from both Radical and Sausage Factory firms, as follows:

I had to pick a career. I knew I was too squeamish to be a doctor, so I just applied for law courses. It was respectable and well paid; or so I thought!

(Eileen, solicitor, *Radcliffe and Musk*, INT)

I took law because it seemed quite a versatile career that could be used as a gateway to different things. I didn't have a clear idea at that point that I wanted to go into the legal profession.

(Thomas, partner, *Swining MacSage*, INT)

By this view, many lawyers entered the legal profession because it represented a sensible career choice; financial considerations were to the fore.

It is, though, well established that criminal legal aid carries lesser remuneration than many other branches of the law. As the previous cohort study considers law students in general, perhaps of greater relevance is the research by Sommerlad and Wall (1999) which focuses only on legally aided lawyers. Their results identify the social agenda significantly trumping financial concerns as a motivating factor. However, the data provided by Sommerlad and Wall (1999) faces the same problem as that in the first section of this chapter. Their lawyers are already engaged in legal aid so might simply have been rationalising the professional situation in which they found themselves. By contrast, studies of law student aspirations are free of this problem, as they have yet to take any particular professional path beyond choosing law academically.

This returns us to the notion that lawyers were engaged in a lower waged area of the law because they were not able to do anything more lucrative. Lawyers might have missed out on obtaining training contracts from commercial firms; there is intense competition for these places so that only the ablest students from the most prestigious institutions can be successful – and even they face a challenge (Shiner, 2000: 106–17). In this research, no solicitor offered academic inadequacies as influencing their entry into this branch of the profession. However, one clerk, who had been practising longer than most of the solicitors, did go some way to recognising these factors in her own career path:

> I got into the job because I was a massive under achiever and I failed my A-levels fairly dramatically. I went to rather too many parties so there were entertainment issues, whereby I didn't quite deal with revision, exams. Anyway, I fell into working at the County Court which made me realise that the only way I was ever going to get a half-decent job was to do some exams as I was working, which meant either banking, accountancy or law. So I started doing my course and got a job. Originally, I was going to do matrimonial law as I could divorce someone with my eyes shut, but that didn't happen so I got offered a job doing crime. Now, I knew absolutely nothing about crime, but in those days, back in the 1980s I started here, the requirements for legal advisers were very open and easy and I ended up being taken on but I'm not quite sure I would have employed myself – on my first day here, I hadn't a clue what the difference was between the Magistrates' Court and the Crown Court. I knew even less than the average person on the street knows. I started here and I had absolutely no knowledge as to what crime law was all about.
>
> (Evelyn, police station clerk, *Swining MacSage*, INT)

While no lawyer attributed their own presence in this lower paid area of law to their own limitations, several acknowledged this was a factor inherent in legal aid remuneration – one increasingly prevalent as the system was squeezed tighter. As such, while lawyers were loath to see themselves as deficient, the interviews showed that 25 out of the 35 – from all firms – believed criminal legal aid attracted lawyers who were not good enough to find employment elsewhere. They identified that other solicitors might be practising because they lacked the talent to engage in better remunerated branches. In the participant observation, lawyers were quick to point out solicitors who they saw as lacking, for example:

> There just aren't many decent young solicitors coming through. You can see them here, a couple of them, just not up to it. It makes me sad to see the standards drop like this.
>
> (Leo, senior partner, *Radcliffe and Musk*, IC)

> That solicitor there – he's one of that new breed of civil servant lawyers. It's just a job to them and it shows; they don't have the skills to pull it off, lack that special something which can really help a client.
>
> (Dale, senior partner, *Swining MacSage*, IC)

> It's a little bit depressing to see the other lawyers around here; you know they only do it because they're too useless to do anything else. Legal aid is becoming a graveyard for the also rans.
>
> (Bob, solicitor, *Radford Hope*, IC)

These views were later substantiated in the formal interviews as in the following quotes:

> I think the quality of representation will be affected by legal aid cuts. I've seen a few young people that don't seem to have the fire in their belly that we had when we were that age. It's not quite the same. Whether they get to the soul of the client and understand why that person did what they did and manage to put that across in language that will make the magistrate sympathetic, that's another thing altogether.
>
> (Norma, solicitor, *Radford Hope*, INT)

> The reality is we're not getting the best service from the criminal defence advocates, which just doesn't attract the best people now. Which is very sad.
>
> (Gordon, solicitor, *Radford Hope*, INT)

> I think you will find that it will be dumbed down – you will not get the people coming in. You might get the odd one, who is completely dedicated to the idea but I think the majority will be just people who, frankly, can't cut it in any other area of law. I won't name names but there are some youngsters I have seen around recently who I think, you know, this was clearly the last resort for you; you're not a good lawyer, you're not a good advocate, you've been around for a fair old time but you're still not a good advocate. They're still not a good lawyer and they never will be and it's just because they don't have the ability. Now, I think this will just become the melting pot for the mediocre, I really do.
>
> (Mike, senior partner, *Radison and Muddle*, INT)

The readiness of these lawyers to identify others engaging in this area because they could not practise elsewhere works to highlight their rationalisation. Most lawyers were aware that their branch of the profession was populated by supposed 'lesser lights'. However, they would not see this in themselves. Instead, they protected their own ego from the threat posed by the valuation that lesser remuneration placed on them, and thus maintained their self-image. The financial indictors may have pointed to criminal legal aid being constituted by a cadre of lesser professionals, without high status, but these lawyers were shielded from seeing that in themselves.

Whether considered a genuine conviction or an act of rationalisation, the social agenda seems to have operated to safeguard these lawyers from the judgement implicit in their lesser remuneration. Despite this valuation, it gave them a claim to assert their worth as professionals, premising their high status on fulfilling a societally important role. However, affording this significance to the social agenda seems every bit as problematic as remuneration was in maintaining the self-image of these lawyers. While the association with the type of clients that the social agenda demanded might have been supposed to elevate them, it appears that others actually saw it to have relegated them further.

Lawyers' Self-image and the Legal Profession

The social agenda did not appear to carry much weight within the wider legal profession, a field that Goriely (1996: 48–49) shows to have historically denigrated legally aided criminal defence. Indeed, this has been captured by a survey of lawyers' perceptions of relative professional prestige (Sandefur, 2001: 386–87); criminal defence ranked thirty-first out of 42 areas of practice. That research was conducted in the United States (where legal aid rates are worse still), locating criminal defence behind branches like personal injury and labour law while only ahead of areas such as immigration and juvenile. This situation is reflected by White (1975: 233) who identifies the 'element of distaste, sometimes even of disdain which is to be found amongst some solicitors of standing for those who do legal aid work'. These attitudes existed prior to legal aid as we know it and back to its roots in the Poor Prisoners Defence Act 1903. This would be the impression provided by one clerk to the Old Bailey (cited Goriely, 1996: 48) who, in 1904, was said to have contemptuously professed that these lawyers would become the 'lowest class of professional'.

There can be little doubt that the aforementioned financial considerations played their part in these circumstances. It has also been suggested that there operated an 'ideology of triviality' (McBarnet, 1981: 143) where the problems presented were dull, ordinary and tedious: beneath the expertise of a qualified lawyer (Bottoms and McClean, 1976: 226). This reflects the 'professional purity thesis' of professional prestige (Sandefur, 2001: 391–94). However, McConville et al (1994: 128–30) problematise this contention, suggesting that lawyers themselves choose to make the work routine.

As such, a third possibility can be entertained: lawyers were denigrated through association with their clients. In this vein, Larson (1977: 221) highlights the role that a client's socio-economic status has on the ranking of the profession, meaning, as Eraut (1994: 5) articulates, 'the importance of the clients affects the status of the professional providing the service'. Accordingly, for these lawyers, Sommerlad (1996: 298) posits that low status among peers indicates a 'clear reflection of the connection between the status of the client and the lawyer'. The association between lawyers and clients, then, leads to the former being tainted along the 'client-type thesis' of professional prestige when the latter are considered somewhat lowly and undesirable (Sandefur, 2001: 391). This is a judgement of relative levels of 'honour' which lawyers dealing in areas concerned with 'prestige clients' are particularly want to make of those supposed inferior to them (Heinz and Laumann, 1982: 61–65). The contact lawyers had with their clients, then, degraded them, and here a parallel can be drawn between two of the original professions: legal and medical. When the post-war Labour Government outlined plans for the National Health Service, there was vehement hostility from within the profession, primarily channelled through the British Medical Association (Rintala, 2003: 59–60). This opposition seems to have been, at least partly, premised upon class; medical practitioners feared the degradation of association with the masses, *the great unwashed.* This would counteract their high status as a gentlemanly profession.

The introduction of legal aid, of course, meant lawyers dealing with clients who could not afford representation from their own funds. As a result, there was a shift from predominantly middle-class patronage to a working-class cadre, a move which Sommerlad (2001: 359–60) links to a 'discursive shift'. These lower class clients were demonised and, concomitantly, so were the lawyers who worked with them. It seems self-evident that this would reflect a sharper decline than that anticipated by the medical profession, as these legal professionals would not simply be working with the proletariat but their most ostensibly unpleasant element: the criminal classes. Any class distinctions, then, would be exacerbated. So it is that the social agenda of these lawyers involved their perpetuating the low status accrued through lesser remuneration. It does not seem to have been enough to earn them the rank of professional; thus, McDonald (1982: 273) is able to characterise the English legal profession as:

> A core of high status practitioners, concerned chiefly with the functions of capital, surrounded by a peripheral majority who deal in personal services for private clients . . . they [criminal lawyers] represent a lower form of legal practice somewhat similar to social work.

Studies of such peripheral lawyers have documented an awareness of this position (McConville et al, 1994: 24–26; Sommerlad, 2001: 355–60; Mungham and Thomas, 1979: 174). There were comments made throughout my own participant observation to the same effect, such as the following:

> I don't know how Harold [partner, *Radford Hope*] must feel: someone of his stature and experience, having to deal with cases down here [Magistrates' Court].
>
> (Shelly, solicitor, *Radcliffe and Musk*, IC)

> I hate having to come down here and work in the Magistrates' Court; it's so depressing. This isn't lawyering, it's social work; you're just dealing with people's little everyday problems. That's not what I want to do. I'm a lawyer; I should be using my brain and actually having to work through legal problems. I just feel like this is all a big waste of my time.
>
> (Teresa, solicitor, *Radcliffe and Musk*, IC)

> [Lawyer One] Are you down the Mags [Magistrates' Court]?
>
> [Lawyer Two] Yep. Worse luck. No one wants to do that!
>
> [Lawyer One] I wouldn't do it. I'm better than that you know?!
>
> [Lawyer Two] I wouldn't do it unless I had to. Don't have a choice though.
>
> (Gordon and Harry, solicitors, *Radford Hope*, OR – Gordon had recently left criminal defence for a civil department in the firm)

It can be said, then, that the lawyers' attempts to realise the perfection demanded by their ego-ideals was again faced with failure. The social agenda would not allow them to be recognised as the high status professionals they thought themselves to be. However, just as rationalisation protected them from the realities of financial remuneration, lawyers needed to utilise another Freudian defence mechanism to shield them from the consequences of the social agenda's reality: this time, *displacement.*

Displacement is a 'neurotic defence', entailing the redirecting of pain and displeasure caused by a dangerous object and onto a safer one (Vaillant, 1992: 257). This process of transference prevents the ego from having to deal with the real trauma, reducing the anxiety experienced. The recipient can be understood as a scapegoat. These lawyers avoided facing the pain and displeasure of their social agenda failing to attain them the self-image they sought and instead transferred these feelings onto the lawyer–client relationship.

Before turning to that displacement effect, however, it is important to note that at an intellectual level the lawyers identified several other factors underpinning challenges to their claims to be high status professionals. Many criticised the media and the government for the populist line both followed, and which the public consumed unquestioningly, ensuring the legitimisation of their devaluation. A flavour of this can be gleaned from these examples:

> Part of the problem has to be that, I think, the government would like us to be public servants that, in a way, we are as we are dependent on the public purse. But they do not want the expense of having to treat us like civil servants – give us that status and having to give us flexitime, pension, all the benefits that go with being a civil servant. They won't give us that respect.
>
> (Leo, senior partner, *Radcliffe and Musk*, INT)

> The public doesn't appreciate our public service role, in the wider sense – getting all these people off, having them found not guilty when they're guilty, or whatever. But I do – it's a necessary part of society that people are represented through a well-manned criminal justice system and part of that are solicitors provided through legal aid. We're a part of that, so I think that for the greater good, it is part of the system. People don't. If you did a poll in *The Sun*, they would bring back hanging and would also get rid of us, because it's not perceived to be good.
>
> (Shelly, solicitor, *Radcliffe and Musk*, INT)

Similarly, some lawyers displayed frustration for lawyers from other branches of the profession. In particular, this involved indignation at their, supposedly underserved, inflated remuneration casting the profession as a whole in a bad light, as in this quote:

> Despite what the public are led to believe, we are not the fat cat lawyers that the government go on about. And the government know we're not. Alright, that greedy so and so might be taking the piss but okay, do something about him then. If they think the QC is paid too much, don't pay him so much but no, no, no: 'We'll keep paying top end and keep chipping away at the bottom because you're earning bugger all anyway'.
>
> (Mike, senior partner, *Radison and Muddle*, INT)

As such, there were lawyers from both Radical and Sausage Factory firms who recognised the role that all these groups played in ensuring that they were not high status professionals. In addition to these, I have suggested that the lawyers' own, largely unacknowledged, shortcomings contributed to their presence in this branch of the profession. All these factors seem to have contributed to the position the lawyers faced; their self-image was threatened and they faced pain and discomfort from failing to meet their ego-ideals. None of the above, though, became the targets for the displacement that the lawyers engaged in to protect their egos. All were either too dangerous to attack (antagonising their peer groups, hating themselves) or simply beyond effective reach (the media, government and public opinion). In their place, then, the lawyers seem to have directed this pain and displeasure onto their clients.

Their clients presented a safe and accessible target. They were the proverbial dogs to be kicked. Further, social psychological research has suggested that commitment to a cause among such professionals wanes without social validation (Parker, 1999: 229–31). The lack of status afforded to lawyers facilitated their moving, seamlessly, from seeing the clients in a positive light to something altogether darker. Accordingly, the particular form this displacement seems to have taken was embittered resentment of their clients. The lawyers had convinced themselves that these clients were the reason they practised and, therefore, they were also the reason for all the pain and discomfort they so encountered. This resentment was commonplace as the lawyers went about their business in the participant observation, evinced most clearly in conversations such as the following:

> After you do this job a while, you don't feel like you're serving justice anymore. Not helping people. What about helping the victims? Prosecuting seems more appealing, to help someone. You just realise that our clients are usually guilty, most of the time you're working to protect scumbags. It gets to you.
>
> (Harry, solicitor, *Radford Hope*, IC)

> Do you know what horrifies me most, about all of this? Between you and me, parting shots and everything; it's the horror of how seriously everyone has to take everything about the main criminal players. They all bow down to them, the more serious the criminal. And I'm not into that at all. And actually, it's just a job. It makes me so sad. I feel kind of quite sorry for them. I see someone that, in terms of like the criminal world, it's like the more criminal you are, the more status you're given. That's not me, not what I wanted to do. I can't wait to leave. Do something worthwhile, you know?
>
> (Audrey, solicitor, *Swining MacSage*, IC)

> I guess I should do Watson [client], shouldn't I? He's such a pain in the arse, keeps whinging and bending my ear. I almost don't want to, but at least it'll get rid of him. But then there'll be another one biting my ear. They always want something.
>
> (Denise, solicitor, *Radcliffe and Musk*, OR – to a colleague)

Displacement allowed lawyers to proceed with their valorisation of the social agenda, and to believe that it entitled them to be considered high status professionals. Their egos were unaware that they were being shielded from the reality that it actually degraded them in the eyes of their peers as the pain and displeasure that would ensue were removed and targeted upon their clients. Through a combination of both rationalisation and displacement, these lawyers were able to, effectively, delude themselves and maintain their self-image as high status professionals in the face of external challenges.

Positive and Negative Attitudes

This presentation, then, has offered an account whereby these lawyers ultimately came to take out the pain and displeasure caused by the challenges to their self-image upon their clients. With this so formulated, we can return to the issues of attitudes themselves and that initial contradiction. The question posed at the beginning of this discussion remains: how can lawyers claim to hold positive attitudes yet display negative attitudes?

That one party was lying can still be offered as an answer. That I might be lying remains with those of you reading; while, I recognise that, the supposition lawyers were lying in the interviews could still be said to carry at least some weight. Lawyers might have grown to resent their clients, blaming them for things that were not their fault, then lied to me that this was a healthy relationship in order to protect their careers and standing. As before, though, this understanding still appears somewhat impulsive to me. More pertinently, though, it would make little sense for lawyers to use the interviews to feed me the received line. They will have been aware that I had borne witness to what occurred behind the scenes over the many months of preceding participant observation. Rather, the alternative offered in this research is that lawyers could hold to both positive and negative attitudes simultaneously, not necessarily conscious of this distinction or its contradictory nature.

At this point, Jung's approach to attitudes seems to offer promise in understanding the situation we have seen. For Jung (2009: 414), an attitude can be understood as, 'the readiness of the psyche to act or react in a certain way'. This aspect of his theory is not far removed from the position of mainstream psychology, as represented by Bohner and Wanke (2002). However, where this more controversial, psychoanalyst diverges, moving beyond even Freud, is in Jung's (2009: 415) supposition that attitudes are generally constituted in pairs: one conscious, the other unconscious, a distinction which means that, 'consciousness has a constellation of contents different from that of the unconscious, a duality particularly evident in neurosis'. From the Jungian perspective, a neurosis is an unresolved tension between opposing attitudes of the conscious and the unconscious. Neurosis arrives when the conscious attitude is unable to recognise or effectively integrate elements deemed important to the unconscious attitude (Jung, 2009: 415). In the process, one of the dualities that can be drawn is between 'abstractism' and 'concretism' (Jung, 2009: 409–10, 420–21). For our purposes, these represent two ways of thinking and feeling – the former more sophisticated, rational and logical and the latter primitive, based entirely on perception through sensation. Concretism is useful for the manner in which it allows recognition of external reality; however, it is deficient in how that is subsequently interpreted.

The theory of Jung (2009) offers insights which, as with Freud's (1989c) ego, might be appropriated in lay terms and used as a heuristic device to provide some explanatory potential for the divergent accounts of these lawyers' attitudes. The lawyers conceivably suffered from a neurosis, a split between their consciously espousing positive attitudes to clients and unconsciously disseminating negative attitudes. This can be characterised as their distinguishing between the client and a client: the general and the particular. The client was that experienced in the abstract, viewed in theoretical terms through the prism of access to justice and thus representing the social agenda discussed in the formal interviews. On the other hand, a client was the concrete experience, that client dealt with in the here and now, associated with all the pain and displeasure of their position; that which they resented throughout the participant observation. When thinking objectively, detached and reasoning, the lawyer still held positive attitudes towards the client, as in the interviews. It was only when lost in the moment, acting on subjective impulses that the lawyers displayed these negative attitudes towards a client. This is a position encapsulated in the following contrasting examples from Laura, one *Swining MacSage* solicitor. In the interview, she stressed positive attitudes:

> I only ever wanted to do crime. I wanted to do law but crime was the only area that interested me, I liked the idea of working with people. I have quite an altruistic attitude, so I wanted to make a difference – I wanted to help the underdog. It's just something I've grown up with, my mum did a lot of charity work, I worked with a lot of disadvantaged people when I was growing up, and I suppose I just wanted, in my own little way, to make a difference.
>
> (Laura, solicitor, *Swining MacSage*, INT)

In the participant observation, she revealed negative attitudes:

> I hope this man gets prison. He's a nasty piece of work. You didn't hear that! But, urgh, thinking he can talk to me like that.
>
> (Laura, solicitor, *Swining MacSage*, IC)

> I'm quite glad he hasn't turned up; he's a whinging little git.
>
> (Laura, solicitor, *Swining MacSage*, IC)

> I've had enough of him, fuck him. Someone else can do him, I don't care.
>
> (Laura, solicitor, *Swining MacSage*, IC)

For Laura, the social agenda and willingness to work for the client appeared strong; however, her resentment and frustration at having to deal with a client seemed just as powerful. Despite this, in the formal interview, she came across as comfortable with her practice and at peace with herself.

This process, clearly, required another act of rationalisation on the part of these lawyers. In order to reconcile the negative attitudes they displayed as they went about their everyday business with the loftier ideals positive attitudes represented, the lawyers engaged in a fantasy. The lawyers could, thus, treat clients they encountered without respect, displaying derision and a willingness to dismiss and degrade them with ease but, as long as they felt they were doing their job to the best of their abilities, they could claim positive attitudes. As such, these lawyers might have believed that they possessed positive attitudes and met the social agenda that, thereon, allowed them to satisfy their ego-ideal. They attained their perfection, meeting the rules and standards so set down, feeling pride, value and a sense of accomplishment. As a defence mechanism, then, rationalisation protected the lawyers from the reality that they failed doubly (neither being paid well nor being valued for their social agenda), meaning that their ego could function relatively free from pain or discomfort.

Rather than lying in a conscious, and malicious or duplicitous manner, it is possible they were lying without realising it, to themselves and thereon to me. Regardless of whether I went native, the lawyers appear to have seen me as native by the time of the interviews. They spoke to me as they would speak to one another, *on the inside*: displaying a professional attitude in theoretical terms but quite the contrary in reality. As such, when provided with the time and space to muse upon their attitudes towards clients, they thought in the abstract, and convinced themselves that the abstract was more than just a myth. However, I also saw the concrete, and that there was a disparity between the two.

Whether or not the lawyers realised it, then, they displayed negative attitudes to their clients. This must be indicative of a strained lawyer–client relationship, and so highly concerning to those who believe in the principle of access to justice and the rights of defendants to be afforded dignity. More so, with these clients so reliant on the lawyers to realise their right to a fair trial, the prevalence of these attitudes raises daunting questions about the further impact these attitudes may have had on their practice. In his discussion of 'cop culture', Waddington (1999: 302) notes the distinction between the *canteen* and the *street*; the negative attitudes police display in the former should not be assumed to have an impact on what they do on the latter. In this research, the lawyers have been shown to disseminate their most negative attitudes while actually on *their* street. In either case, though, that negative attitudes can be identified should raise the question of how they might thereon be manifested in behaviour. This is the topic to which any such interested research need apply itself next. So, it is that in the following chapter I move on to consider one aspect of that behavior: how lawyers managed contact and access.

4

Behaviour

This chapter explores the manner in which lawyers behaved towards their clients, building on the analysis of attitudes presented in the preceding chapter. That chapter created a need to address whether the negative attitudes lawyers displayed were reflected in their actions. This directs attention towards how lawyers interacted with clients, focusing on features of what can be called 'procedural justice' (Tyler, 1988: 128–31). By this line, dealing with behaviour requires addressing something other than the substantive handling of a case: those factors responsible for the end result. Rather, it centralises the process in its own right. Clients are often chiefly concerned with how they are treated, not least that this is respectful, rendering it a significant thread to pursue in and of itself. The focus of this chapter, then, is on behaviour, with specific regard to the contact and access lawyers were willing to grant their clients. Contact and access are essential to foster rapport and enable communication and, as such, should be considered elemental for any functioning relationship.

However, as with the preceding chapter, the ethnographic data has not created a coherent image of the issue. Rather, two competing pictures emerged. In the formal interviews, lawyers talked of treating clients with *respect*, which suggested they acted in a way that showed a positive feeling of esteem towards clients. This would be indicative of a healthy lawyer–client relationship. In the participant observation, though, it is shown that these claims were far removed from what was actually seen. Lawyers appeared to treat the clients in a *disrespectful* manner, rather engaging in rude conduct with a lack of courtesy pointing to a strained lawyer–client relationship.

In this chapter, I address both perspectives in turn before drawing them together. The first two sections refrain from a close engagement with either the lawyers or the literature and, instead, space is provided in which to present some of the major themes to emerge from the research. This involves the selection and dissemination of examples that reflect commonly held positions among the lawyers and regular occurrences in their work. In the third section, both elements are brought together into a more critical discussion of the impact this behaviour appeared to have on the lawyer–client relationship. Overall, I claim that the issue of behaviour demonstrates a strained lawyer–client relationship. I start by turning to the formal interviews.

* * *

SECTION 1 – WHAT LAWYERS SAID ABOUT BEHAVIOUR

In this first section, I begin exploring behaviour by focusing on the views lawyers expressed in the formal interviews: their claims about behaviour and how they described their interactions with clients. Lawyers suggested that contact and access arrangements were respectful of clients and their needs and thus augured a healthy lawyer–client relationship. Lawyers took pride in their claims to treat clients well.

To give voice to these lawyers, this section abstains from detailed analysis. Rather, representative excerpts have been chosen to provide a flavour of the interviews, organised along the following lines:

1. *Consistency and Time* – lawyers identified these as the most important qualities of representation.
2. *External Pressures* – the difficult conditions lawyers saw themselves operating within.
3. *Resistance* – the manner in which lawyers dealt with these pressures, for their clients.

Consistency and Time

To understand how lawyers viewed the lawyer–client relationship, it is important to identify those features they considered necessary for its good health. In interview, lawyers held personal factors as more important than strictly legal consideration. These included developing good rapport, honesty, accessibility and communication. The ability to individualise service is key. The lawyers claimed to hold a particular conception of contact and access to be crucial in dealing with clients. This is the ideal by which lawyers provide consistency in representation to the client and, thereon, affording them the time they desire. The lawyer works for the client. Accordingly, an overwhelming 35 out of the 35 lawyers expressed sentiments similar to the following:

> The lawyer–client relationship is at the root of everything we do. Clients have to trust us and be able to have confidence in us. So much of our work is repeat work, clients who keep coming back to us. We do see ourselves at the heart of the community here and our reputation is important. Word of mouth, recommendations, people who keep coming back. Clients know they can rely on us.
>
> (Leo, senior partner, *Radcliffe and Musk*, INT)

> Some clients just can't be pushed through quickly. For whatever reason, they need more time. They need a solicitor who can spend time with them, go over their case and, maybe as important, get to know them as individuals. Because that's what they are – individuals. No two clients are the same . . . ideally, the solicitor will have time to build up that relationship.
>
> (Catherine, solicitor, *Radford Hope*, INT)

> Some clients just require more time than others. Suppose you're dealing with someone whose first language is not English, a simple process could take forever. Supposing you're dealing with a client who is educationally disadvantaged, or has a learning disability, as opposed to a client who is able to do a lot of their work himself, and comes in with a chronology the first time he sees you. They're chalk and cheese. It is not like making widgets within the car manufacturing industry, where I know that every widget looks exactly the same and takes me five minutes to make. Because people aren't the same.
>
> (Bobby, partner, *Sosig and Sage*, INT)

These features were considered particularly important by my lawyers for the role they played in developing 'rapport' with clients. Some 25 out of the 35 lawyers – across the firms – displayed these views, said to be necessary in order that the client would trust them. This can be seen in these examples:

> Building that relationship with the client is the most important part of the job. I think it's number one to be honest. If they don't trust you I don't see how you can represent them to the best of your ability. I see my role as obviously having to build that trust up. I have to make the client comfortable in my presence, to feel some sort of rapport.
>
> (Laura, solicitor, *Swining MacSage*, INT)

> It's about a personal bond, really. The actual offence might be quite straightforward but it's a social thing, I suppose. They need to feel that you're on their side and that you'll help them. They may look back on it – they may be guilty – but it's still about showing them that you're there for them . . . I think it's important to build up rapport.
>
> (Dick, partner, *Swining MacSage*, INT)

Most lawyers thus emphasised the role contact and access played in establishing what they considered to be the foundations of the lawyer–client relationship. One police station clerk, Johnny from *Radford Hope*, aptly articulated this approach as signifying a display of respect:

> You've got to have trust with a client. He's got to have faith in you. You have to build up rapport, so you need to spend time with them, you have to. You've got to treat them with respect. At the end of the day, it's all about respect. My father always told me to respect other people and that's what I try to do with my clients.
>
> (Johnny, police station clerk, *Radford Hope*, INT)

Many lawyers professed this approach as an ideal to strive for, albeit one they saw challenged by external pressures.

External Pressures

In identifying the importance of consistency and time, lawyers in these interviews tended to do so in juxtaposition with the reality they perceived: that external pressures restricted their ability to achieve such standards. The majority of lawyers – 31 out of the 35 – from Radical and Sausage Factory firms alike expressed this belief.

Moreover, all but one of those lawyers did so with a palpable sense of disappointment, as in the following:

> It's very pressurised, because often you are seeing a number of people in a morning so you can't waste any time. For example, you can't waste any time on niceties with the client; just straight in the room, you've got to get the client focused and tell them what you've got and deal with all these issues. You feel sometimes like you're a machine when you've got three or four of these people; it's quite disheartening. It's not a very pleasant way of working. There is human contact but there's not as much of it because we're all having to do more and more cases in less and less time. So there isn't time to get a real knowledge of somebody and really understand what makes them tick. It's very fast – in/out – you can't do the job properly, or as well as you used to be able to do, because you can't take the time and the trouble and the care. It's just rush, rush, rush, rush.
>
> (Norma, solicitor, *Radford Hope*, INT)

> The quantity and the quality of contact has diminished and part of the reason for that is that there is so much pressure on solicitors now to deal with a case on the day . . . doing a high volume of cases on any given day and that limits the time available for each individual case.
>
> (Leo, senior partner, *Radcliffe and Musk*, INT)

> It's not like it used to be. You can't enjoy it as much; everything is just so quick and basic. It's like someone is pressing fast-forward on the video recorder sometimes.
>
> (Nadine, partner, *Swining MacSage*, INT)

Lawyers identified two sources of this pressure. The primary concern in all firms was with legal aid funding, with 30 out of the 35 interviewees talking of the negative effect this had on their work. Lawyers of every variety felt this apprehension, as visible from these examples:

> Legal aid is going to become a third rate service . . . The client will have to wait, they're going to have to be used to making appointments at courts. You know, anyone who hires a solicitor privately, can be assured of when they want to see the solicitor they generally can, the appointment will be kept, the solicitor will have reviewed all the papers by then, they will get some sort of personal service and likely to get the same lawyer all through all the hearings, if they want that. Legal aid clients are going to get whoever is available, who won't have time to give a personal service because it just won't be feasible to do it because the only way to operate legal aid is going to be by volume it seems to me. There's a point where you can make efficiencies and it doesn't affect the quality because, actually, it drives out the inefficiencies. But there comes a point when it downgrades the service. And that's where we're going.
>
> (Dennis, solicitor, *freelance*, INT)

> There's always pressure with the Legal Services Commission cutting down finances. They are bound to have an effect because when you deal with the longer jobs in custody, you get your fixed fee of £200, then nothing until you've gone over £600 or so; you lose all that money before the £600 or so. It comes down to business, at the end of the day; the longer you're in the police station, the less money you make . . . so they encourage you to do things quickly whenever possible.
>
> (Johnny, police station clerk, *Radford Hope*, INT)

> There are situations where a lot of solicitors, and this does not include our firm, I hasten to add [laughs], but there are a lot of solicitors firms who will say that, 'we don't get paid for sending a caseworker to court, therefore we are not going to send a caseworker into court'. And that has resulted in there being an awful lot of problems in cases, because a caseworker hasn't been there from a firm of solicitors, and the solicitors therefore don't know what's happening, they get the wrong end of the stick.
>
> (Josie, barrister, *Swining MacSage*, INT)

In addition to legal aid, the interviews saw 24 out of 31 solicitors problematise the drive for efficiency within the Magistrates' Court, known as 'Criminal Justice: Simple, Speedy, Summary' (see Department for Constitutional Affairs, 2006b). This scheme sought to reduce the time between charge and disposal, cutting the number of hearings and facilitating early guilty pleas. This concerned lawyers in both Radical and Sausage Factory firms, as seen in the following:

> With CJSSS [Criminal Justice: Simple, Speedy, Summary] there's terrible pressure at court. Sometimes you can do things quickly at court, sometimes you have clients that you see regularly, you represented them last week, it's a straightforward guilty plea and you can work at top speed. But, if you're pleading not guilty, you cannot be expected to prepare in five minutes and we are being forced into situations which are not in anybody's interests . . . Moves towards efficiency don't always result in more efficiency – they might result in a bit more speed, but it's not justice.
>
> (Donna, solicitor, *Radcliffe and Musk*, INT)

> I see CJSSS [Criminal Justice: Simple, Speedy, Summary] as a measure to get cases through the system more quickly and save costs generally in the whole system. The Labour Government appears to be ideologically opposed to what they perceive as a complicated, expensive, burdensome legal system. They want to try and slim it all down, make it less expensive, make it more immediate. I think there will be more miscarriages of justice, it isn't possible to say how many but I think there will be more as a result of pressures to move cases through quickly.
>
> (Thomas, partner, *Swining MacSage*, INT)

Combined, many lawyers presented a bleak trend regarding contact and access. However, this was a situation that most also claimed to resist.

Resistance

In the face of the claimed pressures, the majority of lawyers – 33 out of the 35 – were resolute that they fought to resist these for the clients.

Pressures from the court were, apparently, easier to overcome. Several lawyers talked proudly of 'standing up' to the courts, as represented by statements such as the following:

> You have a duty to your client. You have a duty to the court, of course, but if the court is putting undue pressure on you to do something too quickly which is not in the interests of your client, whilst not being disrespectful, you are perfectly entitled to stand up and say that, 'this is not the way it should be done'. We do that quite frequently.
>
> (Harold, partner, *Radford Hope*, INT)

> I think you have to be fairly robust. And I think you have to stand up to situations more . . . Courts making requirements of you that are, actually, not in the interests of your client, but are consistent with your code of conduct. In other words, you're not doing anything that is unethical and you're not doing anything that is not appropriate but the court requires expedition and therefore occasionally you just have to say: 'Actually, no'. And a simple 'no' actually works.
>
> (Bobby, partner, *Sosig and Sage*, INT)

In the light of these problems, lawyers talked of their developing alternative coping methods. A good example of this was in relation to CJSSS's encouragement of early pleas, as explained below:

> You have to stand your ground. There's been occasions where you are pushed into such a corner that there's no way – you know someone perhaps needs to plead guilty and you to have to advise them to enter a guilty plea, but you're pushed into such a corner that you have to enter a not guilty plea just to allow yourself some time to perhaps listen to interview tapes and do a basis of plea. We're not provided with the papers before court . . . often the CJSSS [Criminal Justice: Simple, Speedy, Summary] packs don't have everything we need to have anyway, and we're getting pressure on to enter pleas at the first opportunity – but to do so, I think you could be bordering on negligence if you allow your clients to do that, especially entering a guilty plea, which is why, if pushed, if the magistrate won't back down and they won't listen to reason, you enter a not guilty plea then change your plea later on.
>
> (Laura, solicitor, *Swining MacSage*, INT)

However, their accounts suggested that the pressures of legal aid appeared more difficult to resolve and thus exerted the greatest force. Some non-solicitor lawyers were adamant that they would simply ignore such pressures and provide the ideal service to the client:

> I don't find the way in which I do my job has changed at all. If you've got a case that requires extra time because you've got a client with special needs, or needs a bit of extra attention, you take that time. It certainly hasn't changed the way in which I deal with clients. A client deserves the time they need. I still give the clients the service I gave them before; I'm not going to change that. That should never change. That's why I do this job, it's why I do a good job and I don't want the client to be short-changed simply because we're only getting paid x amount for being there. Some clients still need a bit more TLC and you need more time to go over things.
>
> (Maddie, police station clerk, *Radcliffe and Musk*, INT)

Solicitors, though, declined to express such stubbornness. It did not appear that they viewed this as a viable option. Police station clerks were only expected to deal with one case at a time and in-house barristers at Crown Court did not have the long lists of the Magistrates' Court, so each could spend more time with clients. In addition, they were also more likely to be involved over the life of a case. Both were able to maintain a greater level of contact than were solicitors.

In place of outright resistance, a handful of solicitors suggested that they were able to adapt to the circumstances of reduced contact and access. They offered their experience and skills picked up over years of practice, as in the following:

> I've been in business for such a long time that I'm a lot quicker working than somebody who's new to it or newer to it. And so I can pick up a set of papers and go straight to the important part of it . . . the tendency is to try and pick up a case at court, look at the papers and try to advise your client, all at the same time, in say 15 or 20 minutes, that could lead to bad advice being given. I'm possibly more skilled at it than other people because I've been doing it for so long.
>
> (Windom, solicitor, *Swining MacSage*, INT)

> Experienced lawyers like myself, and there are loads of us, can deal with that because we don't need to do an awful lot, we've read the papers quickly; we know pretty much what it is about.
>
> (Mike, senior partner, *Radison and Muddle*, INT)

Following this, most lawyers appeared to take the view that clients, in turn, also had to adapt to circumstances of contact and access that were not ideal. By this line, the clients had to trust that lawyers were attempting to work 'in their best interests'.

On the issue of behaviour, then, lawyers from all firms presented an image of a healthy lawyer–client relationship. They discussed the importance of good contact and access arrangements in demonstrating respect for clients. Lawyers identified problems in maintaining these arrangements but professed the intention of overcoming them as best they could. In the following section, I present data from the participation observation that paints a rather different picture.

* * *

SECTION 2 – WHAT I SAW ON BEHAVIOUR

This section complements the interview data with material from the participant observation, documenting the behaviour of lawyers and how they interacted with clients. Following these lawyers revealed that, in the realm of contact and access, they behaved disrespectfully towards their clients, suggestive of a strained lawyer–client relationship. Their approach appears to impact adversely on the treatment clients received.

At this stage, the activity of these lawyers is detailed without recourse to critique. Instead, specific situations and statements are presented to demonstrate their everyday doings. This data is structured into the following three areas:

1. *Organisation* – the manner in which firms were premised upon discontinuous representation.
2. *Continuity* – the effect this had on consistency of representation.
3. *Time* – the concomitant impact on when and for how long clients were seen.

Organisation

The three firms studied were all centred on the organisational practice of discontinuous representation, which entailed clients being habitually dispersed between lawyers as and when it worked to the lawyers' convenience. This was established in the weekly diary meetings. In these, several lawyers gathered together to tally the clients who were due to appear (at court, police station or for interview) plus courts and duty slots which had to be covered with the lawyers who were free and/or inclined to take them on. Allocation was most frequently determined by ensuring that each lawyer had an even spread of duties; less so by whose expertise might best suit the client's needs and less still by which lawyer had dealt with a client previously. This process can be appreciated from the following brief excerpt of a routine meeting:

> [Lawyer One] Right, we've got a trial on Tuesday. Brett Lee [client], assault. Audrey, do you fancy doing that?
>
> [Lawyer Two] Yeah, sure, I don't mind.
>
> [Lawyer One] Okay. Now, Laura – Youth Court?
>
> [Lawyer Three] That's alright. As long as there isn't too much, I need to go early. I put it down as half-day.
>
> [Lawyer One] There isn't much in, to be honest.
>
> [Lawyer Three] That's fine then.
>
> [Lawyer One] Great. Now, if I put Nadine [partner] down for the list. Audrey, if your trial goes short, will you be able to help Nadine?
>
> [Lawyer Two] Yeah, sure.
>
> [Lawyer One] Right, so that's Tuesday. Wednesday, how about the list?
>
> [Lawyer Two] If my trial is short and I help Nadine then do it, that's three days in a row. I don't really want to do that.
>
> [Lawyer One] Okay.
>
> [Lawyer Two] I mean, if I need to then I will, I was just saying that I'd prefer not to.
>
> [Lawyer One] No, that's okay. I could put you down for police stations?
>
> [Lawyer Two] That's great.
>
> (Ed, senior partner, Audrey and Laura, solicitors, *Swining MacSage*, OR)

Despite such forward planning, lawyers routinely picked up case files on the afternoon before or the morning of their having to deal with the client. Moreover, any notion of planned scheduling was regularly thrown out of the window, as lawyers exchanged cases with one another at court, for reasons of pragmatism and expediency. Above all else, lawyers sought to work through lists of clients as quickly as possible. A flavour of this is provided in the following exchanges at the Magistrates' Court:

> [Lawyer One] Right, so that's four overnights [Court Two], two in [Court] Three, then there's a couple in breaches [Court Eight], one in [Court] Six and in [Court] Seven. What do you fancy?

[Lawyer Two] I don't mind. Whatever's best for you?

[Lawyer One] Well, it makes sense if someone takes [Courts] Two and Three.

[Lawyer Two] I can do that.

[Lawyer One] Are you sure?

[Lawyer Two] Yep, that'll be alright. Which are they?

[Lawyer One] These ones. If I take the rest, and come find you when I'm done – these shouldn't take that long. Are you sure you're okay with all of those?

[Lawyer One] Yep.

(Catherine and Leland, solicitors, *Radford Hope*, OR – they brought a large pile of files, found out which court each was in from reception then divided them up in the foyer)

[Lawyer One] I am busy, if you're going to ask. Want to take something off me?

[Lawyer Two] That busy? Oh! God. I guess I could if you need me too it's just I'm snowed under myself.

[Lawyer One] I've asked Ben [partner] if he can come down to help. I've got far too much going on.

[Lawyer Two] What's Teresa [solicitor] doing?

[Lawyer One] She's stuck in a trial. If it's still going ahead.

[Lawyer Two] I mean, I've only seen one of my overnights, I've still got to see the other two. But it's not like I'm going to be here forever.

[Lawyer One] No, it's okay. I'll palm some off on Ben. In the meantime, I've got to go and see some of these.

(Leo, senior partner, and Ronette, solicitor, *Radcliffe and Musk*, OR – running into each other at court)

These lawyers, then, offered clients a fragmented service as standard. In the previous section, lawyers identified this approach as functioning to the detriment of the lawyer–client relationship in two key ways: consistency and time.

Consistency

Clients would see several lawyers over the course of their case. Lawyers from all firms accepted this as standard, and it was expected that the clients should as well. This can be seen in the following quote:

> We make it clear in the initial letters we send out that the client cannot expect to be represented by the same solicitor every time. It's just not realistic. We have to manage expectations because some of them come in thinking they should be able to see the same solicitor.
>
> (Ed, senior partner, *Swining MacSage*, IC)

It was said that 'regular clients' also accepted this approach. The following lawyers attested to this:

> Some of the older ones, who haven't been in a while, don't understand. They expect personal service. But most of those who are in here regularly understand; they just accept it, it's just how we do things these days.
>
> (Leo, senior partner, *Radcliffe and Musk*, IC)

> I popped in to try and settle him down, but obviously I can't reassure him that someone who picked up his file the day of the trial is going to do the best job they could. Because they're just not. But I tried to explain to him that we're professionals and that's our job. We're used to picking up cases and then getting straight on with them. I told him that I had to go to the Magistrates' Court now and deal with a bunch of clients who I'd never met before. It's just what we do; we're used to it. Most clients are used to it. But I can see why a person who doesn't know the law might not be overly convinced by that.
>
> (Teresa, solicitor, *Radcliffe and Musk*, IC – at the Crown Court. The client had an anxiety disorder)

However, some clients did complain. The following exchanges – involving clients meeting lawyers for the first time in the Magistrates' Court cells, several hearings into their case – demonstrate such discontent:

> [Client] I was telling the last solicitor that, and the one before.
>
> [Lawyer] I know. But you have to listen to me now.
>
> [Client] You're missing the point. I've had so many solicitors. I get sick of having a different solicitor every time.
>
> [Lawyer] Alright. But that's how it works.
>
> [Client] Look, don't take this the wrong way but I don't know who you are and I still don't know what you're doing here. Who the fuck are you?
>
> (Rene Farrell, client, and Teresa, solicitor, *Radcliffe and Musk*, OR)

> [Lawyer] My name is Audrey, have we met before?
>
> [Client] No.
>
> [Lawyer] Why are you in today?
>
> [Client] Where's my, are you a solicitor?
>
> [Lawyer] Yeah.
>
> [Client] I thought there was gonna be *Swining MacSage*?
>
> [Lawyer] Okay. So tell me about your case.
>
> [Client] Are you from *Swining MacSage*?
>
> [Lawyer] Yes.
>
> [Client] But you don't know what I'm in for?
>
> [Lawyer] I haven't, couldn't read the papers.
>
> [Client] The solicitor I had at the police station said she'd tell them.
>
> [Lawyer] Who dealt with you at the police station?
>
> [Client] Charlie [police station clerk]. Where's my normal solicitor?
>
> [Lawyer] Who's your normal solicitor?
>
> [Client] He's got glasses.
>
> [Lawyer] Thomas [solicitor]?

[Client] Yeah. Where is he?

[Lawyer] I don't know. Why?

[Client] He helped me last time and I'd rather him.

(Audrey, solicitor, and Mark Waugh, client, *Swining MacSage*, OR)

Though some clients questioned the lack of consistency, most lawyers were able to placate them with ease, as shown in these extracts:

[Client] Have you actually read my file?

[Lawyer] Not personally, no. My colleague has though.

[Client] Okay.

(Cameron White, client, and Leland, solicitor, *Radford Hope*, OR)

[Client] Will you meet us here next time?

[Lawyer] Well, you might not see me. We don't work like that. You'll see whoever is free. We don't give personal service. No one does.

[Client] Oh, that's a shame but okay.

(Bob Massie, client, and Ed, senior partner, *Swining MacSage*, OR)

This inconsistency of representation went hand-in-hand with the lack of time lawyers afforded to clients.

Time

Most lawyers felt that they did not have the time to devote to clients. Across the firms, the consensus appeared to be that the lawyers' time was their own – thus, precious – and that clients wasted it. Many lawyers were adamant that clients should be made to wait until it suited them, as the following quotes reveal:

What, does he think I have nothing else to do apart from deal with him? I'll see him when I'm ready.

(Harold, partner, *Radford Hope*, IC)

Oh, let him wait. He usually keeps us waiting, anyway.

(Leo, senior partner, *Radcliffe and Musk*, IC)

I'm not going to wait around for them to turn up. Can't be bothered. I'm going back to the office.

(Laura, solicitor, *Swining MacSage*, IC – at the Magistrates' Court around eleven o'clock in the morning)

A large number of lawyers also displayed a preoccupation with time in regard to the amount they were willing to spend with clients, once they had decided to see them. Lawyers from Radical and Sausage Factory firms alike begrudged devoting more time to clients than judged to be strictly necessary. Clients frequently wanted more time than lawyers would accept, as shown by these examples in which lawyers bemoaned the demands of clients:

> I could do without this today. I could do without all the tears and sob stories. You always get that with benefit fraud; they always have all these excuses, it drags on and on. They can never just accept that what they've done is a criminal offence and get on with it. I just want to tell them to hurry up!
>
> (Maddie, police station clerk, *Radcliffe and Musk*, IC)

> [Lawyer One] He got 12 months.
>
> [Lawyer Two] Good, I'm pleased for you. He's been a headache hasn't he? Real drain on your time.
>
> [Lawyer One] At least there won't be any more phone calls for a while! I can relax now. No more excuses to think up [to avoid dealing with him]!
>
> (Dick and Thomas, partners, *Swining MacSage*, OR)

Clients were often aware of the lack of time devoted to them and would sometimes complain, as exemplified by the following:

> [Client] Where have you been?
>
> [Lawyer] Where have *you* been; been so quiet lately!
>
> [Client] No, not that. Where have you been all morning. *Radcliffe* have chosen the worst possible day to slack off. You're usually on the ball. But it's 11.50 and you've only just come to see me. You've lost it *Radcliffe*.
>
> (Ed Manua, client, and Ronette, solicitor, *Radcliffe and Musk*, OR – in the Magistrates' Court cells)

> [Client] Right, I want to talk about what happened.
>
> [Lawyer] We can talk about that again. Let's just get today done first.
>
> [Client] You never have time to talk to me. Always fob me off. Last one was the same.
>
> [Lawyer] There's just no need yet. We will send you a letter.
>
> [Client] Always say the same thing!
>
> (Kris Britt, client, and Shelly, solicitor, *Radcliffe and Musk*, OR)

Again, though, lawyers were usually able to pacify clients.

Despite this, it should be apparent that this organisational practice meant contact and access did not work for the clients. This demonstrated the lawyers' disrespect towards their clients, a stance encapsulated by one solicitor, Audrey, *Swining MacSage*, and her reaction to a client concerned that she did not know his case. Audrey had not met the client before encountering him at the Magistrates' Court, and had told him that she had not read his case and was too busy to spend much time with him prior to his first appearance. The client appeared scared:

> [Client] Can't I speak to someone from the office? Sending someone who doesn't know anything about me, about my case! Where's Dick [solicitor]? Can't you ring the office? Can't you get someone that I know?
>
> [Lawyer] I shall go and find out where Dick is because, to be honest, I'd rather him have to deal with you, anyway.
>
> [Client] To be honest, it looks like you don't even care about my case.
>
> [Lawyer] Excuse me! You don't know how good I am or not.

> [Client] But you know nothing about my case? Tell me I could go back to prison but you don't know my case? I want my solicitor, knows my case. Why did they send you, you know nothing about me?
>
> [Lawyer] Well, that's not my fault is it?
>
> (Michael Clarke, client, and Audrey, solicitor, *Swining MacSage*, OR)

Audrey grew increasingly frustrated as the client continued to complain, eventually raising her hand to indicate she was not listening. After around three minutes of silence, the client left. Audrey drew a long breath before commenting:

> What an arse. I'm not going to deal with him, he'll just criticise me. I can't be arsed with people like that. I hate people like that, it really upsets my day.
>
> (Audrey, solicitor, *Swining MacSage*, IC)

This approach to contact and access should be recognised as emblematic of that taken by lawyers throughout the participant observation. Most lawyers were irritated by clients who wanted better treatment than they were receiving so acted in a manner that suggested clients got what they deserved, even though that was far from ideal.

When it came to contact and access, lawyers from all firms behaved disrespectfully towards their clients. They accepted organisational practices that precipitated ill-treatment of clients, expecting clients to accept them as well. As such, this participant observation data has provided a contrast to the formal interviews on the issue of behaviour in the lawyer–client relationship. This is addressed in the next section.

* * *

SECTION 3 – BEHAVIOUR

As with attitudes, the issue of behaviour has entailed the presentation of two competing narratives. While addressing the management of contact and access, lawyers in Radical and Sausage Factory firms alike used the formal interviews to claim their acting with respect towards clients. The participant observation, though, suggested quite the opposite, as they were shown acting disrespectfully. In this discussion, both positions are drawn together into a more engaged analysis, raising the question: how were clients actually treated?

I begin by reflecting on the gap between what was said in the interview and shown in the participant observation. This is presented as the difference between lawyers claiming to react to external pressures and appearing to act of their own accord. Whatever the cause, it is thereafter suggested that the effect was the same: lawyers were engaged in a volume business. As a result, I claim that clients were dehumanised. Looking at contact and access, then, ultimately revealed lawyers treating clients with disrespect bordering on contempt. I suggest that this undermines the health of the lawyer–client relationship.

Action and Reaction

The formal interviews and participant observation provided competing accounts of behaviour. When the lawyers talked of respecting clients in the former, they perpetuated a discourse that any difficulties in this regard reflected unfortunate but necessary reactions to external pressures. In the latter, though, the disrespect they displayed made it seem that, to some extent, lawyers were acting of their own volition. When addressing the issue of behaviour and how lawyers used the organisational practice of discontinuous representation to manage contact and access, it is important to acknowledge the balance between action and reaction to legal aid remuneration.

In the formal interviews, lawyers from all firms presented a united front that they were reacting to external pressures, with a clear majority of 30 out of 35 taking such a position. The most significant of these threats was expressed as that pertaining to legal aid remuneration. Lawyers framed their behaviour within the attempts of successive governments to curb the criminal legal aid budget. This was an expenditure that, then Justice Secretary, Jack Straw (1999) had infamously condemned as extravagant, claiming it to be the largest in the world. These lawyers had witnessed various reforms introduced to restrict their remuneration, including fixed fees, contracting and tendering proposals. This amounted to what Cape (cited in House of Commons Constitutional Affairs Committee, 2007: 22) labels a 'revolution' in funding: 'something which has such potential for destruction of the legal aid profession'.

Some lawyers in my study believed that this destruction was the ultimate objective of the government, others that the government simply held no regard for the lawyers or their role. Accordingly, lawyers argued that it was not they, but the public and the government who really disrespected their clients. This was articulated by James, senior partner, from *Radford Hope*:

> The problem is that politicians don't see any votes in the work we do. I think, for that reason, they are entirely unsympathetic; they are only interested in whether they get votes. The public just look upon it as 'the criminal classes' and not 'us'. I think, generally, people don't understand how deprived many of the clients we deal with are, how they have missed out on education, how they have been inveigled into drug use or how they just function on a level that many people wouldn't recognise as normal . . . Nobody really recognises the tremendous worth of what we do and the need for someone to help such people.
>
> (James, senior partner, *Radford Hope*, INT)

Many of these lawyers duly forwarded the line that no one cared about criminals, locating legally aided criminal defence as the 'least loved branch of the welfare state' (Freeland, 2006). This can be seen in the following quotes from within both Sausage

Factory and Radical firms:

> I'm not sure where the legal aid situation leaves clients. I'm not sure that the government know and I'm not sure that the government cares, frankly. The deterioration is very much long term. There has been no new money that has been introduced. There doesn't appear to be any political will to put money into the system or, indeed, to maintain the status quo and most people don't understand the role that we play within the democratic society. That is, until they are arrested and suddenly screaming for help. That's where we come in and make the difference. We do it because no one else would.
>
> (Garland, partner, *Sosford and Banger*, INT)

> The government can't care about these people otherwise they wouldn't continually erode legal aid rates. There's been no increase in the rates for years. And you wonder what value government puts on it. Clearly not very highly because they've been totally cynical, and I don't think that the type of people getting criminal defence are really at the top of the list for government. They're not going to vote, they're lower end of society, criminals. The government couldn't case less about them . . . What we do is important because we help them whoever they are, it doesn't matter what thanks we get; it's our duty.
>
> (Gordon, solicitor, *Radford Hope*, INT)

The impression many lawyers sought to convey – that they stood up for clients and gave them the respect others denied them – amounted to positioning themselves as akin to heroes. These lawyers, then, appeared to take on a thankless task, helping those who had been left behind by the rest of society, and all for little more than their own sense of duty to a cause they knew was right. They seemed little short of martyrs.

The participant observation revealed this to be a fiction, with lawyers appearing to treat clients no differently from the stance they so criticised in the general public and government. Clients were pushed from pillar to post and rushed through the system as criminals who no one should or did care about. This was evident from the discussions that took place in the offices of these firms before leaving for court in the morning. Most lawyers appeared to see clients as a burden, and were more interested in the way that dealing with large numbers was a personal inconvenience and gave them more to do rather than any impact it might have on the service clients received. This can be seen in the following exchange in the office one morning, where the lawyer's prime concern was that he might have to suffer a long day in court:

> [Lawyer One] Thomas [partner] is in Crown Court with that? I thought it was Magistrates?'
>
> [Lawyer Two] That means we've got no one doing the list then. Thomas was down to do [Courts] One and Three.
>
> [Lawyer One] You're doing overnights?
>
> [Lawyer Two] I'm doing overnights. I've got three so far.
>
> [Lawyer One] So, I'm in [Courts] One, Two and Three.
>
> [Lawyer Two] You're in [Courts] One, Three and Youth Court now.
>
> [Lawyer One] For fuck's sake. Can you go and ask him how long he's going to be? I've got

> to finish this dictation off. I don't like this going off to Crown Court business, leaving everybody else in the shit. What a fucking day I'm going to have now. And I have that mad woman. I'm going to have a shit day today, be stuck there all afternoon. Selfish.
>
> (Dick, partner, and Nadine, partner, *Swining MacSage*, OR)

In interview, most lawyers claimed it was the external pressures borne of restricted remuneration that pushed them into behaving this way – while their behaviour was not ideal, nor was the reality they faced. They simply saw 'no money' in legally aided criminal defence. In order to sustain themselves, many lawyers insisted that that they were forced to compromise their behaviour; discontinuous representation was a necessity to survive. This was reflected in comments such as these:

> You should go through the unused material, chase witnesses up, go the extra mile for the client. But you don't. You realise that you can't do that. At the end of the day, every case has to be about trying to make a profit.
>
> (Ed, senior partner, *Swining MacSage*, INT)

> The way in which my approach has changed is perhaps of interest. I trained at a firm, which you would describe as client-centred and in the early years my first thoughts were always with the case and how it should be dealt with. The question of costs was almost secondary. The position now is that the first question that crosses my mind is: 'How do we get paid for this?' – a sad reflection on the legal aid system.
>
> (Leo, solicitor, *Radcliffe and Musk*, EM)

> Your idealism does take a bit of a hit over the years. It's got to be run now like a business to survive.
>
> (Catherine, solicitor, *Radford Hope*, INT)

In their earlier research, Sommerlad and Wall (1999) present similar findings. The lawyers in that study discuss the need to 'cut corners', which the authors attribute to the encroachment of New Public Management (41–59). The topic of New Public Management represents a long-held interest for Sommerlad (1999), and she has raised concerns that its importation into legally aided criminal defence is changing the character (and diminishing the quality) of representation. The term was coined by Hood (1991) to capture an increasingly consumerist rhetoric in public service provision. It reflects the wave of public sector reforms, implemented since the 1980s, intended to bring greater cost efficiencies for governments. This approach gives governments greater authority to dictate output thus increasing the predictability of budgeting. A ready example of this process is provided by the contracting regime that the New Labour Government introduced to criminal legal aid (Hynes and Robins, 2009: 108–11).

New Public Management, though, has been criticised. Several ways in which public organisations differ from the private sector are outlined by Boston et al (1996: 37–38), including the breadth of their impact, complexity of objectives and evaluation criteria. Such reform tends to ignore these differences. Under New Public Management, individuals are no longer 'citizens' but 'customers' (Osborne and Gaebler, 1996: 579–80). Customers appear 'a means to an end', a necessary stage in the pursuit of profit. It is for this reason that Marquand (2001) implicates New Public Management within a general climate of 'mean-spirited rhetoric' that increasingly casts doubt on the validity of the 'service' element in public services. The moniker customer, applied to lawyers' clients, is problematised by Berlins (2009), who suggests that it put these services on a par with the trivialities of buying a television or a fridge rather than seeking expert professional advice on significant life choices. This, in turn, reflects the concerns of Hoggett (1996: 26–28) that these reforms actually ignored the individual in favour of a fictive universalism, working to provide a justification for an increased intensification of labour practices. As this process subsumes the provision of legal aid, Sommerlad (2001: 359–60) highlights its essentially 'degrading' character for lawyers. The only way for practice to continue is through discontinuous representation, so the service that can be provided is not that which lawyers want to supply.

However, the situation witnessed in the participant observation contrasted somewhat with this depiction. Notably, lawyers did not provide any discernable sense of regret at behaving in the manner they did; rather they appeared to embrace it. This can be seen from the way that a *Swining MacSage* partner, Thomas, reacted to a client phoning him at the office. The client was worried about a letter he had received pertaining to his case that morning. Thomas told him that he was just about to leave for court, when in reality he spent the following half an hour sitting at his desk, largely making chitchat. Thomas saw this as legitimate, commenting:

> Oh God, I've dealt with him for a full two and a half years. He's just this nervous, worried guy; always concerned about something. He just phones up and wants to talk about his case. He's a right pain. Trying to fit him into your working day; such a waste of your time. He just wants to talk about his case. I have to think of all kinds of excuses.
>
> (Thomas, partner, *Swining MacSage*, IC)

Not only did lawyers fail to show regret; in some situations they were positively celebratory at the manner in which they benefited at their clients expense. Consider, for example, *Radcliffe and Musk's* senior partner, Leo, thinking aloud on viewing a television programme that flashed breaking news about a House of Lords ruling:

> Ohh, now that's very interesting. And I'm just thinking of the benefits financially here, not what's good for the client. But, being totally mercenary, we stand to make a nice little earning from that. We have the fee from the first trial, the second trial has already begun and, if they cancel that, then we still get the fee. Then, if they want to start again, that's another fee. And we're talking a not inconsiderable amount of money here. Come on Mr [Jack] Straw, bring on the law change! No, it's not great for the client, he will have to wait even longer, and it might, thinking about it, mean Ben [partner] can't represent him, so he'll have to see somebody else, but there you go.
>
> (Leo, senior partner, *Radcliffe and Musk*, IC)

In their managing contact and access through discontinuous representation, lawyers presented a clear disregard for their clients and, as such, there is a need to regard with scepticism their claims in interview that they were merely reacting to external pressures. It is important to confront the possibility that these lawyers – at least to some extent – chose to behave as they did. This reflects the position taken by McConville et al (1994: 294–98) who posit such behaviour as primarily a matter of values. The prevalence of discontinuous representation appals McConville et al (1994: 271) who offer the conclusion that:

> What is clear is that it is not merely a question of the economic determinants of practice under legal aid, nor of the sheer volume of the casework . . . non-economic factors are of at least equal importance in determining the generally poor quality of criminal defence work.

Perhaps, rather than being pushed into discontinuous representation to sustain themselves, lawyers were willingly pulled towards these practices to maximise their profits. In the previous chapter, it was suggested that an element of greed might exist for lawyers who were so focused on their finances and eager for more than they – or the average Britain – received. This might well be found in their disregarding basic client care in this manner.

For Thomas and Mungham (1983: 147–49), lawyers are fundamentally motivated by self-interest. In their research, they highlight lawyers concerned with potential economic discomfort – specifically, the ending of the conveyancing monopoly – striving to manage contact and access in a manner that maximised their financial reward. Lawyers achieved this by the introduction of the duty solicitor scheme. In an attempt at generating a positive public image, this was spun as a means of improving the service the client received as they had greater access to lawyers. Its management, though, created opportunities for lawyers with little experience of – or interest in – criminal defence to *milk the system*. It was intended as a guaranteed wage earner, and this came before any consideration of what was best for the clients.

With this in mind, it is important to recognise that lawyers used discontinuous representation to manage contact and access long before the present study was conducted. Indeed, the Widgery Report (Departmental Committee on Legal Aid in Criminal Proceedings, 1966: 81–82) had raised this concern in the 1960s:

> There is a widespread feeling among prisoners that the standard of legal aid provided is inferior to that available to persons who pay for their own defence . . . not given a proper chance to instruct their legal representatives and that the opportunity to consult their legal representative was confined to a few minutes in the court precincts before their case came up . . . neglect to prepare their cases properly . . . find themselves being represented by a member of the Bar whom they had not expected.

The research undertaken by McConville et al (1994) was conducted over two decades later, but discontinuous representation is every bit as insidious in their report. The lawyers I observed no doubt had genuine concerns about contemporary developments including fixed fees, contracting and the prospect of Best Value Tendering. However, the literature shows that lawyers have acted in this manner even when these were not considerations. This makes a mockery of some lawyer complaints that they had been forced to change their practices, and of their harking back to halcyon days of yore when they were free to act how they chose:

> I remember the lovely old days. One of the constant complaints clients have, and that people are now getting used to, is prison visits of course, that is a biggie. There was a time when we could afford the luxury of, not doing social calls, but regular prison visits. Nowadays, we have to tell them I am only coming up the once and, at that one meeting, we'll go through everything. There is less face-to-face contact; you have to write letters to them all the time telling them what you are doing, most of which are either never read or can't be read because they can't read. So, yes, there is a big difference in client contact.
>
> (Mike, senior partner, *Radison and Muddle*, INT)

> In those days, criminal defence was a very different world. For a start, you got paid for what you did, which was good because it meant that those that worked very hard and did a good job got paid more. There is no question that the quality of service is diminishing year on year and will continue to diminish while the government continue to put more pressures on us. Even if they were to stop putting pressures on tomorrow, you wouldn't go back uphill again. I can't see us ever going back to the way we were.
>
> (Harold, partner, *Radford Hope*, INT)

Whatever the financial circumstances, it seems that lawyers have frequently offered excuses as to why they acted in ways that deviated from the ideal. So it was in this research. What bolsters the conclusion that these are excuses rather than explanations is the fact that firms have always been, and still are, provided ample opportunities from which to make a profit. During my fieldwork period, the government claimed that legal aid firms could still make a profit under fixed fees despite the reforms, citing that remuneration was reasonable on a 'swings and roundabouts' basis (Ministry of Justice, 2009: 14). It was suggested that lawyers would be paid better in some cases and worse in others, with the overall effect being cost neutrality. Consistent with this, my research appeared to produce numerous examples of occasions on which lawyers could benefit from the current system of remuneration without compromising their behaviour.

There were various means to achieve this in the Magistrates' Court. For example, a particular tactic of Leo, senior partner from *Radcliffe and Musk*, involved clients, already on curfew orders, brought into the cells for new offences. He would find out if there had been a breach and then get clients to fill out two sets of legal aid forms – for the new offence and breach proceedings – before preparing for the sentencing hearing as if there had been no breach. Breaches were charged by a private security firm, not the Crown Prosecution Service. Leo hoped the breach would not appear on the computer system in time for the sentencing, but turn up later, ensuring that they were not prosecuted together and the second fee could be claimed. This activity has been labelled as 'case-splitting' (Gray et al, 1996: 277–78). Leo often joked about his propensity to use this tactic, as in the following:

> Somewhere in the system will be breach proceedings. Get that second fee! 'Whoops, I didn't realise'. Keep quiet, get the fee!
>
> (Leo, senior partner, *Radcliffe and Musk*, IC)

> There are no breach proceedings. What a shame. I feel cheated! I should have a word with her; get those breaches done quicker!
>
> (Leo, senior partner, *Radcliffe and Musk*, IC)

> Oh, I did well yesterday, had a few new ones come into the cells. I got them sorted and billed. I must have made around £1200. Not bad at all. There should be some breaches coming up in the system too!
>
> (Leo, senior partner, *Radcliffe and Musk*, OR – to a colleague)

Another technique some lawyers used was when appointed by the court to cross-examine a witness in a trial, usually for domestic violence. They were paid from Central Funds, by the hour and at private rates. A solicitor, Shelly, *Radcliffe and Musk*, explained how they were able to spend longer than necessary on such cases:

> The partners are putting loads of pressure on me to do more on it. The view is that if they're going to grant us these things we should make the most of it. Which is fine, from a partner's point of view, they obviously want to make as much money from it as possible. But, then, I actually have to do it. It's making work for myself just to claim it back which I'm not sure I'm entirely comfortable with. I've been in court and seen other solicitors – from the firm you are going to next [*Swining MacSage*] – sit in court all day when they're only paid by the court for cross-examination. That's £195 an hour, private fees.
>
> (Shelly, solicitor, *Radcliffe and Musk*, IC)

She told me that she didn't like doing it but did it all the same, and it was not only that other firm which routinely practised the tactic – the others lawyers from her firm did too. A similar approach was often taken with duty solicitor slots, across the firms; lawyers were able to see their own clients but claim the higher, hourly, fees provided for duty cases. One partner in the study was notorious for using this time to write his crime thriller novels. At first, I had assumed he was incredibly diligent – writing reams of notes, reading and re-reading what he had written with great care and attention. I felt a little let down when I realised that he had been stealing every spare moment proofing his manuscripts (he was on his third book in a year).

There were numerous other examples of lawyers 'getting lucky' that were not so habitual, as in one case where Leo, senior partner, *Radcliffe and Musk*, inadvertently became embroiled in a Newton hearing (a 'mini-trial' in which the judge decides whether to allow a guilty plea on a different factual basis) as duty solicitor. The magistrates retired, and Leo came to the back of the court, annoyed, and told me:

> I wish I'd have known that was going to happen. You can't do trials as duty. I'd have got legal aid. Bollocks. That's £350 down the drain. That's ruined my week. I'm really disappointed with myself. I should have seen it coming. Actually, I suppose I could do it now [winks].
>
> (Leo, senior partner, *Radcliffe and Musk*, IC)

Leo explained the situation to the clerk:

> [Lawyer] I've just realised I can't do trials as duty. You'll have to grant me legal aid.
>
> [Clerk] I'm going to tell!

[Lawyer] Oh please, if I'd have realised I'd have said. It'll be alright.

(Leo, senior partner, *Radcliffe and Musk*, and John Wyndham, Magistrates' clerk, OR)

Having been granted legal aid, Leo jubilantly took his form to the legal aid office:

> They made the bloody stupid regulations. As far as I'm concerned, I'll take advantage of them all day. Lovely!
>
> (Leo, senior partner, *Radcliffe and Musk*, IC)

He later discussed it with Hank, the senior partner of another firm, *Radder Try*:

> [Lawyer One] I had a very nice little costs victory just now. In the middle of the case, I hand him the form and said: 'Can you just do a legal aid?' – yes. Very nice indeed.
>
> [Lawyer Two] You've got to make the most of the opportunities.
>
> [Lawyer One] Thankfully it was a reasonable clerk, a pleasant clerk. Could easily have said: 'Bugger off'. I'm pleased with that though.
>
> (Leo, senior partner, *Radcliffe and Musk*, and Hank, senior partner, *Radder Try*, OR)

Fixed fees also presented advantageous situations to firms in police station work, as shown in the following discussion:

> [Lawyer One] At the moment, it's not too bad. Because I've got a lot of files that we've only done 30 minutes' worth of work on and we've got £206 [full amount] for. I've only had one where we've gone over so far, up at £400, all the rest have gone below. So we're doing well from it.
>
> [Lawyer Two] It is swings and roundabouts.
>
> [Lawyer Three] Quick jobs are the best things. When they say they're ready for a quick interview. Loads of shopliftings. All you need is a load of shoplifters. Everyone's going to be fighting over the shoplifters rather than the murderers soon.
>
> (Dave, police station clerk, Norma and Bob, solicitors, *Radford Hope*, OR)

This discussion, then, gives some credence to the government's argument that fixed fees do not necessarily decrease lawyer remuneration, but rather it was an example of swings and roundabouts.

Overall, lawyers did appear to be confronted with an increasingly fragile economic situation. As such, they were reacting to external pressure. However, this does not justify their treating clients with such disrespect. It seems that lawyers were provided with the opportunity to make back some of the money they claimed to lose out on in other ways. They were able to do this in areas that did not impact upon their behaviour towards clients. This suggests that lawyers wanted to act in this manner.

Ultimately, my data does not allow me to reach a definitive conclusion on the impact that economics had on the performance of these lawyers – I did not see pay packets or accounts. Short of that, though, I would opine that the claims of compulsion that these lawyers made in interview should be taken with a pinch of salt and their rationale considered somewhat questionable.

Volume

Whether action or reaction, the effect of these lawyers' relationship with legal aid remuneration was the same; all three firms utilised the organisational practice of discontinuous representation to constitute themselves as volume businesses. The participant observation showed that each firm – *Radford Hope, Radcliffe and Musk* and *Swining MacSage* – provided a lack of consistency in representation and time for clients in a manner which facilitated the representation of a larger number of clients in a quicker period than might otherwise be possible.

This research was established upon a hypothetical dichotomy between Radical and Sausage Factory firms, taken to represent, respectively, client-centred and profit-centred approaches to practice. One of the key aspects of this characterisation was that Radical firms put their clients first – providing consistency and ample time – while Sausage Factories pay no heed to these considerations as they prioritised profits – using discontinuous representation to chase ever greater volume. In selecting firms for this research, I had hoped to establish firms from either side of this divide. It should now be clear that, once in the field, there was little means of readily discriminating between the firms in this manner. All exhibited a factory approach, as evinced by quotes such as the following:

> Compared to how it used to be, it's like a factory these days. You don't spend that much time with people, just deal with them as quickly as possible, rush it all through.
>
> (Nadine, partner, *Swining MacSage*, INT)

> We can only survive by taking a factory approach, and I think the quality will go. We just churn out case after case.
>
> (Catherine, solicitor, *Radford Hope*, INT)

> Is it a factory now? Yes, yes, yes, yes, yes!
>
> (Bobby, partner, *Sosig and Sage*, INT)

However, while achieving the same ends, the particular makeup of each varied. The firm most obviously manifesting volume concerns was *Swining MacSage*, as would be expected from the institution designated as the representative Sausage Factory. So it was that, senior partner, Ed could sum up the philosophy of the firm thus:

> There's no room for idealism in the job, business imperatives get in the way.
>
> (Ed, senior partner, *Swining MacSage*, IC)

Swining MacSage was the largest firm and sent the greatest number of lawyers to the Magistrates' Court, where they also had the longest client lists. Lawyers tended to be assigned to clear particular courts each day. As well as the Magistrates' Court work, though, *Swining MacSage* was the only firm to have delineated their practice into three distinct departments, with one dedicated exclusively to Crown Court matters and another to police station calls. In achieving this, they utilised the largest amount of unqualified clerks. Accordingly, *Swining MacSage* was widely regarded as the most efficient practice, viewed admiringly by administrative personnel and partners at both *Radford Hope* and *Radcliffe and Musk* for their appearance as a fully functioning business entity. This was reflected in the following quotes:

> You're going to see how a firm should be run; a business. You come back and tell me what it's like. I've heard all kinds of stories. They just get on with things there, in-out, no messing about, and everyone knows what to do. That's how we should be run.
>
> (Harriet, secretary, *Radford Hope*, IC)

> I don't know what to make of them over there – they get through an awful lot of work. I think you're going to notice some real differences in how they deal with clients; they can't hang around. I imagine we'll seem pretty laid back in comparison!
>
> (Leo, senior partner, *Radcliffe and Musk*, IC)

Perhaps the most distinctive feature of *Swining MacSage* was the manner in which they used their demarcated constitution and large lawyer numbers. They allowed the organisational practice of discontinuous representation to be fully institutionalised. It seems that this was the difference that saw them recognised as a 'business'. Ed, senior partner, described the situation:

> We do have more lawyers, and I want to make sure they're used to our advantage. Volume has to take precedence over client continuity. It might be beneficial if the solicitor knows the case. That can definitively save time in getting reacquainted with it over a quick skim through of the morning of the hearing. Although sometimes that doesn't even happen! Often you just pick up a case and get on with it. It doesn't make sense to wait around.
>
> (Ed, senior partner, *Swining MacSage*, IC)

Lawyers, then, worked together and took cases from one another at various stages during the process. However, this did not always lead to harmony within the offices, as in the following example:

> [Lawyer One] Can you take [Court] One for me? I'm going to be stuck with this Closure [Order application].
>
> [Lawyer Two] Laura [solicitor] just gave me her duty to finish off. So I've got that with [Courts] Six, Seven and Eight as well. You'll come over if it finishes early?
>
> [Lawyer One] I don't know how long it will be take.
>
> [Lawyer Two] Great. I've been shafted.
>
> (Thomas and Dick, partners, *Swining MacSage*, OR)

This notion of lawyers taking clients from one another, though, was not restricted to *Swining MacSage*. It also represented the defining feature of *Radcliffe and Musk*, in particular through the lack of antagonism and, rather, their fostering a '**team**' mentality. This was outlined by, senior partner, Leo and can be seen as embodied in, solicitor, Shelly:

> We work as a team. I'm very conscious to put that across.
>
> (Leo, senior partner, *Radcliffe and Musk*, IC)

> Let's go check how the troops are doing. See who needs help.
>
> (Shelly, solicitor, *Radcliffe and Musk*, IC)

Radcliffe and Musk were slightly smaller than *Swining MacSage*. However, they still sent significant numbers to the Magistrates' Court and dealt with only marginally fewer clients. Their teamwork meant that they utilised discontinuous representation, with lawyers helping one another and taking clients from colleagues throughout the working day. Senior partner, Leo acknowledged this situation:

> Regulars are usually fine with the system that we operate . . . the message is: 'You won't always see me, but we work as part of a big team'. Of course, there will always be clients who prefer one solicitor or another but as long as they are aware that we cannot promise that, this overcomes the problem.
>
> (Leo, senior partner, *Radcliffe and Musk*, EM)

There was a second policy that the senior partners attempted to imbue within their lawyers at *Radcliffe Musk*, labelled 'trawling', as can be seen in the following:

> Have you been trawling? I have and picked one up already. Let's go and make sure the rest are on the lookout too.
>
> (Donna, solicitor, *Radcliffe and Musk*, OR – to Leo, senior partner, mid-morning)

> You've seen what I'm like, always on the look out for work. It's not poaching; trawling [laughs].
>
> (Leo, senior partner, *Radcliffe and Musk*, IC)

Radcliffe and Musk, then, also prided themselves on being efficient and maximising their volume of clients as Leo, senior partner, espoused:

> I realised long ago that the only way to make money in this business is by being highly organised and efficient which is something that I always try to instil in my employees, mostly successfully I think. We always keep a very keen eye on the finances.
>
> (Leo, senior partner, *Radcliffe and Musk*, EM)

The other firm in this study, *Radford Hope*, presented something of a contrast to *Swining MacSage* and *Radcliffe and Musk*. They were smaller and sent a lesser proportion of their lawyers to court where, once ensconced, either one or two lawyers were expected to manage a greater share of clients themselves. Lawyers from within and without *Radford Hope* were conscious of this distinction, and the extent to which it left those at court to fend for themselves, as reflected in the following quotes:

> I bet you notice a real difference. It's a team there isn't it [*Radcliffe and Musk*]? Everyone for himself at *Radfords*!
>
> (Leland, solicitor, *Radford Hope*, IC)

> It's totally different here [to *Radford Hope*]. Everyone lends a hand.
>
> (Audrey, solicitor, *Swining MacSage*, IC)

> I look at what they [*Radford Hope*] do, and I just don't understand how they can function as a business. They can't do enough cases with just one or two solicitors at the courts.
>
> (Leo, senior partner, *Radcliffe and Musk*, IC)

Radford Hope did not handle a significantly smaller number of clients than the other firms, though, meaning lawyers felt over-burdened with heavy workloads. This situation was epitomised by the fact that they lost half their lawyers in the year between my pilot study and the research proper. Over the course of the participant observation, a solicitor departed, another went part-time and even the one taken on during this period had left by the time of the formal interviews.

The remaining lawyers did not feel that they had enough staff to handle the number of cases expected of them by senior partner James, who was seen as out of touch as he was rarely at the Magistrates' Court. There was a great deal of discontent at these conditions, as seen in these quotes:

> [Lawyer One] This is a nightmare day; monster of a list and we're duty solicitor and there's only two of us. There are about 15 [cases] and Youth Court and then there's the duty, which will be a nightmare.
>
> [Lawyer Two] This keeps happening more and more.
>
> (Harold, partner, and Norma, solicitor, *Radford Hope*, OR)

> [Lawyer One] I was there until half past six last night. I had 16 cases, most of them sentencing. They were waiting for me to lock up. Then when I got back, the office was locked.
>
> [Lawyer Two] I always take the key these days, just in case. You know what it's like here!
>
> (Catherine and Leland, solicitors, *Radford Hope*, OR)

Radford Hope were characterised as somewhat chaotic within the city's legal community, with some justification. For example, Leland, one of the firm's solicitors, was informed by a prosecutor at court that they had a trial that day. It was due to begin at two o'clock, and Leland found out at a quarter to one. The firm had forgotten to assign the case to anyone in the morning leaving an incredulous Leland around an hour to prepare for a trial:

> Can you believe it? Someone is going to find out they've got a trial this afternoon. This is what happens at *Radfords*. It's chaos here. Can you imagine, though, the client – someone's spent lunch time preparing for his trial? Incredible. I can't wait to read your book! This is what it's like, you couldn't make it up. It'd be funny if it wasn't so bad [laughs]!
>
> (Leland, solicitor, *Radford Hope*, IC)

Though the chaotic approach of *Radford Hope* lacked the finesse of the other firms, it presented similarities in the use of discontinuous representation to achieve volume; the only difference was in the spread of representation. All three firms functioned as, more or less, efficient factories.

Dehumanisation

With these firms characterised as factories it can thus be understood that lawyers in this study offered a standardised service to their clients. Factories use routinised practices – along production lines – to process goods as swiftly as possible. As such, one might conceive of lawyers' clients as consumers of mass-produced goods. This approach was encapsulated in a phrase coined by a *Radford Hope* solicitor, Leland, as he went about his work:

> That wasn't lawyering. That was a numbers game. The point becomes to get through as many clients as quickly as I can. That's how it is now. Access to justice? There is no access to justice! There's no time for access to justice – you're just unable to provide any level of service to the clients. All you focus on is working through it as quickly as possible. The client loses out in the need to get through the list.
>
> (Leland, solicitor, *Radford Hope*, IC)

The 'numbers game' meant that providing continuous representation and sufficient time to each client was not regarded as an option; most lawyers sought to clear client lists with minimum effort. As a result, these lawyers offered a depersonalised service. This approach was antithetical to any notion of client-centeredness, thereon contradicting lawyer claims as expressed in the formal interviews. Moreover, it might be considered to have challenged the professional code of conduct (Lord Chancellor's Department, 2001: 8) that warns against 'excessive caseloads', insisting that if a lawyer 'considers that the acceptance of any further instructions is reasonably likely to lead to inadequate representation of existing clients, he or she shall decline to accept further instructions'. The ideal approach, which lawyers and their professional bodies have seemed keen to perpetuate, at least at the level of rhetoric, locates the interests of the client at the forefront (Mungham and Thomas, 1983: 147–49). It is depicted in numerous practitioner guides such as that offered by Cape (2006b: 7) – widely read among these lawyers – which explains that:

> The client may be in a variety of emotional states which will require an approach that is both empathetic and inspires confidence. Empathy may be demonstrated by being willing to listen to what the client has to say even if it does not appear directly relevant to the issues . . . allow the client the time and the opportunity to express how and what they are feeling.

Perhaps the most expansive on this topic has been *Lawyers as Counsellors* by Binder et al (2004). In this text, they urge lawyers to focus on the client as a holistic entity and not view the legal problem in isolation. From this perspective, the lawyer–client relationship should be conceptualised as counselling; lawyers need to be willing to listen to clients' concerns, but also to move beyond that. Showing sensitivity and warmth, lawyers should make an effort to understand life from the client's perspective. The counselling relationship places great value on 'mutualism' (Burnard, 2005: 130–31). This concept of mutualism draws on Buber (2008: 6–12) and his notion of 'I-Thou' – the manner in which a bond develops between two individuals as they come to know each other on a reasonably equal and, thereon, intimate level. Mutualism represents a closeness that can only be achieved when experiences are pooled, as the counsellor shares their life with the client; working from Jourard's (1971: 14) supposition that, 'disclosure invites or begets disclosure'. The idea of a common humanity, coming together, seems crucial.

One need not go that far, though, to recognise the importance of allowing the time and space for connections to develop between individuals; without it their relationship would likely lack rapport, hindering communication and restricting understanding (Tickle-Dengen and Rosenthal, 1990: 286–87). This perspective has been presented as the 'contact hypothesis', which suggests that interpersonal contact is the only way to construct successful, stable, human relationships (Allport, 1979: 261–82). The ideal approach, then, constitutes the client as a human being. However, the lawyers in this study diverged so sharply from this that their approach to contact and access meant that they behaved in a manner that rather dehumanised their clients. In dehumanisation, the notion of a common humanity is lost and so it was that clients were changed in the objects of a cold and impersonal bureaucracy. Clients became names on a list, cases; they were effectively reduced to the status of their *files*.

Both Tuitt (2005) and Scheffer (2007) also see clients being transformed into files; however, they judge this situation quite differently, viewing it as a positive act of client-centeredness. The file is identified as a form of liberation; recording what clients said gives them a voice, thus treating them with respect. As such, Tuitt (2005: 122) and Scheffer (2007: 60) set themselves up against an apparently mainstream, 'standard indictment' of the legal profession, one that Tuitt (2005: 122) suggests is critical of the ' "clinical" treatment of clients, the tendency for professionals to treat clients like hypothetical problems, like bits of memoranda or like fee notes'. By this line, Scheffer (2007: 60) claims that many academics believe that the 'file-bias degrades the client to the file-appendix . . . all his fears, worries experiences and expertise is reduced to an extension of the file (and not the other way round)'.

Scant evidence of this conventional position is offered, though it is unreservedly dismissed by both as somewhat simplistic and unrefined. Rather, they offer a deeply theoretical take, incorporating insight on areas such as critical theory, constructivism and semeiotics. This creates the absurd – near incomprehensible – situation whereby lawyers are urged to abandon Habermassian inter-subjective universal pragmatics, with their minimalist celebration of direct encounters, for a Latourian distributed agency that conceptualises files as constitutive participants in legal discourse.

In both accounts, the implication was that to disagree with this formulation was to offer oneself up as a Luddite. However, in the light of the research conducted for this study, such convoluted aspirations seem wholly unconvincing. It is ridiculous to suppose that lawyers were considering these dense and obtuse philosophical debates as they dealt with clients. The optimism that these authors find in the conjecture of hypothetical argument appears detached from the practical reality of criminal defence, which it can only serve to obfuscate. As such, I reject their treatment of the file and, rather, must insist that it be seen as a problematic feature of lawyers' behaviour. The manner in which clients were transformed into their files was disrespectful, appearing to restrict their voice. It acted to deny their humanity.

A similar process is documented by Goffman (1991), within certain closed communities such as mental institutions, monasteries and boarding schools. With the exception of those already in prisons, lawyers' clients did not find themselves in the 'total institutions' defined by Goffman (1991: 13–115); however, parallels can be made. For example, Goffman (1991: 18–20) identified a definitive split between a small staff and a managed mass, the former conceiving of the latter largely in stereotypes and, thereon, feeling superior. Further, social mobility between the two strata was restricted with the social distance formally prescribed. Talk across this divide worked to serve the purpose of communicating information between the group below and the higher levels to which the staff, in turn, ceded authority. This situation provided staff with much control over information pertaining to the lives of those on the bottom, details that staff need only disclose selectively.

Dehumanisation is identified as intrinsic to such institutions, necessary to maintain the predictability of order, systematically disseminated and propagated (Goffman, 1991: 24–40). Standardised treatment entails that both action and speech are utilised to undermine individual identity. This process was evident in my participant observation, as clients appeared locked into something of a quasi-institution through their reliance upon lawyers. Clients were made to wait until they were granted an audience, and in the process of doing so were passed from one lawyer to another. When presented with strangers, clients were unaware of how much or how little this lawyer knew of them; regardless, they were expected to disclose information about themselves. However, when they were allowed to talk, it was at the discretion of the lawyer as to when, for how long and the nature of what could be said. Thereafter, clients were, again, kept at a distance as lawyers discussed them with colleagues and court staff, leaving them in a continual state of ignorant dependence.

The clients in this research were no more than the elements of their story which lawyers could use in going about their work; the constituent elements of a speech of mitigation, bail application or evidence-in-chief. Anything more that clients said was deemed superfluous, as evident in the following examples from both types of firm:

> [Lawyer One] Oh, he's disgusting.
>
> [Lawyer Two] He's quite naïve, isn't he?
>
> [Lawyer One] He's a whinger. Whinge, whinge, whinge. Always asking me questions, or moaning about his life. I don't care. Be quiet!
>
> (Audrey, solicitor, and Ed, senior partner, *Swining MacSage*, OR)

> I always tell them to remember the advice I gave them, I don't repeat the advice. Especially if they start to blab, and go on and on. I just want to get out of there.
>
> (Laura, solicitor, *Swining MacSage*, IC)

> Look, I'm in control today. I don't care what the last one did. That's them, this is me. You tell me what you want to know, then I will decide.
>
> (Teresa, solicitor, *Radcliffe and Musk*, OR – to a client)

However, the sheer insidiousness of this dehumanisation is, perhaps, best appreciated by a particularly evocative example. This was one of the most personally unsettling events of the participant observation, and occurred during the first week of research, with *Radford Hope.*

A solicitor, Bob, was in the Magistrates' Court with a list of nine clients. He was also covering the Youth Court, where he had four clients. Early that morning, he saw a client in the Youth Court; a 14-year-old boy, Ricky, appearing for a breach of a supervision order after failing to attend two meetings with his youth worker. Ricky's conviction had been for a non-dwelling burglary; his first offence.

Bob greeted the boy's mother, and led the four of us into an interview room. Mother and son sat down, Bob introduced himself and then me, as his 'colleague'. Before I could interject and explain that I was conducting research, Bob told them that I would be taking their 'instructions'. I looked at Bob in surprise, but he quickly tore two pieces of paper from his pad and told me:

> You'll be alright. Try and fill a couple of sides, take about half an hour, and then come down and find me when you're done. I'll be getting on with this list.
>
> (Bob, solicitor, *Radford Hope*, IC)

Bob promptly left the room.

I did not feel that I had the chance to object, and remain uncertain as to what course I should have followed. I explained to the mother that I was a student, not affiliated with the firm and with neither legal experience nor training. She accepted this, but seemed keen to tell me their story regardless. I set about interviewing them, struggling to think of questions but making enough to fill the paper. This took close to half an hour and I left, assuring them that I would find out what was going on from Bob.

I went to the Magistrates' Court, where Bob was working through his list. He took the paper, but made no mention of Ricky's case. Throughout the morning, Bob repeatedly attempted to get his cases heard in the Youth Court, explaining that:

> I want to get these out of the way quickly. Better things to do [at the Magistrates' Court].
>
> (Bob, solicitor, *Radford Hope*, IC)

However, the Youth Court was busy and Bob was left frustrated.

Bob had to leave the court at lunchtime. So, a little after midday, he made a call to the office, stating that he needed to be 'relieved'. They duly sent Harold, partner, to the court. He arrived 20 minutes before the one o'clock break and told Bob that he would take his Youth Court work from him. I accompanied Harold upstairs, informing him that I had interviewed Ricky, pointing him out in the waiting area. Harold greeted him and his mother and the extent of their conversation was:

Hi, my name's Harold. I'll be dealing with your case now. I have all the information here. Hopefully get you on before lunch. Okay?

(Harold, partner, *Radford Hope*, OR – the client's mother nodded as Harold walked past)

Harold attempted to persuade the court usher to put his cases on, but there was no time and the bench rose. We went to the advocates' room, where solicitors took their lunch and chatted. At around half past one, senior partner James came across to the Magistrates' Court and took Harold aside into an interview room to explain that he had taken the rest of Bob's cases. So, Harold and James set their files out on a table and began the process of splitting the cases between them. This was achieved by reference to which courtrooms the cases were listed in and so, roughly, what type of hearings they entailed. As part of this, James offered to take the Youth Court cases:

[Lawyer One] So. if you're going to take those, why don't I take this Youth Court stuff off you?

[Lawyer Two] Okay.

[Lawyer One] Is there much there?

[Lawyer Two] Oh, nothing much.

[Lawyer One] Have you seen the clients?

[Lawyer Two] Yes, before lunch.

[Lawyer One] Well I'll just say hello then.

(James, senior partner, and Harold, partner, *Radford Hope*, IC)

I elected to stay with James. I explained about Ricky and that I was the only one who had seen him, and pointed out that the notes in the file were my own. James had not met me previously, so I reminded him that I didn't know what I was doing. He looked over the notes and didn't pass comment. By the time he had read through all three of the files he had taken from Harold, it was approaching two o'clock at which time the court was due to restart. So James went out to the waiting area, and introduced himself to the clients as I pointed them out. To Ricky and his mother he simply said:

Hi, I'm James. I'm the senior partner. I'll be taking your case, you'll be on soon. Sorry for the delay.

(James, senior partner, *Radford Hope*, OR)

James duly got the cases on shortly after the bench returned. Ricky's case was adjourned.

The following month, Ricky was back in court for the next hearing and he was dealt with by another solicitor, Norma. On meeting the client, the boy's mother had greeted me with some enthusiasm, and confused Norma by addressing me and not her. I explained to Norma that I had seen Ricky previously and, also, that I had taken the notes. Norma told me that she hadn't recognised the writing when she looked at the file that morning. That was the final hearing for Ricky; he was found to be in breach of his supervision order which was consequently extended.

Over the course of Ricky's two hearings, then, he saw four different lawyers (a fifth solicitor, Catherine, had apparently dealt with his original sentencing) and had his instructions taken by a research student. Bob had known that I was new and had no legal background, as he had been fastidious in getting me to explain my biography to him on the way to court. Despite this, he left me to take notes from this boy. Harold and James had known that the boy had only been seen by me, yet they still did not deem it necessary to talk to him themselves. My amateurish questioning constituted this boy's file as far as the breach was concerned, and had been accepted by Norma.

I was racked with guilt to have become embroiled in these events. This might not have been the most important of cases nor complicated of hearings but, all the same, it involved a confused client implicated within the criminal justice system and totally reliant upon their lawyer. And the lawyers just passed him around as if he didn't matter at all. That any client could be treated in this way is reprehensible, and that it could happen to a child is, in my view, totally unacceptable. The youth courts are characterised, by Bottoms (2002: 217–18), as supposedly more humanitarian than those of adults, concerned with helping defendants rather than punishing them. Lawyers have a somewhat more nuanced – and heightened – role to perform within them: ensuring that justice is done both by protecting the welfare of this most vulnerable class and concomitantly facilitating the smooth running of the court (Williamson, 1980: 40–43). The lawyers' role is premised upon an ability to communicate with a potentially awkward client – a more intense relationship than with an adult defendant.

However, even Ricky, a 14-year-old child, was treated as a file to be passed around as if it were of no consequence. What this example expressed was degradation to the level of an inanimate object. Dehumanisation is Montagu and Matson's (1983: xi) 'fifth horseman of the apocalypse', capable of inestimable levels of damage. When people become things, they become dispensable and any action towards them can be justified. This dehumanisation, then, presents a self-perpetuating cycle as, once clients are no longer individuals, it becomes ever more natural to continue to treat them so. Even a child's humanity is lost.

Respect and Contempt

This presentation, then, has shown that lawyers managed contact and access to suit the pursuit of volume and the maximisation of profit rather than to benefit their clients. Whether reacting to external pressure or acting to utilise circumstances to their advantage – and the reality is likely to be that they did a bit of both – lawyers caused the clients to suffer. More than simply behaving badly towards their clients, though, the lawyers conducted themselves in a manner that worked to degrade them. To return to the question I posed earlier: how were clients actually treated? My answer is, as if less than human.

The first two sections of this chapter presented divergent accounts. The interviews showed lawyers claiming to behave with respect, while the participant observation documented their behaving disrespectfully. Lawyers, then, clearly did not act with respect. That they had claimed to do so may have been subterfuge or might have constituted self-delusion, as suggested in the preceding chapter. The reasons that underlay the discrepancy, though, should be seen to constitute a subplot, as the main point of this account must be that lawyers behaved disrespectfully towards their clients.

Disrespect has several layers to it – most benignly, elements such as disdain, dishonour and disgrace. However, lower levels reveal increasingly disagreeable thinking in terms of inferiority, debasement and, ultimately, worthlessness. The process of dehumanisation in which these lawyers were engaged should leave little doubt that their feelings occupied these murkier realms. Indeed, I believe that the degree of this disrespect amounted to contempt.

The process of developing contempt might be regarded as somewhat reflexive. For Bell (2005: 88), contempt involves the contemptor perceiving some deficiency in their contempted: a judgemental response premised upon the failure to attain some standard – moral, personal or social. It has a primary role in ordering the moral condemnation of others (Schnall et al, 2008: 13). The contempted is attributed a lesser standing, until they finally assume object status. The comparative element of contempt is drawn out by Hume (1969: 437–41), who highlights the resultant 'positive self-feeling' which can be located in the contemptor. Both Bell (2005) and Hume (1969) reveal the perceived negative qualities of the contempted, which they suggest precipitates a psychological withdrawal. Contemptors distance themselves from the object and cease to identify with it; rather than engage with it, they retreat (Wolfradt et al, 2003: 523). In order to communicate this separation, the contemptor makes their feelings known to peers, but does not necessarily attempt to do so with the object itself; instead, the contempted are often simply neglected and it is hoped that they will react by removing themselves from the contemptor (Brewer, 2007: 704–06).

Applying these ideas to my own study, the lawyers displayed their disregard for clients through their behaviour towards them. They talked to each other in disparaging terms about these clients and effectively cold-shouldered the latter in their daily interactions. This may have created a need to reconsider the differentiation in practice upon which the Radical/Sausage Factory firm dichotomy has been arranged. Rather than seeing an opposition between client-centred and profit-centred approaches to legally aided criminal defence, it seems apposite to suppose that these lawyers all presented a lawyer-centred practice. Contact and access were managed in a manner that suited the lawyer so, when positioning profits ahead of clients, the lawyers were choosing the course of action which brought them greatest benefit. Whether acting or reacting, it is important not to lose sight of the extent to which lawyers opted to behave in the manner that maximised the positive consequences they experienced and minimised the negatives. It would seem churlish to automatically chastise lawyers for seeking some measure of pleasantness in their working lives. However, the manner in which these lawyers went about achieving these advantageous situations can be criticised. Lawyers displayed disregard for the vulnerable individuals who relied on them: those whose rights of access to justice had been entrusted to them by the state.

A lawyer-centred approach allowed them to behave with never a hint of shame or embarrassment at not meeting the ideals set out in the interviews, professional code of conduct (Lord Chancellor's Department, 2001: 8) or practitioner guides they consulted (Cape, 2006b: 7). It meant that lawyers displayed no compunction in advising clients despite knowing little or nothing about them or their case. This was evident from routine exchanges like the following:

> There is one other alternative [to a bail application]. You could enter a guilty plea now, spend a week in custody and then get it over with. Of course, I haven't read your file so the decision's up to you really.
>
> (Bob, solicitor, *Radford Hope*, OR – this client was curled up in a ball, sobbing, on the floor of her cell. The security staff deemed her mentally unstable)

> Hi, my name is Leo. Now I know very little about your case, having just been given the papers by my colleague but I'm sure we can get you dealt with quickly. What is it?
>
> (Leo, senior partner, *Radcliffe and Musk*, OR)

> [Lawyer] Hello, I'm Ronette, I'm a solicitor with *Radcliffes*.
>
> [Client] Hi. Will I be on before lunch?
>
> [Lawyer] I don't know. Look, let me tell you what will happen. Eileen [solicitor], who is another one of our solicitors, is doing some cases in Court Three, and I have a few to do in another court. Probably, I'll just go over your case with you now and then she'll represent you in court. So don't be surprised if you don't see me standing there for you! Now, let's have a look at what the file says, shall we?
>
> (Ronette, solicitor, and Sarah Coyte, client, *Radcliffe and Musk*, OR)

Some lawyers were unconcerned at admitting the extent to which their knowledge of the clients lagged behind that of a temporary – non-legal – research student, as in these examples:

> You see, you know what's going on more than we do. There's nothing about this in the notes, so I don't know anything. I'm relying on you to tell me.
>
> (Leland, solicitor, *Radford Hope*, IC)

> Dan is going to help me with her. He knows her better than me.
>
> (Shelly, solicitor, *Radcliffe and Musk*, OR – to an usher)

> She's had four of us now. I need you to tell me about her. Someone like her, she's complicated. Reading through her stuff, she needs continuity somewhere in her life, that's why she's so messed up. It's confusing. I need you to put it together for me.
>
> (Teresa, solicitor, *Radcliffe and Musk*, IC – on a juvenile client)

Many lawyers even found these situations amusing, as displayed in the following quotes:

> So, what's she like, Dan? Maybe you should be doing her trial for all I know of her [laughs]!
>
> (Teresa, solicitor, *Radcliffe and Musk*, IC – on a youth who had a trial that morning)

Do you want to take a couple of these from me, Dan? I'm sure you know more about them than me by now [laughs]?!

(Leo, senior partner, *Radcliffe and Musk*, IC)

So, Dan, are you going to tell me about her? I know nothing! You're the one who should be representing her [laughs]!

(Ed, senior partner, *Swining MacSage*, IC)

I did not see the humour though, admittedly, I was unsure how best to act; to ingratiate myself with lawyers by laughing or try to help the clients by solemnly explaining what I knew. In the event, I tended to smile, vaguely in acknowledgment, and blurt out the details as best as I could remember. Lawyers, though, were ever unperturbed. They appeared similarly bereft of empathy on those occasions when clients expressed concern or opted to question the treatment they received. Clients were expected to accept lawyers' behaviour. Anything else was to risk their ire, as in these examples:

[Client] Who's going to be doing my sentencing?

[Lawyer] I don't know. It might well be me.

[Client] Who's that guy, is it Leo [senior partner]?

[Lawyer] Leo, yes.

[Client] Yeah, I want him. I don't want no more time [in prison]. I'm doing long enough already. I'm not saying you're crap or anything. I just know him, he's good.

(David Warner, client, and Teresa, solicitor, *Radcliffe and Musk*, OR – Teresa's response to me was: 'What an arsehole. Did you hear him; asking for Leo? I can't believe that')

Who does he think he is? He thinks he can just demand to see me anytime he's in court. He'll see whoever is free. Who does he think he is, asking me?

(Harold, partner, *Radford Hope*, IC)

What does he expect? He can't just pick and choose who he wants to represent him.

(Leo, senior partner, *Radcliffe and Musk*, IC)

It seemed apparent that lawyers were largely focused on themselves, and that clients tended to get in the way. This can be seen from participant observation and interview alike, in quotes such as these:

I'd like to get McGrath [client] done quickly. On and gone. I want to go next door to Court Two – James [senior partner, *Radford Hope*] is making a cracking speech on a bail application for a murder client. I tried to get in but it was full. Get this out of the way then try again.

(Donna, solicitor, *Radcliffe and Musk*, OR – to a colleague)

The day is coming when we won't be in police stations, that will go full circle, I'm quite certain about that and if you think about it, this was only 1984. That's 30 years of duty solicitors and boom, out the window. I can't say that on a personal level I would be disappointed because I am quite fed up with being woken up in the middle of the night and

> having to cart myself down to the police station even though police stations are actually the places where we can do the most good.
>
> (Eileen, solicitor, *Radcliffe and Musk*, INT)

All this behaviour can be considered emblematic of a lawyer-centred approach. However, it found its apotheosis in the manner in which many lawyers had become so laid back as to express total detachment from the consequences of their practice. Several lawyers defined their role as 'puzzle solving', a 'detective story' or a 'game'. To some extent, then, it was a bit of fun for them. The application of this philosophy, and the low-stakes gambling it facilitated, can be witnessed in an experience at the Magistrates' Court with *Radford Hope* solicitor, Leland. On the way into the courtroom he gaily whispered:

> I haven't got the file, but luckily I heard James [senior partner] mention it in the diary meeting yesterday. So I'm going to try and bluff it.
>
> (Leland, solicitor, *Radford Hope*, IC)

With the hearing concluded, Leland came to me at the back of the court. He was laughing and clearly pleased with himself:

> Did you see me? I played the game, kept my head down, stayed at the back of court, hid. I let them do the talking, pretended I knew about the case and didn't really say anything. I bluffed it. I've never even seen the file.
>
> (Leland, solicitor, *Radford Hope*, IC)

He later explained that:

> You have to do that a lot, pretend to know the case. Over time, I've learnt to do it well. You try and let other people tell you the information, sit back a bit. I don't know what the client would have thought about it, he probably didn't have a clue what was going on [laughs]. Like me [laughs]!
>
> (Leland, solicitor, *Radford Hope*, IC)

The complete indifference towards the client should be palpable.

The lower status of the clients suggests that there was great strain on the lawyer–client relationship. Contempt has been placed on the same continuum as resentment and anger by Solomon (1993: 233–35). Those emotions were identified in the previous chapter on attitudes. Having now considered behaviour, parallels can be drawn as we have witnessed negativity in both attitude and behaviour towards clients. For Solomon (1993), resentment and anger were aimed at an individual's equals and betters, but the previous chapter highlighted the manner in which these were displaced downwards onto clients. In addition to this, clients bore the full brunt of the contempt Solomon (1993) believes to be reserved for those of lower status. The strain this might place on the lawyer–client relationship can be seen from the work of the psychologist Gottman (1995). He prides himself on 94 per cent accuracy in using snippets of behaviour to predict the status of a relationship 15 years' hence (Gottman, 1995: 20). Of the four categories of negative emotional behaviour posited to exert the greatest impact, the most destructive is said to be contempt (Carstensen et al, 1995: 146–47).

However, we cannot yet settle upon an assessment of the lawyer–client relationship without considering one further issue: outcomes. In defining access to criminal justice, Young and Wall (1996: 4–5) suggest that the purpose of the criminal process was to produce authoritative conclusions of legal guilt and innocence. As such, access to justice is concerned with ensuring that the criminal process attains its goal fairly and legitimately. While attitudes and behaviour are important considerations along the way, the criminal process is ultimately judged on the outcomes it produces. Accordingly, the discussions of these two chapters might be seen as directing us towards that which follows. So it is that, in the next chapter, I move on to consider the manner in which the negativity that has so far been discerned impacted upon the outcomes of clients' cases.

5

Outcomes

This final substantive chapter follows lawyers' attitudes and behaviour to their logical end-point: the outcomes obtained for clients. It is intuitive to suppose that justice should be judged on what happens to a case: the verdict of guilty or not guilty. Due to my lack of legal training, it would not be appropriate for me to draw such conclusions meaning that, in this book, outcomes would be better suited by the development of an alternative evaluative criterion. To these ends, the somewhat superficial focus on matters of truth can be disregarded in favour of understanding the practice of law as essentially one of language, wherein lawyers are engaged as 'translators' (Cain, 1983: 110–13). From this perspective, clients do not understand the language of the courts and require lawyers to change their wants into a form that constitutes comprehensible legal discourse. This role attributes great responsibility to lawyers, trusted to even-handedly transmit the views of their clients. This chapter, then, is concerned with outcomes but, in particular, the role clients played in deciding the direction of their own cases.

As with the two previous chapters, though, the ethnographic data collected has not allowed one, straightforward, means of understanding the issue. Instead, it has produced two perspectives, somewhat at odds with one another. In the formal interviews, lawyers presented a healthy lawyer–client relationship. They talked of *giving voice* to the clients, allowing clients to have their say in what happened to their cases. The participant observation suggested that the reality was quite different. There seemed a strained lawyer–client relationship, as lawyers moved beyond translation, *speaking over* their clients. In so doing, lawyers appeared to subordinate the client's voice with the result that lawyers tended to tell the clients what to do.

This chapter explores each position individually before bringing them together. The first two sections are designed to allow an appreciation of key themes that emerged from the research. Specific examples of opinions and events are presented with minimal critical engagement, so that the everyday reality of the situation becomes clear. The third section sees a change of gear, with a more rigorous analysis, considering the impact of the foregoing on the lawyer–client relationship. I conclude by suggesting that the data provided on the issue of outcomes offered a strained relationship. To begin, I offer data from the formal interviews.

* * *

SECTION 1 – WHAT LAWYERS SAID ABOUT OUTCOMES

I commence this investigation of outcomes by presenting the claims made by lawyers in the formal interviews. Most stated that clients decided which direction a case would follow, a role that could be described as giving voice to clients. This suggested a healthy lawyer–client relationship wherein lawyers emphasise their desire to empower clients.

I refrain from critical commentary in this section in order to allow the standpoint of these lawyers to come to the fore. To achieve this, I have selected a series of representative quotes, organised under the following headings:

1. *Advisers* – the role lawyers played in determining clients' pleas.
2. *Clients' Choice* – the extent to which clients were responsible for the direction of their case.
3. *Prosecutors* – the manner in which lawyers engaged with the prosecution to aid the clients' choice.

Advisers

At the outset, it seems appropriate to consider a point on which lawyers in these interviews were unanimous: all of the 35 interviewees identified their role as something akin to 'advisers'. This was conceptualised under several epithets; lawyers posited themselves as variously 'informing', 'educating' or 'translating' for clients. They positioned themselves able to facilitate clients' access to justice, as shown in the following responses to my questioning of how they saw their role:

> Our role is to educate them, definitely. Help them as well. Guide them. I'd say all of the above! Most of them don't know about the law and the ones that do are possibly in difficult situations, very emotional, are probably not thinking right. So all of it really, we get involved.
>
> (Leland, solicitor, *Radford Hope*, INT)

> We're making sure they're fully aware of everything that's going on in court and obviously what happens next – they want to know the risks, best case scenario or worst case scenario – it's really about providing lots of information to them.
>
> (Laura, solicitor, *Swining MacSage*, INT)

> Guide them is possibly a good word, hold their hand, see them through. You have a professional skill, a legal qualification, therefore you are learned in the law and you have a role to advise them well.
>
> (Eileen, solicitor, *Radcliffe and Musk*, INT)

In attributing themselves such a role, lawyers appeared to invoke the notion that knowledge is power. Their acting as advisers was considered of great importance; lawyers tended to believe that they enabled clients to choose what happened in their cases.

Clients' Choice

An informed client, then, was deemed able to make a choice – within certain parameters – as to the direction in which their case proceeded. As such, 31 out of 35 lawyers described how choice rested with the client. Lawyers prepared clients so that they could properly make this choice, as evinced by the following quotes:

> Our job is to advise on the options open – at the end of the day it's up to the client which course of action he takes, we simply allow them to make that choice. You could say we are officers of the court – that sounds very grand.
>
> (Jerry, Crown Court clerk, *Swining MacSage*, INT)

> Whether they choose to take your advice or not is up to them. You have to make sure they are making informed decisions, so you advise them. You advise them of the consequences of the various options that might be available to them; you never make a decision for them.
>
> (Eileen, solicitor, *Radcliffe and Musk*, INT)

Lawyers from all firms were adamant that, in fulfilling this duty, they provided nothing stronger than advice. They were attuned to accusations of their exerting a greater influence but did not see validity in this course of questioning. The lack of response it elicited made me feel increasingly awkward in pursuing this topic as the course of the interviews went on. As a result, the most demonstrative discussions were with those working in the firm that was my initial interview site, *Radcliffe and Musk*. That said, a majority of lawyers from all firms – 23 out of the 35 – presented views to the effect that they did not push a client to plead guilty, albeit that most put the point tersely. Some of the more effusive denials can be seen in these examples:

> I've not come across lawyers pushing their clients. There might be people that are doing it, but no that's not something I've really come across here, I don't think. I have advised people of the strength of the evidence, and on the credit that they'd get for a guilty plea, but I also think that you can get yourself into quite dangerous territory if you start telling people to plead guilty to things that they haven't done.
>
> (Ronette, solicitor, *Radcliffe and Musk*, INT)

> The way I present the case to them will leave them in no doubt as to what my favourite choice is and I will also say: 'Look, you have got to be realistic, it's got to be your decision, it's your case; it's your ass on the line'. And I quite often use that line with clients and say: 'It is your decision; you tell me what you want me to do'. Even if I don't think that's the right way to go.
>
> (Leo, senior partner, *Radcliffe and Musk*, INT)

> I don't see lawyers dominating clients. Not for me, personally, no. I always think it's important to allow clients to understand that my job is to advise them, not tell them what to do. I advise them what might be the best course but I make it very clear that any decision is their own and I'm only there to facilitate them understanding what they're doing. I just don't feel it's a situation where we should dominate the client.
>
> (Teresa, solicitor, *Radcliffe and Musk*, INT)

Several lawyers went on to emphasise how they would put the prosecution to proof if this is what the client wanted, even when they did not believe this to be in what they deemed to be the latter's best interests. These lawyers explained that, in such circumstances, they had discharged their professional responsibility by ensuring that the clients had made an informed choice:

> There will be some where you really feel that it's not in their interest to pursue this and they are going to end up in far more trouble at the end of it because of their inability to face up to their problems. But, I think, if you are doing your job properly you say that, 'well if you want to fight this that's fine, as long as you're aware'. Your job is to make them aware of the consequences but it's their choice. And if you have to go to a trial where you know they are going to be found guilty, that's what you do because it's down to them not to you. It's their life and their case.
>
> (Shelly, solicitor, *Radcliffe and Musk*, INT)

> We shouldn't ever try to influence them unduly – you have to give clients advice, and clients have to understand that if evidence is very strong against them. And they have to be advised on credit for a guilty plea, for example. But, at the end of the day, you just have to act on their instructions, so people that say they are not guilty despite overwhelming evidence still ought to have a trial. I think, most of the time, we just do what the client instructs us to do.
>
> (Ronette, solicitor, *Radcliffe and Musk*, INT)

With the client apparently given the choice, lawyers were thereon tasked with ensuring that they had the opportunity to progress in the direction they wanted. In order to allow this, lawyers had to mediate with other individuals involved in the criminal justice system, including the agents of the prosecution.

Prosecutors

Some lawyers asserted that most clients wanted to plead guilty, especially after being advised of their position. Though just under half made no comment about this issue, some 21 out of 35 lawyers, from all firms, described this as the reality of the situation, as reflected in this quote:

> When you think of a criminal solicitor you just think of people who don't ever accept anything. And certainly all my friends always think that everything is contested and everything always results in a trial. Whereas, actually, probably 95 per cent of the cases end up as guilty pleas.
>
> (Annie, solicitor, *Radcliffe and Musk*, INT)

In these circumstances, some lawyers explained that the client's choice was only infrequently concerned with finding grounds to contest a charge. It was said to be more likely that this involved finding an acceptable basis on which to plead guilty. This entailed the lawyers negotiating with the prosecution, and engaging in some manner of plea bargaining. While many seemed uncomfortable discussing this, around two-thirds of lawyers from across the firms – 24 out of the 35 interviewed

– highlighted bargaining as a significant feature of their practice. This is depicted in the following quotes:

> I think there are times when plea bargaining is the most sensible course for all concerned. You are looking at a way to resolve it in the best possible way for the client, but that probably means that there's some scope for negotiation rather than necessarily pushing everything to trial and arguing. Because, quite often in trials, you end up with everything coming out which can be terrible for the defendant. Whereas, if you can agree that they just accept x, y and z and it's just read out in very short pithy terms, it can be much better.
>
> (Shelly, solicitor, *Radcliffe and Musk*, INT)

> If you walk in with an attitude that it's 'them and us' then it's going to go nowhere.
>
> I've seen it in the past. If you've got a hostile relationship with a police officer it's going to get you nowhere. I certainly know that you can strike better deals with officers . . . Negotiation is very important. I think a good relationship with police officers is very important because, if you're hostile, it's going to affect the result you get for your client. Most clients are sensible enough to see that, in fairness – it's just the odd one or two who complain! If a client ever questions that, I have to say: 'Look, if I didn't get on with these officers I wouldn't have half the information in this case that I have got'.
>
> (Maddie, police station clerk, *Radcliffe and Musk*, INT)

In this vein, 30 out of 35 lawyers stressed the importance of their relationship with the prosecutor, as can be seen in the following:

> I think it's very important. I think that often, some defence solicitors and some prosecutors forget what our roles are. Some defence solicitors think that our role is to 'get people off', so to speak, some prosecutors think it's about getting convictions. That's not how I see it; I see my role as being there to protect my client's legal interests. The majority of prosecutors respond very well if you go and speak to them one-on-one. If you speak to them one-on-one then you develop a relationship. Often you can try to negotiate so, even on cases which seem lost, you can sometimes get surprising results.
>
> (Laura, solicitor, *Swining MacSage*, INT)

> You do have to get on together; solicitors should try to work with the prosecutors. They're not the enemy. Defence solicitors would be stupid to act like they were. It would only harm their client's case and reduce their chances of making an acceptable deal.
>
> (Harry, solicitor, *Radford Hope*, INT)

> It's good to get on with the prosecutors and you do notice if you get a good relationship with particular prosecutors then it is easier to negotiate things with them. There are some prosecutors that just aren't approachable and that you just can't really negotiate with and that's awful because that doesn't really benefit the client either.
>
> (Ronette, solicitor, *Radcliffe and Musk*, INT)

These good relations with the prosecution were claimed as crucial in allowing clients to follow the course they chose. Indeed, many lawyers suggested that they fostered such relations for the benefit of the client.

When it came to outcomes, then, these lawyers described a healthy lawyer–client relationship. Lawyers from all firms claimed that they worked to give voice to their clients, to allow them to make informed choices. Even good relations with prosecutors – though some clients found them objectionable – were said to function for the clients. However, a different perspective is offered in the following section, which presents data from the participant observation.

* * *

SECTION 2 – WHAT I SAW ON OUTCOMES

In this section, the interview data is supplemented by that drawn from the participant observation, concerning how lawyers tackled questions of outcomes when going about their work. When deciding the direction of a case, it appeared that lawyers often spoke over their clients, pointing towards a strained lawyer–client relationship. My research depicts a pervading ideology in which lawyers tasked themselves with securing guilty pleas from clients.

As with the interview data, particular extracts from the participant observation are presented here – subject to minimal analysis – to provide a candid depiction of the situation witnessed. For ease of understanding, though, this is organised into the following areas:

1. *Standard Guilty Pleas* – the extent to which lawyers routinely expected clients to plead guilty.
2. *Pressure* – the level at which advice to plead guilty became coercion.
3. *Prosecutors* – the degree to which lawyers were complicit with the prosecution in ensuring guilty pleas.

Standard Guilty Pleas

In the earlier chapter on attitudes, most lawyers were shown to display a presumption of guilt regarding their clients. That the lawyer–client relationship might be infused by such a philosophy challenges the autonomy of clients in the decision-making process. This ethos, then, was also present in the outcomes of cases, shaping and restricting the choices that clients could make. This can also be seen in my own research. All the lawyers were observed to operate in a default mode, whereby they assumed that clients would plead guilty, and thus helped ensure that they did just that. Displays of this position were often muted, drawn out in ostensibly neutral statements and rhetorical questions. The following quotes, drawn from the beginning of consultations with clients at the Magistrates' Court, are illustrative:

> So, what will it be today, guilty pleas?
>
> (Leo, senior partner, *Radcliffe and Musk*, OR)

[Client] It's a criminal damage. The thing is, I was so drunk that I can't remember.

[Lawyer] I think you're happy to plead guilty, Mr Warne.

(Shane Warne, client, and Thomas, partner, *Swining MacSage*, OR)

[Client] What's going to happen today?

[Lawyer] Let's just fill out the legal aid [form] first.

[Client] Okay, but what's going to happen, an adjournment or what?

[Lawyer] I think you might be dealt with.

[Client] Dealt with?

[Lawyer] You might be.

[Client] What, sentenced?

[Lawyer] Yeah.

[Client] What about the plea?

[Lawyer] Well, you'll be entering a plea.

[Client] What, for this? For an assault on a policeman?

[Lawyer] Yeah.

[Client] No, I'm not pleading guilty.

[Lawyer] Oh, right. Well let's discuss what you'll plead in a minute. Do the legal aid first.

(Shaun Tait, client, and Denise, solicitor, *Radcliffe and Musk*, OR)

Lawyers seemed reluctant to recommend openly that clients pleaded guilty. As such, there were awkward moments on the occasions that clients repeated their subtle encouragement back in unambiguous terms. This can be appreciated in the following extract – one of many similar incidents from across the firms – involving an office meeting between a *Swining MacSage* partner, Thomas, and his client. It took place at half past four, the afternoon before the client was due to face trial for charges of assaulting police officers. Thomas had spent over half an hour 'going round in circles' as he asked the client if he wanted to plead guilty; the client steadfastly replied in the negative. Thomas explained how weak his case was and then again asked the client if he wanted to plead guilty. Eventually, the client realised that Thomas was trying to tell him he should plead guilty:

[Client] So you're recommending that I go guilty?

[Lawyer] I am going to say to you that, well, your chances of success in a trial are extremely slim. And, well, if you were saying that it may have happened, sort of, not intentionally, but, maybe that you, sort of, I don't know, maybe urinated and then you caught him accidentally then, well, you could plead guilty on that basis. And you were spitting, not intending to spit directly at them, but you just wanted them away out of the cell and it, maybe, caught them. Accidentally.

[Client] So if I do what you say, would the court see it as bad that I didn't plead guilty straight away?

[Lawyer] Well, I don't think, if we notify them, sort of, fairly soon then I don't think it would be too much of a problem at all. I think, with this, that the court expected a plea on the first occasion. Which, maybe, leaves you in a situation where you feel rushed.

[Client] Yeah.

[Lawyer] Well, we didn't have all the information. You obviously felt rushed in to it. So I think if we vacate now then it won't be a problem at all. And I would hope that, well, the court have got a number of options.

[Client] Right, if you think that's the right thing to do, I'll say it's guilty then.

[Lawyer] Okay. As long as you're certain then. Guilty.

(Justin Langer, client, and Thomas, partner, *Swining MacSage*, OR)

Lawyers from all firms framed their discussions with clients within the basic premise that they would plead guilty. Ideally, most lawyers sought to proceed under an unspoken agreement. However, clients did not always conform and some circumstances required lawyers to exert greater pressure.

Pressure

When clients did not react to subtle encouragement, many lawyers adopted a more explicit approach. In the majority of such cases – including those rare few in which the lawyer eventually accepted the client's story and a trial date was set – there was a stage when lawyers exerted tangible pressure on a client. Lawyers from all firms pushed clients to plead guilty. Sometimes, of course, this was deemed in the client's best interests, whether the latter knew it or not. Some lawyers might also have wanted to do this because it saved them time and effort or, occasionally, because it was more profitable. This temptation is recognised in the professional code of conduct (Lord Chancellor's Department, 2001: 4) which expressly forbids putting pressure on clients to plead guilty for such selfish purposes, insisting that lawyers 'shall not advise a client that it is in her interests to plead guilty unless satisfied that the prosecution is able to discharge the burden of proof'.

Those lawyers who sought to exert pressure were, then, in a potentially difficult position. One method of applying pressure without doing so too overtly was to use scare tactics or inducements. This can be seen in the following extracts from consultations at court, wherein the client was not given the opportunity to express their views before being warned off anything other than the guilty plea the lawyer appeared to favour:

[Lawyer] So, how are we pleading? Oh, I should warn you that the judge you'll be appearing before is very tough on public order offences. He's also very tough on breaches, and he's been sending people down all day for failures to surrender.

[Client] Oh, right. I wanted to go not guilty, I didn't do anything.

[Lawyer] I think you need to think very carefully about this before you come to a decision. There might be a deal on the table.

(Harold, partner, and Mitchell Johnson, client, *Radford Hope*, OR)

So, how are we going to proceed? Obviously, if there was a guilty plea today you would be given credit and any sentence you receive would be reduced. But it's your choice; I'm just

> letting you know the situation. I'm not being funny, but you had away with the gear, didn't you?
>
> (Bob, solicitor, *Radford Hope*, OR)

This encouragement even went so far as to contravene the convention that a lawyer should not directly ask their client whether they are guilty. Lawyers who want to go to trial are generally loath to risk being explicitly told of their client's guilt; their attempt to put the prosecution to proof would be hampered, and compromised, by such disclosure. However, lawyers in this study, keen to conclude a case quickly, showed little compunction about doing so if they felt the client needed to be pushed, as in the following:

> Look, mate, you just need to plead guilty. You did it, didn't you? No messing around.
>
> (Windom, solicitor, *Radford Hope*, OR)

> My colleague tells me you aren't sure about plea. I'm not sure why, bit of a waste of time. It seems to me that you have to plead guilty. You will plead guilty, won't you?
>
> (Ben, partner, *Radcliffe and Musk*, OR)

> Right, so it's four thefts. You did it, yeah? If you say yes, we can get it over with nice and quickly. There's no need to mess about.
>
> (Ed, senior partner, *Swining MacSage*, OR)

Seemingly aware of the need to not say something that could later be used against them, some lawyers seemed somewhat uncomfortable in my presence during such interactions. I can only speculate what happened on the occasions when particular lawyers, from *Swining MacSage*, asked me to leave the room on some errand or other, and I would usually return to find a client had changed his plea to guilty.

It was only infrequently that I saw lawyers lose their cool and transparently tell clients to plead guilty, as reflected by the following examples:

> Look, you can do nothing but accept it. You really should just plead guilty. Listen to what I'm telling you.
>
> (Leland, solicitor, *Radford Hope*, OR)

> [Clerk] How do you plead?
>
> [Client] Not Guilty.
>
> [Lawyer] Guilty!
>
> [Client] I did not assault her.
>
> [Lawyer] Look, if you plead guilty, then I'll explain why later, okay? Trust me.
>
> (Alfred Bester, magistrates' clerk, Matthew Hayden, client, and Thomas, partner, *Swining MacSage*, OR – at the beginning of the hearing, as magistrates sought to discern the client's plea)

While usually careful to maintain their professional persona in the presence of clients, most lawyers displayed no embarrassment about revealing their guilty plea ethos to their peers, as shown by these extracts from both sides of the Radical/Sausage Factory divide:

> [Lawyer One] Now, you might wonder why I have this computer? It's to show him just what he has done.
>
> [Lawyer Two] Is the whole assault on there?
>
> [Lawyer One] Oh yes. And I'll make sure he sees it all too! Properly.
>
> (Harold, partner, and Catherine, solicitor, *Radford Hope*, OR – on the way to the Magistrates' Court for a trial he hoped to 'crack')

> Hopefully, I'll be able to crack this trial – it isn't anything. Then I can come and help you okay?
>
> (Shelly, solicitor, *Radcliffe and Musk*, OR)

> Our job today will just be persuading the client to plead guilty. It's an assault. So, really, our job today is to explain to him that there's no point in having a trial and he might as well plead guilty. He's usually alright, usually listens.
>
> (Ed, senior partner, *Swining MacSage*, OR)

This openness extended to their relations with the prosecution.

Prosecutors

The lawyer–prosecutor relationship appeared every bit as important as the lawyer–client relationship. On average, all lawyers seemed to spend as much, if not more, time discussing cases with prosecutors as they did with clients. In addition, most lawyers tended to talk to prosecutors before they talked to clients. As a result, many lawyers' views of cases seemed to be shaped to a greater extent by the prosecutors' understandings than those of their clients. A little of the significance of this relationship can be seen in the following exchanges where lawyers collected their disclosure from prosecutors in the courtroom:

> [Lawyer] What do you think?
>
> [Prosecutor] Looks like he did it to me.
>
> [Lawyer] There's not really a deal to be done, is there?
>
> [Prosecutor] He either pleads and gets seven months or goes to trial and gets nine.
>
> [Lawyer] Right, okay, thank you. I'll put that to him when I see him.
>
> (Shelly, solicitor, *Radcliffe and Musk*, and Frank Herbert, prosecutor, OR)

> [Prosecutor] Do you know anything about it?
>
> [Lawyer] I don't yet, but I'm sure I soon will.
>
> [Prosecutor] He's in on a warrant.
>
> [Lawyer] For what?
>
> [Prosecutor] For theft.
>
> [Lawyer] Aww. Did he do it?
>
> [Prosecutor] Yeah. Hasn't admitted it.
>
> [Lawyer] Great: straightforward shoplifting.
>
> (Jeffrey Eugenides, prosecutor, and Eileen, solicitor, *Radcliffe and Musk*, OR)

Prosecutors appeared to share the lawyers' presumption of guilt. As such, the collusion of the two parties, usually meant that both assumed, and favoured, guilty pleas as an outcome. Accordingly, when in the presence of prosecutors, most lawyers made no attempt to disguise the pressure they customarily exerted on clients. This was true across the firms, but can be appreciated in the following examples when *Swining MacSage* lawyers returned to the courtroom after having talked to their clients:

> [Prosecutor] What's happening with it, then?
>
> [Lawyer] Oh, we're really putting pressure on him to plead guilty. Really putting pressure on.
>
> [Prosecutor] Will he?
>
> [Lawyer] I don't know, he should.
>
> [Prosecutor] Yeah.
>
> (James Ballard, prosecutor, and Laura, solicitor, *Swining MacSage*, OR)

> [Lawyer] He's pleading not guilty.
>
> [Prosecutor] Why!?
>
> [Lawyer] Because, well.
>
> [Prosecutor] Oh, go on, make me laugh. Well, I just really wouldn't have expected him to go guilty.
>
> [Lawyer] I know.
>
> [Prosecutor] What a twat.
>
> [Lawyer] I've talked to him, he won't listen.
>
> (Thomas, partner, *Swining MacSage*, and Philip Dick, prosecutor, OR)

In these circumstances, decisions over whether to pursue a plea bargain appeared to owe as much, if not more, to discussions in the lawyer–prosecutor relationship than those from the lawyer–client relationship.

Combined, the foregoing has shown that many lawyers from all firms sought to speak over their clients. This can be viewed in an exchange between a *Radcliffe and Musk* solicitor, Teresa, and a youth client, ahead of her trial that afternoon. She faced two charges of common assault – one racially aggravated – and two of assault on a police officer, following an incident in a takeaway restaurant. Teresa had not met her client before the trial date, and had gleaned her information on the girl from the prosecutor as they discussed what should happen. In her police station interview, the girl claimed that she did not assault anybody until the police attended whereupon she acted in self-defence as they manhandled her. Teresa and the prosecutor had laughed about this. Having listened to the prosecutor, Teresa attended the client in her cell:

> [Lawyer] Look, Jodie, I've talked to the prosecutor. I don't think you should plead guilty to the racially aggravated [assault] as the evidence isn't there. If I can make a deal with them, where they drop that one, would you accept that? Would you plead to the others?

[Client] Let me see the [charge] list. That one [an assault on a police officer] is a load of rubbish.

[Lawyer] Look we've accepted that, I told them you would. I think you need to accept that the evidence is quite strong.

[Client] Come on. The evidence isn't strong on that? The police are obviously going to stick up for each other.

[Lawyer] But you still weren't pleasant. Listen to me, Jodie, I'm going to explain. If you plead guilty on that, we can explain to the court that what was happening made you respond in a certain way.

[Client] But they'll just say I had no excuse for spitting. I was pushed to the ground! I still have the marks.

[Lawyer] It's called mitigation. It means we can tell them what you say happened afterwards.

[Client] No, I'm not having that.

[Lawyer] Look, Jodie, I will tell them what you say happened.

[Client] Hang on, hang on. Let me say something. Because this is the only time I get to actually say something. I never get to say anything.

[Lawyer] Later, Jodie. Just listen to me for now.

(Teresa, solicitor, and Jodie Fields, client, *Radcliffe and Musk*, INT)

After two more discussions with the prosecutor, Teresa persuaded the girl to plead guilty to all the assaults and had the racially aggravated charge dropped. However, the client still protested her innocence – to Teresa, her youth worker, the clerk and the bench – even as she was sentenced.

The participant observation, then, appeared to present a strained lawyer–client relationship. Most lawyers spoke over their clients, persuading clients to take cases in the direction that the lawyer chose. This meant the outcomes sought were not necessarily those that clients had wanted, as lawyers from all firms would push clients towards guilty pleas. This stands at odds with the formal interviews, an inconsistency pursued in the following section.

* * *

SECTION 3 – OUTCOMES

Outcomes followed the issues of attitudes and behaviour in generating two alternative perspectives. The formal interviews saw lawyers from all firms emphasise that they worked to give voice to the clients' wishes. In contrast, the participant observation showed that, when it came to outcomes, lawyers attempted to speak over the clients. This discussion adopts a more critical tone, analysing both accounts together and posing the question: who actually chose the direction to follow?

I begin exploring this question by addressing the professionally prescribed role of the lawyer to give advice and take instructions. In reality – and in line with previous research in this area – I argue that they actually appeared to impart both. I go on to show that the typical academic assessment of this situation has been critical, positing that lawyers controlled clients. I then acknowledge that lawyers might make the plausible sounding claim in response that these academics are out of touch, and that lawyers know what their clients want better than an academic ever could. However, it is shown that lawyers ultimately sought to fool their clients into opting for the course of action favoured by the lawyer, or, when that failed, manipulating the impression the client formed of the lawyer's, often ineffective, efforts on their behalf. These results were achieved through confidence tricks, most notably *spooking the client* and *pyrotechnics*. As such, I conclude that lawyers were able to take advantage of their clients' vulnerability, so that the influence they exerted over choices presented a threat to the lawyer–client relationship. Indeed, I suggest that it can be conceptualised as a form of client abuse.

Advice and Instructions

In the formal interviews, many lawyers discussed their role as facilitators, allowing clients to act as informed agents of their own destiny. In making these claims, these lawyers appeared to revert to the social agenda stressed in the attitudes chapter. Most lawyers presented themselves as concerned with helping people achieve what they wanted. This position tallies with the 'classical' picture of lawyering, long and widely disseminated (McConville et al, 1994: 18–19). It has been suggested that lawyers, and their professional bodies, have worked hard to foster a public image that emphasises their humanity and selflessness (Fennell, 1980: 22–24). So it is that Thomas and Mungham (1983: 134–35) are able to examine the outpourings of the Law Society, identifying their self-descriptions of a profession premised upon service, public protection, trust and being much more than a business transaction. For Thomas and Mungham (1983: 135), this is underlined by the supposition that, 'the Law Society is anxious to distinguish between professional services and business, to promote so vigorously an altruistic conception of the lawyer/client relationship'. So it is that the professional code of conduct (Lord Chancellor's Department, 2001: 4) describes a lawyers' function, whereby the 'primary duty of a professional employee is to protect the interests of the client . . . A professional employee shall provide the client with fearless, vigorous and effective defence'.

In relation to the direction in which cases proceed, lawyers have two vital roles to fulfil in order to meet these ideals: they must give advice and take instructions. This forms a basic standard of competence, recognised by the Law Society (2011: 7) in their duty solicitor accreditation, wherein lawyers must 'allow the client to explain his or her position . . . give appropriate advice to the client in a form that assists them to decide upon the best course of action'. The onus, then, is on working *for* the client, allowing *them* to make decisions. As such, this advice must not extend beyond informative guidance. Thus, the professional code of conduct (Lord Chancellor's Department, 2001: 4) reminds lawyers that, 'a professional employee should not put a client under pressure to plead guilty'.

Practitioner guides present similar messages. This can be seen in advice centred on police station interactions, as that provided by Cape (2006b: 4–5), which instructs lawyers that:

> A lawyer must treat the interests of the client as paramount... While, for example, a client may be advised in strong terms of the advantages of admitting an offence to the police, whether to do so is a matter for the client and the lawyer should not impose any undue pressure to accept their advice. After all, it is the client who has to live with the consequences.

This attitude is also to be found in work focused on the courts, as that offered by Ede and Edwards (2008: 92) which insists that, 'your client must take the decision; you must assist him to reach it by advice'. Lawyers are, in other words, responsible for ensuring that clients make informed decisions.

Such is the stance that lawyers took in the formal interviews, and they were adamant that they would not cross this boundary. This position can be appreciated in the following quotes:

> I think everyone needs to know that in that court, no matter what else is going on, we are actually speaking for them. We might be the only person speaking on their behalf, but they know that they've got a voice, and that we're working as hard as we can to get their case acquitted for them. Our role? Everything – explaining the procedures to them, lots of them need that; explain to them what I think is likely to happen – be their legal adviser.
>
> (Denise, solicitor, *Radcliffe and Musk*, INT)

> Well, you always have to advise clients properly, go through the evidence with them, and tell them what your view is on how the witnesses will come across, if you can get any indication of that, how many witnesses there are, what you think the strengths are in their evidence, what you think the weaknesses are, so you always need to advise them on all of that. Then you can advise them on their own – what they're saying, whether it's consistent with what they're saying in interview, whether there are any problems with what they're saying. So you, kind of, have to go through it with them but they have to make the final decision and if they want a trial then they should have a trial.
>
> (Ronette, solicitor, *Radcliffe and Musk*, INT)

However, in her practitioner guide, Davies (2007: 34–39) notes that lawyers must tread a fine line:

> If you suspect your client is not telling you the truth ... you may want to give him robust advice ... but do not 'lean' on the person. There is a fine line between robust explanation and leaning. It is not your case it is his.

These norms reflect the important plea bargaining case of *Turner*.[1] In this judgment, the Court of Appeal developed what can be seen as a set of rules for plea

[1] *R v Turner* [1970] 2 QB 321.

negotiation, chief among which was the recognition that, in some situations, defence counsel might encourage clients to plead guilty and, in so doing, provide advice *in strong terms.* The extent to which this plays off due process principles against competing crime control practices is highlighted by McConville (2002: 354–60). Lawyers are implicated within a functionally crime control system and, thereon, tasked with transmitting certain systematic imperatives, including the sentence discount for pleading guilty. However, this system concomitantly attempts to maintain its legitimacy by claiming that this does not amount to improper pressure, and that the plea remains voluntary and premised upon factual guilt.

That there is a form of improper pressure implies that some manner of pressure is acceptable creating a situation rife with ambiguity over just how much is too much. This grey area is evident in returning to the practitioner guide of Ede and Edwards (2008: 99), which implores:

> Do not necessarily accept your client's denial at face value: enquire as to his reasons. If the prosecution evidence appears strong, challenge your client with it . . . Cross-examine him as robustly as appropriate . . . Do not let your client think you are hostile or no longer on his side.

Their text suggests that lawyers might conceivably be so forceful as to risk the client forgetting that the lawyer is working for them. This eventuality appeared to be accepted by many lawyers in this study. In interview, 23 out of the 35 lawyers, from all firms, discussed interactions with clients in which it would not have been unreasonable for the latter to have felt some level of uncertainty, as in the following:

> If he'd said he wanted to go not guilty, I'd have said: 'If you think you are going to win a trial on this you are stark raving bonkers'. Oh, God, yeah, I'd be frank with him. I would have said: 'You are crazy'.
>
> (Shelly, solicitor, *Radcliffe and Musk*, INT)

> You have to make sure that they have a voice if they want particular things said but also try to not let them run it. So you say: 'Look, I think this approach is slightly better, let's do it this way'. That kind of thing.
>
> (Denise, solicitor, *Radcliffe and Musk*, INT)

While such an approach might be sympathetically described as 'firm' or 'robust', an alternative perspective was offered by a *Radford Hope* solicitor, Leland, during the participant observation:

> I would love to see Bob [solicitor] dealing with a client like this. He doesn't like it when they have their own opinions on what they should do. Bob does not take instructions and give advice, he gives advice *and* gives instructions. Anything else is a big waste of time. He'd have gone mad with that client, climbing up the walls at all the time it'd take! A lot of solicitors are like that.
>
> (Leland, solicitor, *Radford Hope*, IC)

In contrast to the interviews, and the general presentation of the profession, lawyers were regularly seen throughout the participant observation giving both advice and instructions. This represented an ethos that can be appreciated from the following quotes in which lawyers from all three firms refer to situations in which their clients would not change their pleas to guilty:

> That client, he's a difficult one. He insists on going to trial. He won't take it, he just won't take instructions.
>
> (Ed, senior partner, *Swining MacSage*, IC)

> I thought he was going to agree then. He's so frustrating, he just won't listen!
>
> (Harold, partner, *Radford Hope*, IC)

> Pressure from solicitor is not necessarily wrong if client is being unreasonable... needless to say, my advice is usually fairly robust!
>
> (Leo, senior partner, *Radcliffe and Musk*, EM)

The following examples show situations in which the lawyer was giving instructions to the client. Each dialogue is a snippet from a conversation in which the lawyer was persuading the client to change their pleas to guilty. Both clients were reluctant but each lawyer was insistent. The clients eventually agreed to plead guilty, though without admitting to the lawyer that they had done the acts they were charged with:

> [Client] No, I'm staying not guilty, Leo.
>
> [Lawyer] Well, it's your choice. But you really have to choose to plead. There's no way you'd win a trial.
>
> [Client] I want to give it a go, though, isn't it?
>
> [Lawyer] Listen to me, just plead guilty.
>
> (Travis Birt, client, and Leo, senior partner, *Radcliffe and Musk*, OR)

> [Client] I want to say not guilty. I didn't take anything.
>
> [Lawyer] Right, look, you need to stop messing about. Just put your hands up to it.
>
> [Client] But, I didn't.
>
> [Lawyer] I'm reading it, and it says to me that you did it. That's what anyone would think who saw it. It's what they'll think in there. You might as well just admit it.
>
> (Callum Ferguson, client, and Bob, solicitor, *Radford Hope*, OR)

The role of the lawyer in my study, then, should be seen to have extended beyond giving advice. They exerted a greater influence, appearing to overstep the role traditionally ascribed to them; sometimes the lawyer decided the direction of the case.

Control

The notion that lawyers persuade clients to plead guilty has become a prominent concern of socio-legal literature addressing the lawyer–client relationship. Indeed, Mulcahy (1994: 411) suggests that, 'few aspects of the criminal justice system have generated more controversy than plea negotiations . . . their prevalence in English courtrooms is undisputed'. The prevailing academic interest lies in the notion of control; an imbalance of power allows lawyers to dominate clients. That thesis forms the backbone of much sociological enquiry into the professions generally. In this manner, Johnson (1972: 45) suggests that the professions are premised upon defining both the needs of the consumer and how those needs should be met. Similarly, for Hughes (1958: 79) professionals can be identified seeking to 'presume to tell society what is good and right for the individual and for society at large in some aspect of life . . . set the very terms in which people may think about this aspect of life'. Professionals hold a monopoly of specialist knowledge, which ensures their hierarchical superiority over those clients dependent on their services. With this consideration in mind, White (1990: 861) looks at lawyers, in particular, and contemplates the origins of the word client, highlighting that it derives from the Latin *cluere* – to be named, to hear oneself named. Ancient Rome saw those under the patronage of patricians labelled *clientem*; they were known by the names of their patron. This perspective duly informs her understanding of the lawyer–client relationship; the former can subordinate the latter, with lawyers substituting clients' interests with their own.

This situation has well been documented with regard to divorce lawyers. For Mather at al (1995: 306–07), clients are reduced to the status of passengers. Their study is premised upon lawyers' reports of their dealings with clients, positioning the lawyers as taxi drivers who choose the route along which they take their fare. However, Sarat and Felstiner (1988: 742) move beyond this, suggesting that the lawyers they observed often controlled the destination as well as the route, leaving clients to talk past lawyers as the latter make up their own minds about the course of action to be taken. As a result, Sarat and Felstiner (1986: 96) identify that the most common pattern of lawyer–client interaction present in their research involves lawyers persuading 'a somewhat reluctant client to reach a negotiated settlement'. Indeed, Sarat and Felstiner (1995: 115) found that lawyer and client interests are fundamentally at odds so that time and time again they 'observed lawyers attempting to focus their client's attentions on the issues the lawyers thought to be major, while the clients often concentrated on matters which the lawyers considered secondary'. The authors equated the place of the client to that of slaves, prisoners, students and wives subjected to patriarchal hegemony. The more critical timbre of their work likely derives from the ethnographic method they utilise which does not take lawyers' words as gospel in the manner that Mather et al (1995) do. This provides a warts and all experience verifying the findings of Davis et al (1994: 69) on divorce lawyers, who are said to have 'brought considerable pressures to bear on their client to accept a settlement which the client regarded as unfair'.

A pair of ethnographic studies into legal aid lawyers more generally presents similar sentiments: lawyers rarely ask clients what they want to do. In Israel, Bogoch and Danet (1984: 270) find lawyers reluctant to listen sympathetically to clients' stories, repeatedly challenging their version of events. These authors suggest that lawyers' interests are pitted against those of the clients, as the former use language to control the latter's presentation of cases. A similar process is outlined by Hostika (1979: 607) with regard to the situation in the United States:

> The general picture that emerges from this analysis is one of lawyer control over the process of interaction, reflected in control over the definition of the situation; that is, the description of what happened, the evaluation of what ought to happen, and the prescription of what is going to happen.

As such, clients' problems become routinised, stereotyped into standard definitions of maximum convenience to lawyers. This echoes research into the criminal process wherein Cunningham (1991–92: 1299) describes lawyers as 'oppressors', silencing those below them, engaged in the routine domination of clients. In Carlen's (1976: 91–92) assessment of the Magistrates' Courts, their central purpose is to maintain social control, treating those who pass through them with neither humanity nor justice, presenting 'a secretive, collusive but creative information game whose rules were forever being adapted to further the interests of the professional contestants'.

It is in these circumstances that Worrall (1990: 22) is able to claim that clients' feelings and emotions are objectified by lawyers who bestow upon them a mere 'unitary value' as a 'privileged discourse is constructed from the broken utterances of the powerless'. Based on her interviews with female offenders, it appears that lawyers are able to make decisions for clients, controlling the direction a case takes in the criminal process. This has been demonstrated as a widespread phenomenon in the research conducted by Baldwin and McConville (1977: 83–100). Many of the Crown Court defendants they talked to did not perceive themselves to be genuine parties in the decision-making process, feeling estranged from the lawyer who was supposedly representing them. In the majority of cases involving late guilty pleas, Baldwin and McConville (1977: 45) identify pressure from lawyers as a major influence behind the change and, in a large number of these examples, they claim 'evidence that the advice counsel gave was of such a nature that no reasonable person could say that it was fair or proper that the final decision to plead guilty was made voluntarily'.

This 'routine dependence' on guilty pleas in the criminal courts is explored by McConville et al (1994: 182–210) who largely attribute them to the earlier cited presumption of guilt lawyers adhere to. These authors suggest that this presumption leads lawyers to deem clients unworthy of trial. In the United States, these shared values have been said to bind together defence and prosecution (Grossman, 1978: 72–73). The two are locked into an 'exchange relationship', premised upon the mutual goal of processing defendants through the system as swiftly as possible (Cole, 1970: 338–42). These circumstances can be understood to involve all participants engaging in a common *courtroom culture*. In this environment, Heumann (1978: 84) identifies the lawyers' mindset shifting from the presumption of trial to a presumption of plea bargaining.

Globalisation has seemingly transported these values, as we witness something akin to the Americanisation of legal jurisdictions around the world. Indeed, Mulcahy (1994: 426) highlights the trend to be present in this country, with lawyers more closely allied to the prosecutor than their client. When discussing plea bargains, Mulcahy (1994: 412) suggests that, 'legal practitioners involved in these negotiations are more concerned with punishing the guilty than with safeguarding defendants rights . . . these representations represent common attitudes and a co-operative ethos among local practitioners'. His fieldwork was reported in 1994. Conducted some 15 years later, my own research confirms that this trend has continued, notwithstanding the efforts that have been made in the interim to promote active defence such as introducing the police station accreditation scheme (see Edwards, 2008). My own research also found that guilty pleas are favoured for financial reasons. In the preceding chapters, lawyers claimed that increasingly restrictive legal aid remuneration placed economic pressures on them. Under fixed fees, a guilty plea meant they were paid the same for a single court appearance as for a handful. Accordingly, it was most profitable for them to conclude cases quickly when most were terminated by a guilty plea anyway. I felt awkward raising this subject with lawyers lest it seemed I was casting aspersions on their professional integrity. Nevertheless, several discussed it during the participant observation, as the following quotes from each firm illustrate:

> Of course, now we don't get paid for travelling and waiting we have to make sure we recoup our costs somehow, so we have to get through as many cases as quickly as we can.
>
> (Harold, partner, *Radford Hope*, IC)

> As a result of the changes the government have made to legal aid, we have got to, really, make sure that we get in and out of the case as quickly as possible.
>
> (Ed, senior partner, *Swining MacSage*, IC)

> It pays to have someone who can just deal with guilty pleas, so we have Donna [solicitor] who can just churn them out. That's how you make the money.
>
> (Leo, senior partner, *Radcliffe and Musk*, IC)

In addition, this factor was alluded to by a handful of the lawyers in the formal interviews, as evident from the following:

> Obviously if we can get a case dealt with quickly, then that can be advantageous and I don't think that we generally want to adjourn cases as we will rack up costs. Because we are on a fixed fee and it doesn't really matter whether it's, say, three hearings or four hearings; we get paid the same.
>
> (Thomas, partner, *Swining MacSage*, INT)

> Of course, it's an advantage to get things dealt with quickly, particularly in the Magistrates' Court. You have to be happy if you can conclude a case early as those are the ones you can make money on. It's the cases that drag on, going nowhere, where clients can, perhaps, be seen to be messing around, which you want to nip in the bud.
>
> (Ben, partner, *Radcliffe and Musk*, INT)

> I do feel under pressure to cut corners, we all do in this line of business now. That's accepted . . . Solicitors are turning up at court regularly and carving everything up, because it's not in their interest to take things to trial because, with the limited resources they have within their firm, it's far more expedient to get people to plead and move on to

> something else. So it's a factory approach isn't it? You get a lot of guilty pleas and your firm is getting the benefit.
>
> (Jerry, police station clerk, Swining MacSage, INT)

Some lawyers were willing to use the clients to achieve their own ends. In reporting the most common complaints made by clients against lawyers, Gibb (2007) has located this aspect at the forefront, as clients 'feel alienated by jargon and frustrated at their levels of control'.

A solicitor from *Radcliffe and Musk*, Eileen, recognised this as a bone of contention in her interview:

> One of the biggest complaints you will ever get from clients, is the feeling that: one, they are not being listened to; two, they are being brow-beaten into making a particular decision, and; three, that it wasn't explained to them, they didn't understand.
>
> (Eileen, solicitor, *Radcliffe and Musk*, INT)

In this research, I did not discuss with lawyers whether I could talk to their clients and, as such, it would have been wrong of me to question them. However, I was often left alone with clients and allowed them to lead conversations. This involved occasions when lawyers had persuaded them to plead guilty and they shared with me their disgruntlement. In the following examples, the lawyers from Sausage Factory and Radical firms respectively had gone out to finalise the terms of a deal with the prosecutor:

> The thing is, they're lying. And I have to plead guilty to something that's a lie. It's not fair.
>
> (Jason Gillespie, client, *Swining MacSage*, IC)

> I hate this. This is how it is. You know I'm telling the truth right? But I have to pretend, just go with them. It's shit, mate, sorry to say.
>
> (Doug Bollinger, client, *Radford Hope*, IC)

There was also one memorable occasion in which a *Swining MacSage* partner, Thomas, had been attempting to persuade a client to plead guilty to criminal damage. The client had been resistant, but Thomas was persistent and thought he had convinced the client. However, when the clerk asked for the client's pleas and Thomas said 'guilty', the angry client retorted:

> Mate, you're sacked. I'd rather represent myself. You don't listen to me. Not guilty! I did not do it!
>
> (Adam Voges, client, *Swining MacSage*, OR)

The participant observation data in this research, then, reiterates that which has characterised much of the existing socio-legal literature: lawyers had extended their role beyond giving advice. I interpreted the practices I saw as a form of domination.

Choice

However, the idea that lawyers controlled clients has been dismissed by Travers (1997b: 105–06) as an academic stereotype. He contests the supposition that clients who were persuaded to plead guilty were rendered powerless, insisting that lawyers would not recognise such interpretations (Travers, 1997a: 370–71). Talk of control is said to be alien and unfamiliar to those actually located within this branch of the legal profession. In the formal interviews for this study, the question of control was put to lawyers, but found little response. Rather than dismiss it, lawyers tended to sidestep questions that pertained to it; it was occasionally implied that others might do it, though never the lawyer themselves. For many lawyers, the divergence between academic discussions of control and their own self-perceptions might be borne of the distance between theory and practice – it was often suggested that those outside the legal profession did not understand their job. This was usually discussed in relation to the government or public, as in this example:

> Most people don't find out what's going on in the system. I'm not saying that everybody should become a defendant but to take them around court, you know, follow people, see what actually happens. When I first started listening to Jack Straw, I found out about his being a barrister, I was surprised. But, from my limited knowledge of him, I don't think he practised for that long within legal aid. I don't think he did that for that long enough to understand the situation. Defence solicitors know that. It shows you that people who make decisions, they haven't been there.
>
> (Leland, solicitor, *Radford Hope*, INT)

This sense that the world of the defence lawyer could only be comprehended from within could be extended to academics: the distance separating those who write about lawyers' work and their actually being engaged in it. Perhaps, through politeness, this matter was little discussed around me. However, it was well articulated by a *Radcliffe and Musk* solicitor, Shelly, in relation to a prominent legal scholar who had once been a lawyer in her firm:

> It's amazing that he can write so much about representing clients, it's been such a long time since he's done it himself. Every so often he'll come back, have a look at the Crown Court, keep his toe in. But he doesn't get involved in the everyday things. He might phone up to ask a question, the impact of this or that, but he hasn't actually done it for so long. The thing is, there's such a huge gap between theory and practice. You can have a long book about representing clients but reading it doesn't help you. It's all about experience. Doing it first-hand, you learn more than you ever would just by reading it. You can get too bogged down in the theory; you need to actually do it to understand it. We know what we're doing, and we do what's best for the clients and don't need to be told how by someone who just writes about it.
>
> (Shelly, solicitor, *Radcliffe and Musk*, IC)

There was apparently a gap between academics and lawyers. This has been observed by Podmore (1980: 14–15), who suggests that this divide has allowed the former to become increasingly critical of the latter, with the result that:

> An example of strain and segmentation arising from different work settings can be seen in the rift that has developed between some academic lawyers (teachers and researchers) and the professional bodies . . . Increasingly acrimonious disputes arising out of the essentially 'liberal' state of academic lawyers and the 'profit interested' standpoint of private practitioners.

Most lawyers in this study, though, did not appear to be aware of the fault-finding timbre of the existing literature. They were frequently surprised when I quoted it to them in the formal interviews:

> It doesn't sound that this [previous] research comes out very favourably for lawyers at all!
>
> (Teresa, solicitor, *Radcliffe and Musk*, INT)

During the participant observation, I was only once confronted about the criticism present in many academic accounts. This was by a lawyer who had gone back to university and undertaken additional courses, so was exposed to the academic critique. In the first fortnight of the research, I had accompanied the *Radford and Hope* solicitor, Bob, to the Magistrates' Court on several occasions when he had been extremely busy with large lists of clients to work through. We had got on well, and Bob had always been very open and talkative. However, one morning at court Bob began to rant at me, demanding to know what was in my notebooks:

> What do you write in there? You don't understand what it's really like. How can you understand what we have to do? This is my job. You just write it, get to leave it; you don't live it. I have to stay here and do this. It's easy to criticise or pick holes in things from the outside, might not seem perfect. But it's what we do.
>
> (Bob, solicitor, *Radford Hope*, IC)

Though he was confrontational, I judged his tone to be more frightened than aggressive. All the same, it was disconcerting. It was particularly alarming because I could not show him what I had written as I had been criticising him. I had seen him talking in derogatory terms about clients, giving them short shrift and seeming not to listen to them.

At the time, I considered that Bob was trying to cover up practice he knew to be deplorable. However, his concerns should be given credence. He would have recognised my naïvety as I talked in glowing and romantic terms about the lawyer's role. I had amplified my own beliefs and been particularly effusive to ingratiate myself through flattery. Bob was likely concerned that I was not prepared for the reality in which he operated, with the financial pressures lawyers routinely discussed. He did not appear to feel that he would be judged fairly; perhaps only lawyers could understand lawyers.

The view that criminal defence is somehow distinctive can be found to underlie Travers' (1997b: 19–36) work and his espousing ethnomethodological research in Garfinkel's tradition – he places great stock on 'situated local knowledge'. This position is premised upon Garfinkel and Weider's (1991: 203) concerns that the social researcher must address the 'haecceity' of any institutional setting in which they find themselves – they need uncover just what makes a niche unique. So it is that Lynch (1993: 274) deduced that Garfinkel 'seemed to be insisting on a strong participant-observation requirement, through which his student would gain "adequate" mastery of other disciplines'.

The researcher must pay heed to the local knowledge that exists in a specific field. On outcomes, then, it is important to consider that the main difference between lawyers and the academic line offered previously was the concentration on convictions. In academia, this has been a major issue as evinced by the attention given to clients being pushed towards pleading guilty. However, most of these lawyers did not appear to view it as such a salient concern. No lawyer ever told me that convictions did not matter, but they did convey the impression that they did not think them especially significant to most of their clients. Indeed, the interviews saw lawyers reveal several concerns that were identified as more pertinent to clients, most commonly the sentence they would receive and gaining the opportunity to 'have their day in court'. A flavour of this is given in the following quotes:

> Actually, I think, almost, you can make more of a difference on guilty pleas sometimes because you have more opportunity to help people when people can't put forward their own explanations of what happened. I think sometimes you can make more of a difference doing mitigation, and talking people through what happened, than you can actually having a trial; looking at agreeing pleas, like a little plea package or a plea bargain.
>
> (Annie, solicitor, *Radcliffe and Musk*, INT)

> I've done a couple of trials recently where they really shouldn't have been trials and the evidence was very strong but the client was absolutely adamant that they were not guilty and so you really have to have a trial, and they both unfortunately got convicted. But, at least, they had their day in court and sometimes that's what a person needs, is to have their say and to see the witnesses come to court and have their say.
>
> (Ronette, solicitor, *Radcliffe and Musk*, INT)

The position these particular lawyers took is reflected in the practitioner guides, such as Ede and Edwards (2008: 99), which tells lawyers to:

> Give clear advice as to the risks and consequences of losing a trial, i.e. if your client's evidence is disbelieved he risks possible destruction of any mitigation . . . If your client's real concern is the possible sentence, he may be assisted by knowing the sentence the judge actually has in mind.

Throughout the participant observation, lawyers talked of 'regulars', with these constituting the bulk of their court lists. They were repeat offenders, with convictions in double or triple figures. With these clients, there often seemed to be an unspoken understanding on both sides that a guilty plea would be entered. It was not discussed as a live issue. Lawyers were focused on other items beyond the guilty plea: the client avoiding prison or getting the community order that best suited them; taking the opportunity to wipe their slate clean with other offences being taken into consideration when sentencing the matter at hand; maintaining their on-remand status and greater visitation rights, for as long as possible with an initial not guilty plea, and; making sure their possessions and/or loved ones would be safe and in order before going to prison.

On one occasion, a *Radford Hope* solicitor did nothing to prevent a client from being convicted of theft, despite her claims not to have committed the offence. He explained how this achieved what she would have wanted:

> So I got her a conditional discharge. That's a good result. There are some people who wouldn't agree, they'd say it should have been taken it to trial, etc. But that's not the point. She'll be happy with this; it's all over quickly and gives her another chance. I'm pleased.
>
> (Windom, solicitor, *Radford Hope*, IC)

A further example can be seen in the reaction of Laura, a *Swining MacSage* solicitor, to an assault trial. The client was found guilty, but that was not considered the important point to take from it:

> It went really well. He was convicted of the assault, but he was happy with that because, in their findings, they found that the police were completely inconsistent in their statements. Every single police statement was different. The only thing that was corroborated in their evidence was that he used the word 'fuck', but all of them used it in a different statement. Every single one said his behaviour was different, completely different. So, yeah they felt that the police officers' evidence was not consistent with each other but that his behaviour had gone beyond what was reasonable. But that the police didn't treat him as the victim that he was and that, perhaps, if they hadn't have been so heavy handed he wouldn't have reacted that way. He was happy with that; he'd felt aggrieved that the police had treated him the way they had. That really did go very well indeed.
>
> (Laura, solicitor, *Swining MacSage*, IC)

However, I was not simply relying on the lawyers' explanations. The following dialogues show that clients had priorities other than securing an acquittal:

> [Lawyer] The main thing we have to do today is make sure the judge doesn't sentence you. If he does, it'll be prison. You don't want that, do you?
>
> [Client] No, I don't care what happens, I just don't want no prison.
>
> [Lawyer] We have to try and persuade the judge to adjourn it today and send you to Probation for [Pre-Sentence] Reports. Then we've got a fighting chance when we come back in two week' time.
>
> [Client] I just want to be out for Christmas and my kids [cries].
>
> [Lawyer] I know. I want to get you out in two weeks time. You want to get out and see your kids, alright. Any questions?
>
> [Client] Will you try and get me out please? Even if it's tagging or something. Not go to the stores, maintain my script [methadone prescription], anything?
>
> [Lawyer] I will try and do that. So, you're happy to enter pleas, say you're guilty and hopefully go for reports. Is that alright?
>
> [Client] Yeah. Do that.
>
> (Leo, senior partner, and Claire Taylor, client, *Radcliffe and Musk*, OR)

> [Client] Hi, you're *Radford Hope* aren't you?
>
> [Lawyer] Yeah.

[Client] Good. I just need to get it done quickly, I have to be out of here by eleven.

[Lawyer] Why's that?

[Client] For my DRR [Drug Rehabilitation Requirement meeting].

[Lawyer] Okay. So what is it here today?

[Client] It's my first appearance, for a theft from a motor vehicle and it's a simple guilty. I just want it done quickly so I can be away.

(Jason Gillespie, client, and Norma, partner, *Radford Hope*, OR)

Lawyers, then, did not see conviction as the be all and end all, as they did not believe their clients were overly concerned with it. I saw for myself that this belief was not unjustified – at least so far as some clients were concerned. From the lawyers' perspective, then, academics focused on conviction were detached from the real world. Academics might judge clients by their own standards, far removed from the world of regular patrons. Lawyers considered themselves more attuned to these values through the knowledge gained from years of experience. It was the lawyers who witnessed clients returning time after time, laughing even, proud about how long their lists of charges were and regularly asking what the likely sentence was before discussing their plea. They felt close to these clients and so thought that they were able to make judgements about what they thought and what was important to them. As such, they deemed themselves able to provide the clients with something of a mediated choice; it was taken for granted that clients would want to plead guilty, and lawyers tasked themselves with providing options following this acceptance of guilt. By this line, what seems at first glance to be lawyers exerting pressure on clients to plead guilty is reconceptualised as the former helping the latter to achieve ends that are in their best interests, whether or not clients understand the situation. In short, lawyers knew best. This stance fed into their self-professed role as advisers, helping to enlighten clients as to what they wanted, even when they did not initially realise it.

At this point in the analysis it is helpful to draw on Blank's (2004) *Sociological Theory of Choice*. His thesis is largely premised upon hierarchy and Bourdieu's (1984) notion of status. For Blank (2004: 15–16), those with greater social, economic and cultural capitals review the options for those below them. The individuals making the choice defer to those with the superior knowledge and cachet, following their lead. The individual is not alone in making their choice, they make it based on relations with others; it is a social act. To some extent, this approach situates choice as the communal activity that Durkheim (1964: 278–79) seeks to promote, stressing that human contact created association that led, in turn, to the development of 'groups of co-operators'.

Under this practice, choice is a collaborative decision-making process, involving some measure of consultation and agreement with others. An important aspect might involve having another regulate the size of the choice set that can be selected from. Psychological research has suggested that, the larger the set, the more difficult individuals find it to make a choice (Iyengar and Lepper, 2000). At some point, then, choice ceases to be seen as a signifier of freedom and becomes detrimental to emotional and psychological wellbeing (Schwartz, 2005: 2–4). There is a cognitive burden that can be experienced in having too many options, leading to greater stress and a desire to have the field narrowed (Arunachalam et al, 2009: 823–34). Lawyers fulfilled this role as they shaped their clients' choices, and in so doing, they saw themselves as better placed to make these calls than outsiders.

Confidence Game

In order to accept the legitimacy of the greater influence that lawyers claimed, a great deal of trust has to be placed in their propriety; lawyers must be assumed to put their clients first. Observers and commentators need to be convinced of the integrity of lawyers to uphold access to justice but, most importantly, clients themselves must have faith in them. Accordingly, it seems sensible to consider the verdict that these clients offer. However, research into their views has suggested that they are in a perennially poor position from which to evaluate lawyers, unable to judge the service received (Moorhead et al, 2003: 8–9). For Tata et al (2004: 132), this situation is borne of the passivity of clients, their being reduced to spectators rather than players as 'they played only a small part in the process outside of court and were largely silent within it . . . clients readily said that they could not judge the technical aspects of what lawyers did'. As a result, there is confusion over the features that clients defer to. This situation is reflected by various studies with somewhat contradictory messages. To judge from the qualitative study of Ericson and Baranek (1982: 76–92), based on interviewing and observing around 100 criminal defendants, clients are largely focused on the result of the case. In contrast, the quantitative study conducted by Casper et al (1988: 503–04) of over 600 criminal defendants across three cities, reveals that clients care less about outcomes than they do about achieving a sense of fairness. Both of these studies were conducted in North America, in the 1980s. However, more recent research in the United Kingdom asserts that interpersonal criteria are most important of all (Tata et al, 2004: 131–33; Sommerlad and Wall, 1999: 13–17; Moorhead et al, 2003: 19–20).

These later studies appear to show that clients decline to pronounce upon the 'competence' of their lawyer (Moorhead et al, 2003: 14). For Moorhead et al (2003: 29), this could be attributed to the clients' 'inability to understand when an outcome is good, lucky or poor'. In lieu of this, clients bypass the legal aspect, and accept that which their lawyer presents to them. If clients feel a lawyer to be honest, they go along with what that lawyer says and does. They premise their trust upon personality.

Unfortunately, this means that clients are exposed to lawyers' attempts at 'image management' (Moorhead et al, 2003: 5–6). Lawyers know they can influence clients by manipulating their perceptions, leaving the clients primed for exploitation. This is reflected by Welsh's (2003: 10) practitioner guide, which urges lawyers to 'trick' clients to conceal any lack of knowledge or effort. In these circumstances, Blumberg (1967: 23) labels the lawyer–client relationship a 'confidence game'. Lawyering is a hustle. Clients are *marks* ready to be tricked and, as such, lawyers are able to abuse their trust.

For Blumberg (1967: 25), this situation derives from the special problem lawyers' face justifying their fees, as 'much legal work is intangible'. It is relatively straightforward for a plumber to demonstrate the services they render: unblocking a drain earns the instant appreciation of their client. Doctors are presented with a more challenging situation when there is no call for physical intervention; in order to ensure that the client feels tangible gain, they might be tempted to administer a placebo. To justify their own role, lawyers feel compelled to engage in some level of professional mystification. Lawyers are secretive about the legal process to ensure that clients are kept in 'a proper state of tension' (Blumberg: 1967: 26). The increasingly worried client becomes ever more dependent on their lawyer, as Blumberg (1967: 26) suggests that, 'law practice maintains a manipulation of the clients and a stage management of the lawyer–client relationship so that at least an appearance of help and service will be forthcoming'.

The way in which lawyers use this tool to lower expectations has been suggested by Morison and Leith (1992: 70). This practice leads Ericson and Baranek (1982: 99–100) to note lawyers' 'Godfather quality'; making clients offers they can't refuse. This approach was evident from my participant observation, as lawyers from all firms would regularly seek to spook clients into pleading guilty. The most common means of achieving this was to scare clients with talk of the magistrate or judge who would hear their case. At one time or another, nearly every one of these was built up as 'tough', 'harsh' or 'bad' – despite the same individuals being deemed 'decent' or 'fair' in conversation away from the clients. This common tactic can be appreciated from the following example, where a solicitor opened a consultation by warning the client that the judge would accept 'no messing around':

> Hello Mr Clarke, I'm Audrey. Let me tell you from the off, you've got a DJ [District Judge] today, and he's a tough one. He's a tough one. You just need to know that, before you say anything else.
>
> (Audrey, solicitor, *Swining MacSage*, OR)

It seemed that Audrey wanted to ensure that he would plead guilty, and swiftly. She assured him this was the sensible thing to do and the judge would appreciate it. The client pleaded guilty despite having given no comment in his police station interview.

However, the participant observation uncovered another means of manipulation, involving what Mungham and Thomas (1979: 179) label pyrotechnics, 'the demonstration of sustained aggression and a fancy piece of theatrics . . . deliberate manufacture of emotion and display'. Pyrotechnics refer primarily to advocacy, and that image of the lawyer on their feet in the courtroom so valorised in the supposed golden age of days long past. More recently, from the 1970s onwards, advocacy has been held up as an increasingly insubstantial part of the criminal process, exerting little effect on results (Kapardis, 2003: 208–11). All the same, it still appears to dominate lay perception. As such, Mungham and Thomas (1979: 170) define pyrotechnics to mean that:

> It is possible to leave behind a satisfied client after the completion of a case, even though it might be easy to show that the advocate handled the case poorly, and got less for the client than he could have done had he deployed other arguments or resources.

While fear could produce client satisfaction notwithstanding a guilty plea, this alternative confidence trick provided a mechanism by which lawyers could get clients to accept defeat in the rare cases where they had convinced lawyers to run a case. If lawyers faced a trial or bail application they had not wanted, pyrotechnics allowed them a means to mask the fact that they were not really trying to win.

The application of this approach can be discerned from a trial that Harold, partner in *Radford Hope*, was given by his secretary the morning it was due in the Magistrates' Court. I was sitting with him in his office when he received it. The client was accused of assaulting three police officers. He skimmed through the papers and remarked:

> It hasn't got a chance; the magistrates will never believe one toe rag over three police officers.
>
> (Harold, partner, *Radford Hope*, IC)

Harold, then, had neither the ability nor the inclination to thoroughly prepare the case for the trial. With less than half an hour before he would leave for court, there was no time for him to consider it in detail. Regardless, this was deemed fruitless as he stated that the magistrates wouldn't be persuaded on a case such as this anyway. In these circumstances, Harold proceeded to the Magistrates' Court with the intention of persuading the client to change his plea, later explaining that:

> I told the client he had no chance, and that he should plead guilty.
>
> (Harold, partner, *Radford Hope*, IC)

The client refused, and wanted the case fought. In court, Harold put on a show of pyrotechnics, and was extremely aggressive to the police officers in the witness box. He harangued the first officer, reducing him to shaking and meekly squeaking answers. His questioning produced repeated responses of 'I can't answer that' and 'I don't remember'. Eventually, Harold murmured under his breath, 'Well, you're a policeman, you always say that'. The officer seemed confused, asking, 'I'm sorry, did you say something?' but all Harold said was 'Well, yes'. The officer stated: 'I didn't hear it, and I wondered if it was a question'. Harold sneered and barked, 'No, it wasn't a question', after which he left a purposeful silence.

At this point the prosecutor objected that Harold was 'unfairly murmuring under his breath remarks that could be heard by some in the court but not by others'. The magistrates upheld this objection, and reminded Harold that, 'there is no place for muffled asides in the court'. Harold did not apologise and, instead, proceeded to make numerous more such remarks. He eventually lost the trial. However, the client was happy, thanking Harold profusely.

The delight of this client despite being convicted highlights the manner in which pyrotechnics can engender much goodwill. Harold engaged in more obvious displays of pyrotechnics, and more regularly, than other lawyers. Interestingly, Harold appeared to be the most popular lawyer among lay persons at the Magistrates' Court; clients, ushers and those who watched from the back of court regularly appeared wowed by him. He was notorious for his 'hopeless bail applications', in which he made over-the-top speeches in cases that he deemed did not have a chance. Harold would outline the fine details of the Bail Act 1976, weaving long stories together, with verbose and florid language, always ending with a flourish as he would 'commend my client as a prime candidate for bail'. He did all but take a bow. The typical reactions from the lay persons watching were smiles and admiration:

> [Defendant One] You've got to watch him. He's great! He's tearing the police apart.
>
> [Defendant Two] I want him.
>
> [Defendant One] Me too.
>
> (Tim Paine and Marcus North, defendants, OR – at the back of the Magistrates' Court)

> I love watching Harold. He's so eloquent and passionate. Of all the solicitors I've seen here, he's the one I'd want to represent me.
>
> (Haruki Murakami, usher, IC)

> When I was training, I went along to watch him in court, and he's fantastic. When he stands there and makes his speeches. I know that if I ever got in trouble, knock on wood, then he's the one I'd want to represent me.
>
> (Harriet, secretary, *Radford Hope*, IC)

More often than not, Harold's applications were unsuccessful. He would impishly shrug his shoulders, and apologise to the client and any family at the back of court. However, these parties were rarely disheartened or aggrieved, pyrotechnics made them incredibly forgiving and more likely to greet him with gushing praise for trying.

In contrast, lawyers who did not utilise pyrotechnics tended to be more unpopular, and frequently elicited negative reactions. Clients and their families might not have felt the lawyer to be on their side or may have judged a lack of effort. Another *Radford Hope* solicitor, Bob, provided a good example of this – other lawyers were amused by his approach. He refused to engage in pyrotechnics, priding himself on being 'straight' and aiming to simply 'get my head down and get on with it'. Bob showed little desire to win round the clients, rejecting any gloss or charm. He was frustrated at the notion of running trials or making bail applications that he felt had no merit, and sought to speed clients through as quickly as possible. His colleague, Harold, explained that the result of this was:

> Lots of clients just don't want him to represent them, he winds them up; they don't feel as though he's committed to them.
>
> (Harold, partner, *Radford Hope*, IC)

This can be seen from Bob's approach to the case of a juvenile client who was in the cells on a common assault charge. The client had pushed Bob into making a bail application. Bob was not pleased at having to do this, labelling the attempt

Pointless – a waste of my time.

(Bob, solicitor, *Radford Hope*, IC)

Bob was subdued and appeared distracted; it seemed to me that he was going through the motions and wanted to get it over with. This application, though, was adjourned by the magistrates, so that Bob could establish a firm address for the client. Bob was equally unimpressed by this, complaining to me that:

I can't wait to get to the pub. Have you seen the time [four o'clock]?

(Bob, solicitor, *Radford Hope*, IC)

The client's family had garnered the same impression as I did, and confronted Bob on his heading back into the court for the continuation of the hearing:

He's useless that solicitor . . . What a shit job he's doing . . . Just don't care, does he? It's all his fault . . . Oi! You, you're a joker. So, you gonna try a bit harder to get bail this time, then?

(Nathan Bracken's family, clients, *Radford Hope*, OR)

Bob was similarly languid in the second hearing. The client was refused bail, and Bob left to a chorus of jeers.

Considering these two examples, the practice of pyrotechnics can be appreciated as an exemplar of Goffman's (1990: 203–07) impression management: defensive measures used to save their 'show' from unintended slip-ups and deviations from the script. Social performances, for Goffman (1990: 78) are explained as in a play, making heavy use of the dramaturgical metaphor, whereby, 'the world is not, of course, a stage, but the crucial ways in which it isn't are not easy to specify'. By this, the actor puts on a show, forever with the audience in mind. Each performance is tailored to ensure that the particular target is left with an impression consistent with the desired goal of the actor. So it was that the lawyer performed for the client; they are effectively playing to the gallery. Lawyers seemed to recognise this when I asked them about pyrotechnics:

They do provide satisfaction – for the client watching, and the family at the back of court, that's my job. That's what I should be doing.

(Dale, senior partner, *Swining MacSage*, IC)

The client, he appreciates a bit of fireworks in there.

(Harold, partner, *Radford Hope*, IC)

However, performing for that particular audience was not necessarily a positive thing. This was acknowledged by Leo, the senior partner of *Radcliffe and Musk* who, unprompted, used the word pyrotechnics to describe these practices in a negative manner:

Pyrotechnics – usually a complete waste of time and a 'show' for the client.

(Leo, senior partner, *Radcliffe and Musk*, EM)

Pyrotechnics might have done more harm than good in actually attaining a good result for a client, militating against any sort of victory (Kapardis, 2003: 211–19). In addition to closing down witnesses, stopping them talking, pyrotechnics likely worked to frustrate magistrates or judges who would be left unimpressed at the harsh treatment afforded to witnesses or police officers. This is recognised in practitioner guides, such as Davies (2007: 34) which warns that, 'such people do not deserve to be harangued when they are in the witness box, and you will not get the sympathy of the bench or a jury by badgering them'.

By concentrating on making a good impression on the client at the expense of the officials who hear the case, the lawyers put aside any serious attempts to succeed with the court. Instead, they focused their efforts on deceiving the client that they had made efforts to do so. Leo was attuned to this, and in commenting on it made reference to Harold, partner, *Radford Hope*:

> I can think of a solicitor here (whom you would know) who regularly used to use this tactic in bail applications (particularly when he had little to say). My impression was that he did not really want to have to advise the client that the application was hopeless and initially wanted to 'keep the client happy' and that it was easier to make 'a lot of noise' in court than try to explain the realities of the client's situation. This was quite often (in my view) detrimental to the client's case and as a result the client would often get entirely the wrong idea about the merits of his case – this observation based on taking over several such clients later on.
>
> (Leo, senior partner, *Radcliffe and Musk*, EM)

In the earlier example, then, it is likely that Harold knew that ranting at police officers would not be conducive to achieving a not guilty verdict in the trial. In the same way, he was probably aware that his bail applications had very little chance of succeeding. This can be seen in the following exchange with a prosecutor:

> [Prosecutor] What a wonderful exposition of the Bail Act. It hasn't got a chance though!
>
> [Lawyer] Oh, I know! Sometimes you just have to go off on one.
>
> (Douglas Copeland, prosecutor, and Harold, partner, *Radford Hope*, OR)

Harold's actions were froth, and pyrotechnics can be understood as a lot of sound and fury, signifying nothing. Lawyers were frustrated at proceeding in the direction that the client chose, and could cite strong prosecution evidence, questionable client character or a lack of time to prepare to excuse them from putting work into a case. More so, they could do little and still receive greater rewards in terms of the plaudits that pyrotechnics provided. Clients were distracted from the reality that their cases were treated as hopeless and thus pyrotechnics provided for the obfuscation of poor practice and poor results. Pyrotechnics may have been superficial, but they seemed to exert a considerable sway on clients.

The difference that pyrotechnics could make can be seen from the one client's varying reactions to two lawyers, one of whom engaged in them – Dale, senior partner – and one who did not – Thomas, partner – both from *Swining MacSage*. Thomas had a client, David Boon, for whom he had made an unsuccessful bail application on charges of common assault. Following the hearing, Thomas was confronted by David's family and friends who jostled him into an interview room. Here they shouted abuse at him and he was mocked and threatened with physical violence. Court security staff rushed to the scene and kept guard as the heated exchange continued. The group was livid, claiming that Thomas was:

> Useless . . . not trying . . . didn't care . . . working with them [the prosecution] . . . he should be sacked!
>
> (David Boon's family, clients, *Swining MacSage*, OR)

They complained to the firm about Thomas's low-key, routine bail application and threatened to take their business elsewhere. When Thomas got back to the office that afternoon he was called to see Dale. He read Thomas the – metaphorical – riot act, as David and family provided a lot of business to the firm. Dale subsequently went on a successful charm offensive, persuading the family to retain them. The most important part of this was identified to be the need for pyrotechnics:

> You have to show them that you're trying. They want to feel like you put the effort in. Did you think Thomas did that? He doesn't know how, he hasn't got the personality; head down, too quiet, all that. He hasn't got the advocacy. You have to remember, that it's them at the back, they're the important ones. Just make them feel it. That's what I can do.
>
> (Dale, senior partner, *Swining MacSage*, IC)

Dale duly put on a show of pyrotechnics, he was flashy and entertaining; he impressed the public gallery. However, he did not provide any new arguments, and the content of his application was all but identical to Thomas's. Dale did not expect any success and the first result was duly repeated; the client was remanded in custody. However, the reaction was quite different, as the family was left extremely happy:

> Thank you, Dale, we really appreciate you trying . . . you gave it everything, he knows that . . . you're the best.
>
> (David Boon's family, clients, *Swining MacSage*, OR)

In a conversation over lunch later that week, Dale had discussed Thomas's handling of this case with his other senior partner, Ed:

> [Lawyer One] It doesn't matter whether he gets him out or not, he should still make sure they're [the family] happy with the service they got.
>
> [Lawyer Two] Yes, I just don't think he realises that. I don't think he knows what the job is about.
>
> [Lawyer One] He's too quiet.
>
> (Dale and Ed, senior partners, *Swining MacSage*, OR)

Dale considered that Thomas had an understated, 'civil service approach', antithetical to his, bombastic, 'old school approach'. The popularity of the latter seems to signify that this was simply a victory for style over substance.

It was true, then, that most lawyers in this research appeared to know what many of their clients desired; they wanted a show. That this allowed lawyers to get away without working as hard as they might, disguised incompetent practice, and softened the sting of defeat, does not seem a particularly good advert for lawyers' claims to use their experiential knowledge to the clients' benefit. If lawyers really did work to get what their clients wanted, it seems strange that they would willingly trick their clients into accepting the outcomes they achieved. The presence of these confidence tricks within my data questions the sense in trusting lawyers to look after the best interests of their clients. It suggests that many lawyers are willing and able to control their clients. These findings are more consistent with the academic critique than the lawyers' defence that academics simply do not understand how law works in practice.

Outcomes – Control and Choice

In this discussion, it has been shown that lawyers were able to exert great influence over clients and the decisions made in cases. This went beyond their traditional role of providing advice, as lawyers appeared to give the instructions that are supposedly the domain of clients. I can, then, return to the question asked at the outset of this discussion: who actually chose the direction to follow? The answer seems to have been the lawyers, though they made it appear as though their clients chose.

Two divergent images emerged from each of the opening sections of this chapter. In the interviews, many lawyers claimed to give voice to clients, while the participant observation showed most speaking over the clients. The choices I witnessed, then, owed more to the direction of the lawyers than the clients. Their claims to the contrary might be considered the deception or fantasy ascribed in previous chapters, as the reality was that clients seemed to be controlled. This is a powerful supposition that demands further consideration.

In so doing, it is perhaps useful to turn to Habermas (1999: 88–89) and his 'ideal speech situation'. This device plays a central role in his early philosophy and his attempts to develop an understanding of social interactions. It presents a model by which only reciprocity and communication can provide for a genuine discussion. This idea is premised upon principles of truthfulness, legitimacy, mutual understanding and, perhaps most significantly, the right to speak. As such, Habermas (1999: 89) states that the following rules must apply to achieve ideal speech:

> 1. Every subject with the competence to speak and act is allowed to take part in a discourse.
> 2a Everyone is allowed to question any assertion whatever.
> 2b. Everyone is allowed to introduce any assertion whatever into the discourse.
> 2c. Everyone is allowed to express his attitudes, desires and needs.
> 3. No speaker may be prevented, by internal or external coercion, from exercising his rights as laid down in (1) and (2).

If each of these points is met then there will be a free dialogue. There would be no fear of coercion, and any discrepancies in power, prestige or confidence has no bearing. Free speech allows a true consensus to be reached. Were this discussion to simply draw on my formal interview data, the lawyers might have successfully argued for their achieving this ideal speech situation through activating numbers one and two. However, that would not tally with my experience from the participant observation, where lawyers regularly breached the prohibition set out in number three. Overall, then, there was a situation that appeared far from ideal.

However, it should be noted that the ideal speech situation is a concept rife with problems. That ideal might never exist. It has been shown that there will always be gaps in any ideal speech situation, gaps that allow coercion to operate (Flyvberg, 1998: 215–19). For Rae (1975: 1293–94), the idea that such consensus could ever be reached was misplaced; if a decision had to be made, there was always an implicit threat that this might be carried out were consensus not reached. As such, McGann (2005: 4–9) posits that the ideal speech situation and its vision of consensus are logically impossible. Further, society can be considered filled with individually structured 'fields', each bounded by their own rules and thereon possessed of particular conceptions of what constitutes legitimate opinion (Bourdieu and Wacquant, 1992: 94–100). Within these fields, there will always be experts and those expected to defer to them.

It might, then, be considered natural, even inherent, that lawyers should shape the choice for their clients. Research conducted four decades ago leads Carlen (1974: 101–03) to observe that the Magistrates' Court develops 'remedial routines for the maintenance of control' as the criminal justice system uses situational rules to manage what defendants said. The procedures that she highlighted will no longer be seen in represented cases because defence lawyers maintain order on the court's behalf. The silencing of defendants is now achieved in a more subtle and apparently legitimate way. Under Cain's (1983: 110–13) characterisation of lawyers as translators, there need be no malevolence in the restricted choice they provided to clients. That this practice might be labelled as control is decried by Cain (1983: 111) who argues that it actually amounts to the more positive concept of 'reconstitution'. For Cain (1983: 111), 'clients bring many issues to the solicitor, expressed and constituted in terms of a variety of everyday discourses' and, in turn, 'the lawyer translates these, and reconstitutes the issues in terms of a legal discourse which has a trans-situational applicability'.

However, her research took place when working class clients represented a distinct minority, and she acknowledges that this group might be more vulnerable and contradict her conclusions. So it is that McConville et al (1994: 130) contest her supposition, stating that their subsequent research 'gives little support to the conception of lawyers as altruistic professionals giving effect to the wishes of autonomous clients or . . . translating the needs of clients into the meta-language of the law'. Lawyers, rather, can be seen as 'stealing conflicts, taking the wants of clients and setting them aside if they deviate from their own (Christie, 1977: 4). A mediated choice is scant little choice at all if it entails lawyers denying clients a vocabulary of their own. In this way, clients in my research were silenced and lawyers able to take advantage of them. All of this enabled lawyers to work primarily for themselves and not for the clients.

It is in these circumstances that many lawyers could follow a tactic such as the 'coded' bail application. It was more difficult for lawyers to persuade clients against bail applications than it was not guilty pleas, and there was a lot less work required in a speech than in a trial. As such, lawyers were more likely to make bail applications that they did not want to. However, in these situations, many would deploy certain key words, which Hucklesby (1997a: 278–79) describes as a type of 'shorthand'. Lawyers used this to tell the other court users that they were simply going through the motions and not actually trying. This was discussed by several lawyers throughout the participant observation, as in these examples from both types of firm:

> McGrath [client] is on my back and moaning. He wants me to make a bail application, and it's hopeless. Luckily, it's Judge-in-Chambers, and the client isn't present, so I've written a coded application. Make sure the judge knows I'm only doing it because the client is pushing me so much. You can't really do it in the Magistrates' Court with the client there, but I will in front of a judge. Just so he knows I'm not a complete dickhead.
>
> (Leo, senior partner, *Radcliffe and Musk*, IC)

> [Lawyer One] Can I say: 'I am instructed'? So they know I don't mean it.
>
> [Lawyer Two] No! You can't be that obvious.
>
> [Lawyer One] But I don't want to do it, it's hopeless. She won't listen though. I won't make it too obvious – I just don't want to look like an idiot.
>
> (Laura, solicitor, and Nadine, partner, *Swining MacSage*, OR)

These were, then, bail applications crafted for the lawyers' needs rather than those of the clients; they served the dual purpose of saving face while maintaining business. A similar situation can be seen when some lawyers used unpromising trials as a chance to practise their skills. These lawyers did not feel the need to try, simply using the speeches and cross-examinations as a form of exercise, as described by lawyers from Sausage Factory and Radical firms respectively:

> It was fun, it didn't matter, he was probably going to get convicted, so I could let go a bit. It was good practice, that's why they give you trials that don't matter when you're starting out, so you can make your mistakes there.
>
> (Laura, solicitor, *Swining MacSage*, IC)

> When there's no pressure on a case, you can relax, and have some fun. It's when there's a case that you've actually got a chance of winning, where they might expect a result, that's when you feel pressure. When it's a hopeless case, you can just enjoy. It doesn't matter if you lose a hopeless case.
>
> (Leland, solicitor, *Radford Hope*, IC)

Each of these instances conveys the potential that lawyers had to abuse the trust placed in them.

It has been noted by Galanter (2005: 3–15) that those who must deal with the legal profession are often left wary; there is a lay perception that lawyers can get away with whatever they like. He suggests that lawyer jokes constitute a safe means to vent frustrations, without fear of recrimination from this influential group. Building on this base of distrust and ill-favour, Murphy (2009) offers a means to conceptualise client experiences by dint of a *power and control wheel.* This is one of numerous adaptations of the original power and control wheels developed for domestic abuse, known as Duluth models (see Pope and Ferraro, 2006). A warning has been issued by Dutton and Corvo (2006: 477–79), cautioning that these wheels can be misused to narrow-mindedly ignore wider, sociological issues in favour of focusing on the acts of abuse itself. However, these authors acknowledge that these wheels do form a vital starting point for debate, as a means to highlight problems not yet popularly accepted. In application to the lawyer–client relationship, the wheel posits that the control lawyers could wield as a result of the imbalance of power between them and their clients can constitute a form of psychological abuse. From this perspective, lawyers did not simply abuse trust but, in a grimly real sense, they abused their clients. Various strategies that were witnessed in the participant observation would be construed as client abuse under Murphy's (2009) wheel. These encompass factors from the preceding chapters on attitudes and behaviour as well as the present one on outcomes, including: acting like the boss; making the big decisions; playing mind games; using vague, ambiguous and ineffective language; exaggerating the harmful outcomes to the client; pressuring the client to accept a plea deal, and; ignoring client's instructions, decisions and best interests.

By focusing on outcomes – particularly the question of choice – we are able to see that the lawyer–client relationship could be figuratively, even literally, described as an abusive one. In process as in outcomes, this research has cast a negative light over these lawyers and access to justice. In the final chapter, I move to summarise what has been seen and reflect on the wider implications this may hold.

6

Some Concluding Thoughts: Access to Justice and the Lawyer–Client Relationship Revisited

This research set out to explore the lawyer–client relationship. It has been informed by the supposition that access to justice requires access to criminal defence lawyers funded by legal aid. Moreover, I have insisted that these lawyers need to provide a high quality service dedicated to the clients and displaying strong due process values – active defence. Just turning up is not enough as far as I am concerned – lawyers have to earn their fee (no matter how paltry they deemed it). These factors have been taken as markers of a healthy lawyer–client relationship that properly serves justice. However, the ethnographic data disseminated in the preceding chapters revealed a dispiriting picture that did not meet such expectations. From the findings concerning negative attitudes, disrespectful behaviour and lawyers speaking over clients, it is evident that the nature of the lawyer–client relationship was such as to place clients' access to justice in jeopardy. There was considerable strain on this relationship – symptomatic of ill-health – and the clients appeared to suffer as a result. It was hardly worth the lawyers being there at all, except to serve the interests of swift and efficient court processing of cases (crime control not due process values).

To conclude this investigation, I reflect on some of the implications of what has been reported. My research built on the foundations laid by the ethnographies of McConville et al (1994) and Travers (1997b) some two decades before, and especially the fundamental contradiction between the various images of the lawyer–client relation they portrayed. The former presented evidence justifying an attack on legally aided criminal defence lawyers, while the latter found grounds to praise them. These works present such divergent accounts of the lawyer–client relationship that I felt they needed to be resolved by a new and up-to-date study – such as my own. I deemed that the best way of achieving this goal was to combine the varying structuralist and interpretivist methodologies used by each of the preceding studies in organising and analysing my own ethnographic data – allowing the lawyer to have a voice in the study I conducted. Despite this, my evidence suggested conclusions more in line with the negative image portrayed by McConville et al (1994).

In designing this study, a theoretical sample of Radical and Sausage Factory firms was devised in order to find the best and worst of legally aided criminal defence;

lawyers who facilitated access to justice for their clients and those who precluded it. I was particularly keen to focus on the former to draw out the positive elements of legally aided criminal defence. Thus, two Radical firms and one Sausage Factory firm were the subject of close scrutiny. As such, a distinct pattern should have emerged across these three firms regarding the highlighted issues of attitudes, behaviour and outcomes. This configuration, though, did not materialise in the manner anticipated.

Rather than the theoretical firms directly mapping onto their real life counterparts in the sample, the two prongs of this ethnography produced a complication. In the formal interviews, the great majority of lawyers from all three firms presented views that could be characterised as Radical. In the participant observation, the bulk of lawyers from all three firms acted in a manner suggestive of the Sausage Factory. Though unexpected, this variation was straightforward. Its simplicity works to emphasise how stark and definitive these results were, as should be evident from the following figures.

Attitudes

I anticipated that lawyers in the firms should display readily distinguishable attitudes to their clients. Radical firms would be positive, Sausage Factory negative:

Expectations	Positive	Negative
Radical	X	
Sausage Factory		X

Figure 1

Lawyers from both firms, though, presented positive attitudes in the formal interviews:

Interviews	Positive	Negative
Radical	X	
Sausage Factory	X	

Figure 2

In contrast, the participant observation showed a quite different situation, as each displayed negative attitudes:

Observation	Positive	Negative
Radical		X
Sausage Factory		X

Figure 3

Behaviour

As with attitudes, behaviour was supposed to generate a clear separation between Radical firms where lawyers treated clients with respect and Sausage Factories where the opposite would be found:

Expectations	Respect	Disrespect
Radical	X	
Sausage Factory		X

Figure 4

The formal interviews saw claims to respectful behaviour by all:

Interviews	Respect	Disrespect
Radical	X	
Sausage Factory	X	

Figure 5

The participant observation, though, contradicted this with universally disrespectful behaviour:

Observation	Respect	Disrespect
Radical		X
Sausage Factory		X

Figure 6

Outcomes

Finally, I predicted that outcomes were to follow a similar path. Radical firms would find lawyers giving voice to clients while Sausage Factories would see clients being spoken over:

Expectations	Give Voice	Speak Over
Radical	X	
Sausage Factory		X

Figure 7

The image gleaned from the formal interviews was one in which lawyers gave voice to clients across the board:

Interviews	Give Voice	Speak Over
Radical	X	
Sausage Factory	X	

Figure 8

Meanwhile, the participant observation suggested that these same lawyers actually spoke over their clients:

Observation	Give Voice	Speak Over
Radical		X
Sausage Factory		X

Figure 9

The Lawyer–Client Relationship

In each issue, then, the formal interviews and participant observation were at odds. Overall, this meant that, while it was supposed that these two types of firm would show divergent experiences of the lawyer-client relationship they actually revealed a similar one. It was expected that the Radical firms would exhibit a healthy relationship, rather than the strained one expected with the Sausage Factory firms:

Expectations	Healthy	Strained
Radical	X	
Sausage Factory		X

Figure 10

The formal interviews documented a healthy relationship all round:

Interviews	Healthy	Strained
Radical	X	
Sausage Factory	X	

Figure 11

However, the participant observation exposed a strained relationship in every firm:

Observation	Healthy	Strained
Radical		X
Sausage Factory		X

Figure 12

On the one hand, lawyers portrayed a supposedly healthy relationship while, on the other, I found this not to be the case and saw a strained relationship.

RHETORIC

It should, then, be clear that the formal interviews produced a picture quite distinct from that of the participant observation and that the former tallied with the theoretical Radical firm, while the latter was consistent with the Sausage Factory. Lawyers spoke as if they stood for active defence, while they appeared to practise something far more passive. As such, it can be said that the lawyers talked the talk but did not walk the walk. This poses a question of deep significance to this research, and left-liberal socio-legal studies in general; is the Radical firm simply a matter of rhetoric?

In addressing this question, I feel it is important to reassert the contention that this book is not in any way intended to be anti-lawyer; quite the opposite it was undertaken to support those who practised active defence and the cause they claimed to work for. As such, it is only fair to acknowledge that there will be systematic reasons why a healthy relationship was difficult to achieve in practice. The most obvious of these are the aforementioned burden of reduced legal aid remuneration. This must certainly have exerted some impact, as spending less on goods of whatever variety almost always entails receiving a lesser product in return, you get what you pay for – less and/or lower quality service. But the devaluing of the apparent commodities offered by these lawyers is only one part of a wider process whereby the structure of the criminal process increasingly appears to stand against enacting adversarial justice. A more procedural example exists in the way that the criminal justice system holds out a discount for defendants pleading guilty which, inherently, makes it harder for lawyers to appear to be practising active defence. Lawyers are ethically obliged to advise their clients that it may be in their best interests to plead guilty. In this manner, the criminal justice system ensures that truly active defence can come at a considerable cost to the client. There are, then, systemic inducements to brevity in dealing with cases, an effective streamlining of the lawyer–client relationship that formally induces lawyers towards passivity rather than contesting cases for their clients. It would be unrealistic to pretend such pressures did not exert some influence. However, these disincentives and barriers do not satisfactorily account for the discrepancy between how the lawyers described themselves and how they actually acted. The majority still talked as if they practised active defence and facilitated a healthy relationship, despite my seeing that this was far from the truth.

Meeting this disjuncture, over the course of the research, I have felt the need to become increasingly sceptical of what the lawyers said. For Shermer (2010), a sceptic is one who takes a scientific approach to evaluating claims; science is sceptical and good scientists are sceptics. The sceptic carefully considers the evidence and willingly follows the facts wherever they lead. This can be contrasted with the denier who has a position set out in advance and sorts through the available data employing *confirmation bias* to find evidence that confirms their pre-existing beliefs. Anything that contradicts their position is ignored, so Shermer (2010: 36) suggests that, 'denial is typically driven by ideology and belief... commitment to belief takes precedence over the evidence'.

It would have been an act of denial for me to produce a book that portrayed lawyers in a good light, and depicted a healthy lawyer–client relationship. This could have been achieved, though, with some highly selective presentation of unrepresentative data. That implies, of course, that not everything that I saw aroused my critical ire. It should be recognised, then, that it would be misleading to proceed as if these lawyers were engaged in a constant and unrelenting war against their clients. Throughout the research, I have highlighted my selective use of quotes and examples, deployed to produce a representative account of the dominant patterns. This should not disguise the fact that there were occasions on which lawyers displayed positive attitudes and respectful behaviour towards clients to whom they gave voice. In other words, there was some, albeit quite limited, overlap between what was said and done. These instances were few and far between, and paled with regard to those already documented. It is important, though, that they are not ignored.

On many occasions, lawyers were neutral about clients and offered no judgement. When they did, it tended to be negative, but there were some positive attitudes expressed. This can be seen across the firms, in the following examples taken following client consultations at the Magistrates' Court. The first dialogue refers to three new Eastern European clients involved in an affray, with difficulties speaking English; the latter two concern young, but regular, clients facing drug-related theft charges. The reactions could be deemed patronising but, all the same, seemed well-intentioned:

> Oh, that was great. I think I really bonded with them. They seemed to like me. Nice guys, lovely. I really enjoyed that. I hope I helped them.
>
> (Laura, solicitor, *Swining MacSage*, IC)

> I really hope he can sort himself out. He's been so unlucky in his life. He deserves another chance. Poor kid.
>
> (Shelly, solicitor, *Radcliffe and Musk*, IC)

> He's a sweet little kid. I really liked dealing with him. I hope he gets on okay. I'll keep an eye out for him
>
> (Catherine, solicitor, *Radford Hope*, IC)

While the lawyers were regularly disrespectful to clients, there were also exceptions to the rule at all firms. In the following example, Denise, a *Radcliffe and Musk* solicitor at the Magistrates' Court, encountered a client who was in court for assaulting his wife. The client would not receive legal aid for his Magistrates' appearance as he was self-employed, had not brought payment slips along and, it was assumed, would be beyond the eligibility threshold in any event. The case was likely to be committed to the Crown Court but, all the same, Denise was distraught that the client would have to go through the hearing on his own. She had spent much time with him in the cells, despite not being paid for it, and passionately complained to all who would listen, as follows:

> It's ridiculous. About as serious as it gets – domestic violence. The fact that he's not got anyone representing him today isn't going to make any difference to the outcome. But that's not the point, he should have the right to representation. Access to justice? This is a case in point; complete lack of. It makes me want to give up the job completely. If we can't represent clients like that, in these circumstances, what's the point?
>
> (Denise, solicitor, *Radcliffe and Musk*, OR)

Similar sentiments were expressed by her colleague, Shelly, who was appointed by the court to cross-examine the main witness in another domestic violence case. She was upset that she was to attend the trial but only undertake that one task and then leave the client to fend for himself, as seen from the following:

> It's crap, absolute crap. And I feel terrible about it. I really hate this. I feel really shit. I'd much rather not be here at all. I just don't want to go in and just do the cross-examination, while he does the bad character, other witnesses and makes his own closing speech. It's horrible and I really wish I wasn't in this position.
>
> (Shelly, solicitor, *Radcliffe and Musk*, IC)

With regard to outcomes, the major theme was for lawyers to push clients to accept their decisions and plead guilty. One solicitor expressed regret at this situation:

> It's not right to push clients to plead guilty, not if they really don't want to. Of course, solicitors do encourage clients to see it their way, when it's in their best interests. But, even then, if the client doesn't want to they shouldn't be made to. Clients should be able to do what they want.
>
> (Audrey, solicitor, *Swining MacSage*, IC)

Beyond this, though, the following examples show lawyers from Sausage Factory and Radical firms alike acting to convince clients to plead not guilty:

> [Client] Why would the police make something up?
>
> [Lawyer] They have been known to do that [laughs]. It might be that he realised he made a mistake and was lying to cover his own back by claiming you hit him first. You should really consider pleading not guilty.
>
> (Peter Siddle, client, and Dale, senior partner, *Swining MacSage*, OR)

> [Lawyer] I want you to think very carefully about this. If you're sure you're not guilty then you have to say not guilty.
>
> [Client] But, the other one, he said I should just go guilty.
>
> [Lawyer] Forget about that. What's important is what you believe. If you think you are not guilty, then that's what we do. Think about it.
>
> (Norma, solicitor, and Ben Hilfenhaus, client, *Radford Hope*, OR)

The foregoing from the participant observation could have been used in combination with the interview data to produce a positive work akin to Travers (1997b). Maybe Travers (1997b) was lucky enough to find a firm that practised active defence all the time. However, the possibility of rhetoric is also writ large; accepting the slant lawyers put on events may have produced findings that owed more to this rhetoric than to any reality. However much I wanted to find similarly encouraging results to support my initial belief that lawyers deserve more support (not to mention, for an easy life in terms of analysis), the need for scepticism was too strong. If I had attempted to give a positive slant to what I saw, it could justifiably be construed as an act of denial, as Shermer (2010: 37) suggests that a 'practical way to distinguish between a sceptic and a denier is the extent to which they are willing to update their position in response to new information . . . sceptics change their mind, deniers just keep on denying'. I was not able to deny the discrepancy between what the lawyers said in interview and did through the participant observation; my own standpoint had to change and I became distanced from the lawyers. This was no easy move, and I was initially concerned that I would upset many of my new friends. While I hoped to improve it, I am aware that this research may further harm the reputation of this branch of the legal profession. However, I am first and foremost a social scientist and so guided by Shermer's (2010: 37) conclusion that, 'scepticism is integral to the scientific process because most claims turn out to be fake . . . weeding out the few kernels of wheat from the large pile of chaff requires extensive observation'.

Over time, completing the research for this book has turned me into something of a lawyer-sceptic (which should not be misread as a *lawyer, septic*; a phrase that some of the less sympathetically minded might wish to use in referring to the lawyers in this study) In compiling this book, then, I have to consider that what the lawyers said about their practice might simply have been so much rhetoric; exaggerated and high-flown language, grandiloquence and bluster, used to disguise and deflect attention away from a lack of meaningful content to support it. Of course, this research does not provide the answer to the question of whether the Radical firm is just a matter of rhetoric. It was conducted with a handful of purposively selected firms in a single area. This represents a significant limitation of the present findings. There is a need to be aware of the possibility for variation between different locations, what Church (1985: 451) labels 'local legal cultures' – lawyer norms governing case handling and activity. Accordingly, Hucklesby (1997b: 130) urges the value of considering the social processes involved in particular criminal justice settings and the importance of relationships for the participants within. There is, then, scope for variation and specificity. Following this, I make no claims that the data offered represents the mass of legally aided criminal defence across England and Wales (no matter what anxiety I posses that it actually may well do).

At the very least, the emergence of rhetoric as a topic that needs to be addressed constitutes an extremely important finding in itself. It has wider implications for what we believe about access to justice and what we could legitimately hope to see in the criminal process. While we cannot judge whether the Radical position was all rhetoric, this study does put us in a position from which to consider that there may have been some element of rhetoric from lawyers in this research. That said, it would be wrong to condemn this rhetoric out-of-hand.

For Billig (1996: 1–2), rhetoric should be seen as a pervasive feature of the way in which people interact and arrive at understanding. Rhetoric represents a public position, often on a matter of controversy, so it is reasonable to expect individuals to justify their own position and criticise counter-arguments. As such, Simons (1990: 11) believes that a key job of the rhetorical analyst is to determine how such 'constructions of the real' are made persuasive. In this light, Potter (1996: 107) suggests that rhetoric need be explored for both its offensive and defensive properties; any description must necessarily work against a competing account. Rhetorical discourse will seek to challenge alternatives, intended to damage, rework, or reframe them, while also seeking to resist being discounted itself.

To follow Potter (1996: 108), there is a fundamental need for a double analytic focus when considering rhetoric. This rhetoric serves two functions – building up factual accounts and undermining them. This first aspect is 'reification' – turning something abstract into a material being. By this, accounts are producing an object, something tangible. It is in this sense that Sommerlad (1996: 294–96) sees validity in the dogmas of lawyers' professional claims. Though they may not have achieved the ideals they professed, they still presented a form of reality. This is the reason that Travers (1997b: 130) places such great stock in giving voice to his lawyers. However, the second purpose, 'ironizing', suggests words are used in a manner that contradicted what was witnessed. This sees rhetoric as undermining material reality, distorting it through knowingly erroneous talk, motivated by a particular agenda. These are the concerns that the authors of McConville et al (1994) express when addressing Travers' (1997b) work, which they fear could be compromised and invalidated by the false claims of lawyers (Bridges et al, 1997: 379). They consider it a mistake to accept an account that might differ so markedly from what it describes.

The lawyers in this study, then, may have been both constructing their own reality and seeking to prevent others from making independent judgements on what they experienced. Either way, some level of persuasion should be recognised as involved in this process, as rhetoric can be considered 'the art of persuasive discourse' (Cockcroft and Cockcroft, 1992: 3). This persuasion could be labelled manipulative; however, it can also be construed as par for the course in dialogue and discussion and an inevitable part of the process in constructing social knowledge. Ultimately, rhetoric should be considered somewhat unavoidable in ethnographic research that relies on respondents' statements to any degree. Under the 'universal rhetorical situation', identified by Nichols (1974: 348), rhetoric is a social fact, common to all:

> The basic function of rhetoric is the use of words by human agents to form attitudes or induce action in other human agents . . . it is rooted in an essential function of language itself, a function that is wholly realistic and continuously born anew.

My lawyers were likely engaged in an attempt to both convince themselves and influence me. That the accounts provided by these lawyers in the formal interview suggest rhetoric, then, should not be used to deny the possibility that the Radical firm and, in particular, the values contained within that definition, did and could exist. Indeed, Sommerlad (1996: 295) urges that such rhetoric should not be written off for not conforming completely to the ideal; for her, it will always be an approximation on the trajectory of the professional project. At the very least, these lawyers sowed the seeds of a Radical discourse, which might flower – given the right conditions.

LEGAL AID

The rhetoric of committed service should be taken seriously – it does have potential. As has already been mentioned numerous times, the lawyers in this study would attribute the paucity of such service in practice to their perceived lack of legal aid funding. Their position is captured in the following quote from James, the senior partner of *Radford Hope*, who saw legal aid cuts jeopardising the whole criminal process:

> Government 'tough on crime' rhetoric just works to allow them to take away more and more money from legally aided criminal defence. I liken it to a man who's got a heart condition and is given medication and is also asked to exercise every day and what is actually happening, the government is removing his medication, and each day he goes on the trainer, his feet have been tied. So, eventually, he will have a cardiac arrest. I think the criminal justice system is very close to that.
>
> (James, senior partner, *Radford Hope*, INT)

Indeed, I should note that it was this theme that first influenced my decision to conduct this research – I wanted to prove the worth of this branch of the legal profession against the naysayers in charge of public spending, to prove that they presented a necessary element of the welfare state. I knew that legal aid remuneration rates were a thorny issue and so it was to be expected that it would also be at the forefront of much of these lawyers' thinking. The dichotomy between rhetoric and reality, then, may well be influenced by such structural factors. Indeed, when considering legally aided criminal defence schemes across time and space, Smith (2002: 3) sees one constant: a good quality of service goes hand-in-hand with high levels of funding.

However, in the present times of economic hardship, remuneration is only likely to worsen as the legal aid budget passes onto a Coalition Government committed to deficit reduction (Watt, 2010). Following the new administration's first Comprehensive Spending Review, the Ministry of Justice was tasked with making some of the greatest savings of all Whitehall departments as its £9 billion budget was cut by £3 billion (Helm, Asthana and Townsend, 2010). Alongside fewer prison places and court closures, legal aid was identified as an area ripe for potential cuts (Hanman, 2010). Legal aid in England and Wales accounts for over a fifth of the total budget and, as then Justice Secretary, Kenneth Clarke was so keen on reminding everyone, a larger amount than any other nation in the world with the exception of Northern Ireland. The first raft of legal aid cuts duly saw the annual bill of £2.1 billion cut by £350 million, with the majority being taken from the civil budget – facing cuts of £240 million compared with just £70 million for criminal cases (Bowcott, 2012). The apparent discrepancy seems even more disproportionate when it is considered that civil cases previously accounted for less than half of the overall legal aid budget, at £985 million, with £1.2 billion being taken up by crime (Newman, 2011). The dismantling of civil provision was enshrined within the Legal Aid, Sentencing and Punishment of Offenders Act 2012 – despite the loud noises made by the opposition of the Justice for All campaign. The latter coalition of charities, advice agencies, trade unions, community groups and politicians attempted to highlight some of the more emotive examples of the impacts caused by the cuts to civil legal aid, promoting heart-wrenching stories by the elderly and infirm.

At first glance, it might seem odd that the Coalition Government would choose to protect criminals over the law-abiding vulnerable. Indeed, hard-line crime stances are one of the simplest means of attaining political capital; giving money to support a drug-addicted shoplifter over a geriatric who cannot afford their central heating is unlikely to go down well in the tabloid press or on talk radio phone-in shows. Despite the prospect of negative headlines, targeting civil legal aid represents a relatively easy choice for the government to take. As the freedom of individuals is at stake in criminal cases, and less likely to be so in civil matters involving benefits, divorce or employment, the European Convention on Human Rights offers greater protection to this fund. Cutting more from the criminal legal aid budget would be difficult without incurring the wrath of human rights challenges, though this should not be ruled out in light of the inevitable attempts of the Prime Minister's attempts to appease the right of the Conservative Party by supposedly standing up to their bogeymen of Europe and the forces of – to repeat that most misused of phrases – *political correctness gone mad.*

An increasingly hard-line approach will likely emerge as the more authoritarian Chris Grayling (who, unlike his predecessors, has never been a lawyer) replaces the rather liberal Kenneth Clarke as Justice Secretary, perhaps shifting any remaining emphasis on justice towards one on crime. For Rozenberg (2012), Grayling's main qualification for the post is that he is right wing – likely to use the post as a means to generate tabloid-friendly populist headlines attacking the supposed liberal incursion of the legal establishment. This process was quickly enacted in his first major comments around the subject of legal aid, attacking the reported £1 million fee incurred in Islamist preacher Abu Hamza's prolonged extradition proceedings – a cause that was, of course, championed by the *Daily Mail* (Doyle, 2012). The inevitable transition from *hug a hoody* to *mug a hoody* will likely take form as the next general election gets closer, and has already been suggested by the reaction to David Cameron's first law and order speech in office, halfway through his administration (Jowit, 2012; Walters and Owen, 2012). Despite claims to the contrary in the actual content of the speech, with its arguments against treating crime as a binary concept (soft or tough), it seems highly likely that behind-the-scenes briefings led a raft of popular punitive stories emerging in the right-wing press – in no small part to appease the increasing clamour of backbench Tory voices calling for a lurch to the right in law and order policy (see Tebbit, 2012). Added fuel to the fire is the underlying law and order agenda that underpins any Conservative government and the distinct possibility that the government's unerring quest to speedily reduce the state's economic deficit is as much ideological as it is pragmatic. In the situation Rose (2010) describes as 'death by a thousand cuts', it is likely that criminal legal aid will be adversely impacted sooner rather than later.

Though the need for cuts offers the opportunity for realignment of the system to better serve access to justice, this is unlikely to materialise (see Garside, 2010). This process will rather likely entail measures such as reduction in eligibility criteria and an increase in telephone advice over that provided in person. For those who still receive representation as we know it, it is possible that they will receive a lesser quality of service. These (dis)incentives might further encourage the practices that have been witnessed in this research: lawyers taking increasingly negative attitudes, treating clients with less respect and providing clients with fewer opportunities still to have their voices heard. It could be suggested, then, that the future heralds more of the same, more of the time.

With this consideration in mind, it is valuable to turn to a recent consultation paper on access to justice produced by the Law Society (2010: 5), which was guided by a similar credo to my own research, namely that:

> Any society that wishes to be thought of as just and fair needs to have mechanisms to ensure that the rule of law is maintained and that its members are able to obtain justice properly: the rule of law is meaningless without justice also being freely available.

This Law Society (2010: 18) review is enthused with a deep concern that the legal aid situation has meant that the current system is at a financial breaking point for lawyers:

> For increasing numbers of lawyers, legal aid is no longer a viable business proposition or an acceptable career path. The rewards have become too low relative to what qualified professionals can reasonably expect. The risks are too great . . . the government is compromising lawyers' ability to do a good job for their clients, thus weakening one of the final remaining ties keeping them in the system.

This situation might be considered inevitable as long as legal aid is provided through the private practice, judicare model; a system which Mackay (2001: 1) believes to be so fundamentally flawed that the system would not likely be considered were legal aid introduced today. For Stein (2001: 25–34), this privatised service inherently works against the ability of legal aid to facilitate justice in society; they provide only 'band-aids' – inadequate to deal with such an important task. A significant aspect of this can be found in Smith's (2002: 8–9) assertion that judicare possesses an inbuilt disadvantage, derived from allowing lawyers to act as arbiters of quality control. As long as firms are expected to maintain themselves as viable businesses, it remains plausible that economic concerns could trump those of the clients, meaning the service clients receive must suffer.

The Law Society (2010) has shown itself keen to explore alternatives – to better serve access to justice. If private practice is the problem, it would seem sensible to consider non-profit options. The most prominent of these has been salaried defenders, introduced as a pilot Public Defender Service scheme following Lord Carter's review (see Lord Chancellor's Department, 2000). Salaried defence might be utilised to provide a distinct and independent, community-minded criminal legal aid service. In this manner, the scheme offers a means to improve quality by freeing lawyers from the burdens of business imperatives and allowing them to concentrate on meeting the needs of their clients.

This Public Defender Service had been a contentious issue among the lawyers in my research. They perceived it as a challenge, one premised upon a misguided drive to cut costs with little regard for quality of service. The following interview quotes provide a flavour of the discontent:

> Salaried defenders are just part of the civil service again, so that must put constraints on them in other ways. I don't think it's actually focusing on the client and on the case. It's just cost-cutting.
>
> (Shelly, solicitor, *Radcliffe and Musk*, INT)

> I think the governments that are coming will still be looking at ways of cutting costs – in the CPS [Crown Prosecution Service] they've got people who are not qualified presenting cases, so if they are prepared to allow that, they'll be prepared to allow it for defence too. I can see dedicated caseworkers. I can see defence lawyers as in America, just somebody appointed by the court – I know they piloted it in areas, and it's still going in some areas . . . so I don't think any government will stop trying to cut costs. It'll drip down and the whole system will become increasingly weak. The defence profession as I knew it will die.
>
> (Norma, solicitor, *Radford Hope*, INT)

While they were against the government's practical application of the scheme, several lawyers were attracted by the theoretical principle of salaried defence. They raised the possibility that it might provide them with more freedom to act for their clients in the manner in which they would want. Such lawyers suggested that salaried defence held the potential to alleviate any current financial pressures experienced, as in the following:

> Being a public defender would absolutely free me from distractions and improve quality, yes. I'd get a bit more than I am earning at the moment, I would get flexitime, I would have a contributory pension, I would have 30 days holiday per year, I wouldn't have to worry about employing staff and paying wages, I wouldn't have to worry about going to get business. Please make me a public defender at £55k per year! I would jump tomorrow and every lawyer I've spoken to – and I've spoken to most in the city – would all jump at that opportunity.
>
> (Mike, senior partner, *Radison and Muddle*, INT)

> I know people who have gone into the public defenders system from private practice when they were doing well and they say it's an absolute delight to work there because they

> have all the benefits of being a civil servant, in terms of flexibility, they don't have to overwork, they don't have to stretch themselves.
>
> (Leo, senior partner, *Radcliffe and Musk*, INT)

> The public defender system? To be honest, it would be great if they wanted to say: 'Right, you're contracted to us'. Some solicitors would gladly say that they didn't want to take the risk any more, it would be: 'You pay me a salary, you pay for all my IT, you set up a pension scheme and you run it then – take all the risk away'. Because we're taking all of the risk at the moment. That sounds much more appealing.
>
> (Donna, solicitor, *Radcliffe and Musk*, INT)

However, reports on salaried defenders in Scotland (Tata et al, 2004: 9–10) and the United States (Gilboy and Schmidt, 1979: 19–21) have presented many of the issues evident in this research. Lawyers adopted negative attitudes to clients, they behaved disrespectfully towards them – discontinuous representation was rife – and, ultimately, outcomes still worked for the lawyers and even more clients were pushed towards guilty pleas. *Plus ça change.* More fundamentally, though, the Public Defender Service could be judged a failure in the terms that the government set out for it – it was not cost-effective, proving pricier than private practice (Bridges et al, 2007: 263–64). For the Law Society (2010: 42), this can be considered inevitable in such a system, with the public sector demanding greater overheads and bureaucracy. It seems this area will not be developed further in the immediate future (Zander, 2007: 612–14).

Accordingly, the Law Society (2010: 42) moves beyond salaried defence and onto the advice sector – schemes largely financed by local authorities or charities. In particular, they focus on law centres and Citizens Advice Bureaux (Law Society, 2010: 65–66). There might be grounds on which to call for an expansion of the services provided by the 52 law centres and 416 Citizens Advice Bureaux which currently provide help across a wide swathe of legal areas. As it stands, these organisations tend to deal in matters such as housing, employment, welfare, debt and immigration. A radical model for improving these services is suggested by Smith (2010: 16), under the banner of 'poverty law'. He seeks to transform these individual, local centres into a broader, national movement, with wider strategic goals (Smith, 2010: 16). The rationale offered by Smith (2010: 19) is that this area could take up the slack from lawyers increasingly abandoning and neglecting less profitable areas of law. Freed from the profit motive, he believes that these advisers could be trusted to put the clients first, suggesting that a more comprehensive integration of legal services will benefit access to justice. To move beyond the proposals of Smith (2010) or the Law Society (2010), there is the potential for a debate on whether such a provision of poverty law could be further extended to incorporate criminal defence work in some way.

In a similar vein, the Law Society (2010: 44) commends the triage system for further consideration:

> Triage is traditionally used in medicine and is the process by which individuals are assisted on the basis of the actual or perceived degree of need by assigning them to the

> most effective and efficient provider so as to ensure optimal care . . . a system of allocating scarce resources, providing the maximum resources to individuals of highest priority.

They cite the Dutch system of Legal Service Counters as a working example of a triage approach to legal aid in operation (Law Society, 2010: 75–79). These high street shop fronts provide readily accessible advice, with call centres and consultation rooms on site. The service is free, and non-means tested, as hour-long sessions are offered with legal advisers, while there is no limit on repeat calls. Clients are provided with information and helped to work through their problems. They might ultimately be referred to a local legal practitioner who specialises in the area of need; this lawyer is registered with the Legal Aid Board, to whom the client makes a small, one-off financial contribution for an appointment.

The appropriation of such a scheme in England and Wales would involve more use being made of publicly funded organisations, legal aid centres and student law clinics attached to universities. The Law Society (2010: 75–76) provides figures based on two such counters over the first six months of their operation, which document crime constituting one of the smaller areas of business. However, this might be due to the ingrained nature of traditional criminal legal aid provision, and the possibility for growth in this area remains.

The Law Society (2010), then, discusses a handful of alternatives to the judicare model that offer potential for greater access to justice. However, in assessing them, they return to the same problem; none offer a system that would definitively improve on a better financed judicare model. Salaried services have been shown to cost more than judicare, while any growth of law centres and Citizens Advice Bureaux or the importation of Legal Service Counters would all require a large amount of funding. Accordingly, the Law Society (2010: 45) finds it difficult to envisage how these schemes would improve on the current system were it 'properly funded'.

The Law Society (2010) suggests that private practice is the appropriate model to persist with. They accept that there are methods that might enhance this – the entry of large organisations into the market and alternative business structures; however, both of these are deemed problematic (Law Society, 2010: 46–48). While a smaller number of large providers might reduce administration costs and new commercial entrants promise greater efficiency, they pose substantial threats to quality. The Law Society (2010) contends that these developments would simply work to increase the drive for savings and further decrease attention on clients. In addition, profitable areas of the law would be cherry-picked at the expense of the less lucrative.

Ultimately, the Law Society (2010: 49–57) concludes that the best way to improve access to justice largely involves improving the remuneration offered to the judicare system that currently operates. The current contracts are not judged to be 'fit for purpose' – deemed a decade out of date (Law Society, 2010: 52). Rather, lawyers need to be provided with appropriate remuneration, and one means of achieving this is offered through appointing an independent body to determine rates (Law

Society, 2010: 54–55). Many other public servants – such as nurses and the armed forces – already benefit from pay review bodies. As there is no general consensus as to the market rate for lawyers' services, this body could develop a formula on which fair pay could be determined.

VALUES

For the Law Society (2010), clearly reflecting the views of the profession it represents, it seems that improving the economic situation faced by these lawyers would alleviate many of the problems currently faced by access to justice. As so often in contemporary society, capital is considered as a panacea. There is likely some veracity in the argument that a better funded legal service would better serve justice – taken at face value, this proposition seems somewhat self-evident. However, more money should not be assumed to automatically herald an increase in standards in and of itself. While lesser remuneration might well precipitate ever greater declines in the service provided, it is possible that improving the situation will take more than financial reward. Whether or not financial considerations got us in this position with regard to access to justice, it cannot be taken for granted that simply reversing the rate of remuneration will undo the damage that has been done to legally aided criminal defence practice. The activity of lawyers in this study seems to pertain to something deeper and more intransient, beyond economics. At this point, it is useful to turn to Nicolson and Webb (1999: 289) and their rejoinder to lawyers that, 'to be involved in a business rather than a profession does not excuse one from the human race'.

The failings displayed by these lawyers cannot be written off as financial necessity, and monetary concerns are not enough to excuse them or detract from their responsibility for their own activity. Instead, we must recognise the roles that values play in the professional development of lawyers. This is the task that Boon (2005: 229) sets himself and, seeing values to represent 'how the world ought to be and what is judged valuable or important in life'. The values that informed these lawyers should take centre stage over and above how they coped financially. To some degree, client-centred principles can be enacted whatever the economic circumstances. This was also the stance taken by McConville et al (1994: 296), whose conclusions I (sadly) must echo – for their lawyers, these desirable values are not realised and this is considered representative of the manner in which:

> Legal education and training . . . has tended to be dominated by teaching about the technicalities of the criminal law and procedure, without sufficient attention to basic principles of adversarial justice and their links to more fundamental values.

They call for a redefining of values to ensure that lawyers are taught to care about clients and offer a better quality of service. However, since their research, Francis (2005: 176–85) identifies an ever-increasing disjuncture between legal training and ethics. Things have been getting worse, not better. The professional identity of these lawyers has definitely moved away from client-centeredness and towards managerial, profit-centred, concerns. This requires a level of ethical reflection that progresses beyond simple compliance with the professional codes.

As it stands, professional service equates to little more than a 'tick-box activity' (Sommerlad, 2008: 186). Ethics have become functional rather than moralistic. For Economides (2007: 162), the absence of these values can be attributed to an 'overly narrow, positivistic legal education'. In this manner, it is useful to consider Chapman's (2002: 68) insight that training institutions themselves actually function to make lawyers cynical and unquestioning. There has been a shift towards a neo-liberal mindset in law schools, in which the accumulation of capital and promotion of the self are downplaying the social role of the law (Thornton, 2006: 14–18). This gives weight to Maharg's (2007: 115–18) suggestion that law schools should integrate themselves into their communities. He believes that law students interacting with those whom they will later serve precipitates the development of a moralistic ethical approach to law through experience as well as education. As such, he cites the need to introduce public spirit, cooperation and democracy into legal training. This idealistic tone tallies with Francis' (2005: 189) insistence that, in the future, there is a need to precipitate a move from existing professional codes towards something altogether more aspirational. Such developments should be deemed crucial in the light of Nicolson and Webb's (2005: 167) observation that, 'no part of the professional socialisation process seems to focus specifically on value formation'.

However, Evans and Palermo (2002: 128–29) have warned that institutional values and ethical rules will not necessarily override individual circumstances and commitments. It is for this reason that Nicolson and Webb (2005: 168) urge the consideration of the character and personal values of lawyers. They are sceptical of the role that professional organisations can play in (re)structuring values. These authors insist that the vague pleasantries of lists including items such as public service commitment, integrity, justice and fairness fulfil an inherently conservative function of preserving professional privilege. Values become detached from that which they represent, empty in practical terms and relegated to a theoretical argument by which to preserve the status quo. Any discussion of realigning the values of lawyers, then, must move beyond the syllabuses of law schools or the strictures of professional bodies. Rather, Nicolson and Webb (2005: 168) show us that:

> The time might be ripe for the commencement of a profession-wide debate, involving individual practitioners, practice organisations, professional bodies as well as legal academics, over the values and ethics to which contemporary practice can and organisations should aspire. At the very least, even if no consensus is reached, this is likely to result in values and ethics becoming more central to the professional enterprise.

It is to such a wider debate that my own work seeks to contribute. Rectifying the shameful way that lawyers treat their clients is partly a matter of ethics but, more specifically, these ethical constricts must be socially located. The ethics need to relate to the real world. Lawyers should be encouraged to consider the cultural position they occupy and, thereon, identify just where the values they should embody derive from. Lawyers, then, require a proper grounding in sociology of law, thus being taught to question their role and critique who they are and what they do. To be truly effective, such analysis must step outside a focus on the law in books and look at the everyday reality of living law, the way that these lawyers are daily responsible for shaping and reshaping the experience of law for themselves and those who come into contact with them. This book can play a major contribution to this process, offering a reference point through which to gain sight of a world that often remains closed off and private. As such, it can help new and old lawyers alike, introducing them to the life of a lawyer as recorded by an impartial outsider. The research might help to rewrite an organisational culture which might be sustaining unpleasant behaviour by means of legitimising some manner of ethical fading (Chambliss, 2010). The data it has generated can inform and stimulate discussion as to what kinds of lawyers we have and what we should want. This research has shown a strained lawyer–client relationship that undermines access to justice, across all its lawyers, despite the sample being weighted towards Radical firms. These results suggest that serious consideration should be given to assessing the meaning of the values that lawyers claim. They merit questioning whether any such theoretical values can be properly enacted in reality and, if so, how.

The findings of this project will, of course, be disseminated to lawyers, held up as a mirror to show them what they say and what they do – whether they happen to pick up this book or, more likely, I need appeal to them directly and present the results. What the lawyers see might surprise some, shock others and could evoke disappointment, dismay or a sense of resignation. I have no doubt that some lawyers (including those I accompanied) will be angry with me, and may try to contest my research. Nobody likes to be criticised, especially not by someone from outside their field (*who does he think he is?*). I welcome the debate, though all I can do is tell it as I saw it – I have no agenda except to help them to do their jobs as well as they can. Whether or not lawyers publically admit to seeing themselves in my research, I hope, privately, they can meditate on it to some extent. As much as being research *about* the profession then, this report can become research *for* the profession, hopefully encouraging reflexivity in their practices. Lawyers need to be educated about how they conduct themselves, and the role that rhetoric seems to play in bracketing off this behaviour from their sense of their professional self.

In this regard, a cue can be taken from other professions. I am firmly of the opinion that public service occupations can be treated as a whole, united by the relationship of server to the served. The latter is reliant upon the former, and thus inherently vulnerable. In this situation, Schon (1983: 3–20) finds an increasing crisis of confidence in professional knowledge, a scepticism borne from professionals taking advantage of their position. These lawyers, then, are not alone in the manner in which they fail to meet the values that society expects of public service professionals.

The most infamous alternative example might be that of the medical profession, notorious for its slang and abbreviations belittling patients (see BBC News, 2003). Under this, 'GLM' means 'good looking mum', the 'departure lounge' is the geriatric ward and 'GROLIES' are 'Guardian readers of low intelligence wearing ethnic skirts'. Some notes are adorned with 'TTFO', signalling that patients were 'told to fuck off'. That medical professionals deem this acceptable implies 'ethical erosion' – the widespread devaluation of patients (Fox, 2003: 181).

Derogatory treatment of patients can be understood to constitute something of a learned activity (Wear et al, 2006: 454–55). Trainees treat current practitioners as role models, so those they follow influence their personal professional identity. The ethos of the community becomes self-perpetuating unless it is challenged. A possible solution, proposed by Wear et al (2006: 461) involves making practitioners mindful of what they say and do:

> The issues raised here go to the heart of professionalism in medicine, yet few of us want to acknowledge them directly. But we suggest that an honest engagement with the realities of clinical training faced by our students, even those realities that make us wince, is necessary. We must forewarn students early and consistently in their training . . . We must alert students that they will hear horrible, disrespectful comments about patients' bodies, about their ability to pay for care, about their addictions. We must impress upon students that there are always choices when these moments arise – to ignore such comments, to laugh or chime in, to talk to a trusted role model about what to do, or perhaps even to risk confrontation with the sources of such humor.

This reflects a wider trend for awareness raising as more and more professions are becoming cognisant of their need to comprehend how they act with their clients. Indeed, Hopper (2008: 711) has issued a plea for more qualitative research into mental health care provision, to enable psychiatrists to understand what they actually do. In this spirit, White (2006: 37–39) urges health and social care practitioners to be more reflexive, encouraging the practice of taping oneself to allow greater self-criticism. Within management education, Cunliffe (2004: 411) suggests that, 'we can develop critically reflexive practice by encouraging students to think about how they, with others, construct realities and identities'. She recommends that students are provided with case studies of situations and told to analyse them using theory and principles, engage in role plays to understand their relations to others or keep journals and learn from themselves (Cunliffe, 2004: 413–22).

With regard to teachers, Day et al (2006: 613–14) believe practitioners are drained by emotional, intellectual and social demands. Values are said to shift and vary across time, dependent on a range of situational factors. The teachers require external support to renew and maintain their original values. For Tickle (2005: 61–64), social commentary has a large impact on the mindset of teachers, and he discusses the need for a politics for professionalism. Teachers, then, require reminding of what they use education for, and this will facilitate a process of self-construction whereby their teaching persona is (re)created (Tickle, 2005: 70–72).

In my research, I hope to make legally aided criminal defence lawyers similarly self-aware. As such, this work could aid them in identifying the values that they seek to adhere to and how these would be reflected in practice. Thereafter, the study may also act as a reminder of the need to check whether they are succeeding or failing in attaining those goals. This work could stand as a warning of the difference between rhetoric and reality. In doing so, this research will live beyond this book and I hope it might actually contribute to improving access to justice for at least some clients.

CLIENTS

Though this research has addressed the lawyer–client relationship from the perspective of the lawyers, it is important never to lose sight of the clients; their rights are the reason this research was commenced. On turning to consider the clients, it is useful to refer to a recent collection of essays edited by Jon Robins (2010) – *Closing the Justice Gap* – which seek to disseminate fresh ideas and rejuvenate the principles of access to justice in the midst of a 'legal aid system in crisis' (Zander, 2010: 2). These authors claim their key task as ensuring that whatever is done prioritises the client. Accordingly, Robins (2010: 6) details that the central criteria by which works were accepted were that they needed to be:

> In the client interest, forward-thinking . . . a positive and very different contribution to a debate that's stuck in something of a rut caught between government intransigence (as lawyers and those working in the advice sector might see it) and professional self-interest (as non-lawyers and ministers might see it).

Clearly, my work has been informed by just such values but its focus on lawyers limits the scope to make recommendations for clients. I judged that the rights of these clients was best explored by following the research of McConville et al (1994) and Travers (1997b) to see which findings held good some 15 years after those studies were conducted. I sought to achieve this by utilising sampling, methods and methodology informed by both – ethnographic study concentrating on lawyers understood through structuralist and interpretivist lenses. I supposed that this was an area lacking in nuanced, contemporary treatment. Accordingly, lawyers had to be the centre of attention. In the circumstances of this study, it was not possible to address the clients directly to any great degree. In theory, I could have adopted a dual approach in which I sought to interview both clients and lawyers; in practice, the impact that a dual approach would have exerted on the ethnography would have been considerable, and likely harmful. There was the danger that my relationships with the lawyers might have been compromised, rendering lawyers awkward and guarded leading to further restricted access and a greater effort to play up to the researcher gaze. Lawyers may have been more acutely aware that judgement was being passed on them, and wary that the opinions of their clients could not be anticipated or controlled. The subsequent research could have lacked both the depth and closeness actually obtained. Thereon, producing that research would have seen greater demands on time and space. The lawyers' experiences would have been neglected and, in turn, so would those of the clients. This compromise would not do justice to either side of the relationship, and therefore, not to the relationship at all.

Notwithstanding all that, my research is informed by the supposition that a fully rounded understanding of the lawyer–client relationship necessitates hearing the voice of the client. To these ends, further research is necessary in order to augment and improve on the value of the findings offered herein. Client-focused research, though, is a contentious area, as highlighted by Moorhead et al (2003: 19) who assert that, 'lay clients are unable to assess the basics of legal competence, gathering pertinent information, providing good advice and suggesting practical courses of action'. However, these same authors go on to insist that clients' assessments can be engaged with, in relation to the factors that clients themselves consider important, 'tangible aspects of personal service' (Moorhead et al, 2003: 19). Ultimately, though, Moorhead et al (2003: 27–29) posit that clients should not be relied on as a gauge of the quality of the service lawyers provide; there are 'benefits to be had from a re-emphasis of the needs of the client within the professional domain, but these benefits are limited'. That said, when placed alongside other markers, it can be supposed that the views of clients can be of value. In their study, Sommerlad and Wall (1999: 1) seek to do just this, suggesting that qualitative research is needed 'to identify the views on quality held by the actual participants in the lawyering process'. They recognise the great difficulties that would face any assessor of legal services, rendering the supposed subjectivity of the client perspective no more limited than any other marker (Sommerlad and Wall, 1999: 2). More so, client contributions can help to improve (verify and authenticate) the understandings available from other sources. These client views are complex and heterogeneous, so do not lend themselves to easy generalisations. Rather, they require that work be done to actively pursue their standpoints. Considering this, I believe that a parallel research project should be carried out from the clients' perspective. This could entail a similar research design to the present one, but with clients inserted in place of lawyers. There would be space for both the voice of clients and authorial opinion, and a purposive sample would allow for the best opportunity of capturing a variety of practice, and ideally good service. This would be the sensible follow-up to the present study, offering a means of triangulation, so that, in combination, the lawyer–client relationship could be fully illuminated. I hope that someone will do just this in the near future.

In the meantime, the present research offers the means to make some limited suggestions for the clients. In addition to educating lawyers as to their role in upholding defendants' rights, perhaps consideration should be afforded to the clients themselves and their understanding of the lawyer–client relationship. They might be better informed of the values that could and should infuse their relations, and of the responsibility that lawyers are tasked with on their behalf. At present, the advice available to clients largely takes the form of leaflets offering procedural and technical guidance pertaining to the process of obtaining legal aid and explaining various elements of the criminal justice system and its institutions. This practical information does not address the principles and ideology at play in this particular enactment of access to justice; it does not empower clients to adequately look after their own interests.

In *Closing the Justice Gap*, Harker and Sandbach (2010: 36–38) propose the development of outreach programmes and remote delivery channels in order to engage with the wider public. They commend the potential for personalisation of service, to tailor supply to the precise needs of the client and encourage a system that is more in tune with local needs and demands. However, this would still largely operate through conventional, high-street means, and in another essay, Trigg (2010: 52–53) problematises such approaches suggesting that not everyone has or wants a high street. Rather, it is suggested that more attention should be given to the internet, as this realm increasingly provides the first source of information that people turn to. However, it is all but ignored as a source of advice or point of contact for legal aid clients. In these circumstances, Trigg (2010: 53) believes that 'for legal aid to survive and thrive we need a radical overhaul of everything we do and how we do it, we need to stop detaching it from society and rekindle the nation's natural affection for its law and those who practice it'.

This is said to require a movement from behind the barricades, talking to ordinary people in a language they recognise. This could be utilised as a source of public legal education, to provide better and more reliable information to clients about their rights. However, another contribution in that volume, from Passmore (2010: 27), suggests that teaching clients in this manner simply functions to make them more like lawyers. Rather, advances in technology provide the opportunity to change legal aid and advice 'to meet clients as they are' (Passmore, 2010: 27). He proposes a large-scale, integrated, telephone and internet service to provide information and advice to clients. This approach would put clients in control by empowering them to access the knowledge they require on their own terms. Either way, it appears that clients are demanding this greater accessibility (see Baksi, 2010c).

In this spirit, then, I would suggest that the findings of this research should also be made available to clients. Rather than restrict it to academic and professional realms, clients should be free to engage with it and draw from it any use they can. Obviously, this book is available for anyone to buy, borrow or download – but markets for such scholarly texts are inherently restricted and I am not so wrapped up in my own self-importance as to assume that the majority of ordinary people I pass in the street will have any idea that the book even exists. As such, a far better way of accessing large numbers will be provided by a dedicated website to provide a ready means of dispersing some of the data. As it stands, internet searches from any of the major search engines reveal little to clients about what they could expect from their dealings with lawyers. If they could have straightforward access to these findings, clients would better appreciate how the lawyer–client relationship may actually function. This research has not claimed the ability to generalise its data and so would not posit that they are necessarily reliable as a gauge for all firms in England and Wales. Rather, they represent the results of a particular study in a specific location at a certain point in time but, in so doing, can offer an indicator of some reality which may or may not be replicated elsewhere. These results have implications that should be able to be appreciated and considered by the relevant parties. Users of such a service could see what lawyers in this research thought about their clients, and how they were discussed behind their backs. Clients could also witness the disrespectful behaviour that lawyers engaged in, and the ways in which lawyers could push their clients towards outcomes other than those they wanted. Clients can decide for themselves whether this constitutes a strained relationship and whether they are willing to accept being treated in that manner. They are empowered by knowledge and, as a result, would be able to use some of the particular insights from this study to inform their own decision-making.

JUSTICE

Overall, this research project has left me disappointed. I am disheartened by the similarities between Radical and Sausage Factory firms and the manner in which all *talked* a healthy lawyer–client relationship but *walked* one that was strained. The nature of this strain could be identified in the participant observation findings on attitudes, behaviour and outcomes, which posed a distinct challenge to the rights of defendants in the criminal process to achieve access to justice. This pessimism is merely amplified by the manner in which this work echoes the damning indictment of McConville et al (1994), notwithstanding the intervening time period during which one of the authors could claim that, 'a significant shift has in fact taken place in the standards and practices of many criminal defence lawyers ... transforming what was previously characterised as a "guilty plea culture" into one based more on adversarial principles' (Bridges, 2006: 100). That rather optimistic statement as to the conduct of the profession seems somewhat at odds with the situation I found in this research. More so, the data produced this depressing picture despite all the efforts that I made in sample, design and methodology, intended to give lawyers the opportunity to redress the balance and present a more uplifting image of their profession akin to that in Travers (1997b). The only hint of positivity with regard to active defence was to be found in the rhetoric that lawyers spoke in interview and the occasional (but resolutely exceptional) example of client-centred practice.

However, I believe that there is a ray of hope in the lawyers' rhetoric all the same. As long as access to justice is talked about, and the notion of providing clients with a good service remains on the agenda, then it can be achieved. This might take reforms to legal aid remuneration and improvements in ethical training, it may also require clients being taught to stand up for themselves; however, the potential remains. As such, I do not feel that this research constitutes a defeat but rather an opportunity: it provides the chance for us to improve our criminal process so the freedom of all is enhanced. In a similar vein, the architects of the freedom approach that I have taken in this book, Sanders et al (2010: 746) offer the means to realise these ambitions in their recommendation that:

> We need a new language in which to express our aspirations, and the language of freedom seems to us to provide a vocabulary most likely to persuade the various entrenched interest groups of the need for change. It is time to set the primary goal of the criminal justice system as the promotion of freedom of all citizens and social groups alike.

Legal aid should be acknowledged as containing the ability to enact this freedom, starting the process by protecting the rights of those suspected and accused of criminal offences. As a force for social inclusion, the fairness it promotes could ensure justice and ultimately precipitate greater freedom for all in society. This sets up criminal justice as a means of achieving social justice. This is the approach taken by Cook (2006: 1) who suggests that criminal and social justice are interconnected – the former primarily involving the exercise of legitimate power, the latter chiefly concerned with citizenship, public service and equality. One feeds into the other. The criminal justice system, and the treatment of those suspected and accused of crimes, should be understood in the wider social context and the manner in which the criminal process impacts upon British society. Accordingly, Rutherford (2001: 8) explains that:

> Considerations regarding criminal policy closely intersect with broader ideas about citizenship . . . and the shaping of criminal justice arrangements should have the purpose of fostering social inclusion by, wherever possible, encouraging a rewarding and sustained membership within the wider community. Given the inherent tendencies of criminal justice towards social exclusion, this presents a daunting challenge to policy makers and practitioners.

Legal aid must be championed as an offspring of the welfare state, as an instrument for social equality that allows individuals to 'protect their badge of citizenship' (Stein, 2001: 1). The authority that the state enacts through the criminal justice system will not be respected if it is imposed, but needs to be accountable, legitimate and justified (Faulkner, 1996: 6). In ensuring that criminal justice can achieve social justice, the role of lawyers is vital. For the good of the wider community, then, defendants reliant on legal aid cannot be denied their access to justice through inadequate representation that hinders their taking an active part in the criminal process. If they are excluded, it harms everyone; by extension, all can benefit from a lawyer–client relationship that better honours the rights of clients.

To achieve this, the plight of these clients must be more widely constituted as a viable topic of conversation. However, a series of seminars convened by the Legal Action Group before this research commenced worked to highlight the predominance of a populist dogma that neglected defendants in favour of victims in the criminal justice debate. The Legal Action Group is a non-aligned organisation, concerned with advancing access to justice for all – they have no particular concern to favour one side over the other. Despite this even-handedness, Cape (2004b: 1) highlights that the discussions were chiefly informed by their being 'disturbed by the growing polarisation of the rights and interests of victims and of those accused of crime in both government rhetoric and in popular discourse'.

It is contended that discourse has been clouded by recent attempts from governments of all colours to paint the interests of victims and defendants as irreconcilable. In this, there has been a totemic quest to support victims of crime concomitant with a discernible lack of effort to protect the rights of those suspected or accused of crimes (Cape, 2004b: 5–7). These victims are themselves supposedly subject to a gap between rhetoric and reality, as a lack of respect or information ensures their needs remain unfulfilled. Even so, Jackson (2004: 7) suggests that the criminal process has become increasingly (re)aligned, meaning any imbalance between prosecution and defence unfairly favours the former rather than the latter.

In this situation, the freedom of those suspected or accused of crime is curbed. This impacts negatively on the freedom of all and, accordingly, *Rethinking Crime and Punishment* (2005: 5) summarises the Legal Action Group debates as suggesting that:

> Neither the interests of victims, nor those of society as a whole, are served by reducing the rights of defendants to make it easier to convict them. Protections for defendants exist for good reasons: no one benefits from a person being found guilty of an offence that he or she did not commit . . . The underlying problem may be that current Government thinking on criminal justice policy is driven largely by managerial priorities instead of being underpinned by a shared public understanding of what is meant by 'justice' . . . high standards of justice must be seen as part of the wider public good.

This is the language that discussions of defendants in the criminal process must be recast into; their treatment should be understood to reflect on society as a whole. Fair treatment can be seen to induce commitment and obligation towards the institutions and rules that constitute society (and, thereon, it renders this support well-placed); it creates a climate of respect. In this book, I have not sought to pass judgement on the effect that the legal advice or advocacy witnessed exerted on the results of cases. I am not legally qualified, so could not have done so with complete confidence even if I had wanted to. However, it is satisfying to note the proposals that were being put out for consultation by the Joint Advocacy Group (2010) while this research was being written up. This follows the recommendations of research offered by Devereux et al (2009), positing the necessity for regular monitoring of lawyer standards. The regulatory bodies representing all three strands of the legal profession support the establishment of an independent adjudicator to judge the quality of lawyers, something of a *legal MOT* (Newman, 2012). Under this process, lawyers would be attributed particular levels of competency at regular points across their professional careers. It was never my intention to make such an attempt at rigorous assessment – though these results will inevitably have knock-on effects for legal conceptions of justice. Rather, this was a study focused on human beings in a social relationship. At its heart, this topic is straightforward and free of the complexities of legal jargon and bureaucratic procedure. I have simply used the functioning of that relationship as a means of dealing with the question of whether a particular group of citizens appeared to be treated justly.

In the light of this, then, those who are aware of these findings face a decision (by the way, that's you, the reader – no pressure). There is the option to read about the manner in which lawyers acted towards clients in this research and say nothing. By this line, perhaps you think it inevitable or deserved; these are, after all, the criminal classes. Alternatively, the data presented in this research might prompt concern at perceived injustice, and the feeling that this mistreatment should not be ignored. Those suspected and accused of crimes are members of society like any other. As such, you might take the view that these individuals should be treated in the same manner in which we would hope to find ourselves and our loved ones treated if we found ourselves in the criminal process. Obviously, considering that I conducted this research, I want you to take the latter position. I care passionately about the perilous position in which some of the most vulnerable people in society are being put. In addition, I firmly believe that, if you hurt society, you hurt yourself. Those who commit criminal acts hurt society and deserve to be brought to justice. But these individuals are still a part of society, so to treat them with wanton disregard for fairness simply means that society is hurt for a second time, adding insult to injury. Only justice holds the potential to heal the harms caused by crime and such callous treatment of offenders is not justice but does further damage to the social fabric. In this way, nobody wins, we all debase ourselves and society is all the poorer for it – how can those from the criminal classes seriously be expected to treat society with respect, when their supposed betters chose not to do so by condoning or turning a blind eye to their mistreatment in the criminal process? No matter how selfish or insular (read, libertarian) a person's worldview, however far to the right of the political spectrum they may be, the potential social damage that compromising those in the position of being suspected or accused of crimes should be a concern at some level. Sooner rather than later, the degradation of society will drag everyone down. Though these are left-liberal values, you should not need to put yoghurt on your muesli, wear sandals and read *The Guardian* to be alarmed by the erosion of justice in our society – and you shouldn't need to be driven by a burning desire for socialist revolution to recognise that fair treatment in a democracy applies to all. No matter your ideology, then, I would hope that these findings alarm you in some way and make you think about what can be done to rectify it.

The best result this book could achieve would be to contribute to the flourishing of a wider dialogue that takes seriously the position of those suspected and accused of crime. Defendants in the criminal process deserve justice, and lawyers should be made to work for their clients and properly enact adversarial principles. In this way, legal aid can be made to ensure that the criminal process works for social justice rather than perpetuating social injustice.

BIBLIOGRAPHY

Abbey, R and Boon, A (1995) 'The provision of free legal services by solicitors: a review of the report by the Law Society's pro bono working party' 2 *International Journal of the Legal Profession* 261.

Abel, RL (1988) *The Legal Profession in England and Wales* (Oxford: Basil Blackwell Ltd).

Allport, GW (1979) *The Nature of Prejudice* (New York: Basic Books).

Anderson, DC and Sharrock, WW (1983) 'Irony as a Methodological Theory: A Sketch of Four Sociological Variables' 4 *Poetics Today* 565.

Archer, MS (1982) 'Morphogenesis versus structuration: on combining structure and action' 34 *British Journal of Sociology* 455.

Ashworth, A (1996) 'Legal Aid, Human Rights and Criminal Justice' in Young, R and Wall, D (eds), *Access to Criminal Justice* (London: Blackstone Press Ltd).

—— (2010) *Sentencing and Criminal Justice*, 5th edn (Cambridge: Cambridge University Press).

Ashworth, A and Redmayne, M (2005) *The Criminal Process*, 3rd edn (Oxford: Oxford University Press).

—— (2010) *The Criminal Process*, 4th edn (Oxford: Oxford University Press).

Asimow, M, Greenfield, S, Jorge, G, Machura, S, Osborne, G, Robson, P, Sharp, C and Sockloskie, R (2005) 'Perceptions of lawyers-a transnational study of student views on the image of law and lawyers' 12 *International Journal of the Legal Profession* 408.

Atherley, GRC and Hale, AR (1975) 'Pre-requisites for a Profession in Occupational Safety and Hygiene' 18 *Annals of Occupational Hygiene* 321.

Atkinson, P (1983) 'The Reproduction of the Professional Community' in Dingwall, R and Lewis P (eds), *The Sociology of the Professions* (London: Macmillan Press).

Arunachalam, B, Henneburry, S, Lusk, JL and Norwood, FB (2009) 'An Empirical Investigation into the Excessive-Choice Effect' 91 *American Journal of Agricultural Economics* 810.

Baksi, C (2009a) 'Fraud case judge slams solicitor-advocates for "incompetence"' *Law Society Gazette* (23 April).

—— (2009b) 'Chancery Lane hails scrapping of best value tendering pilots' *Law Society Gazette* (18 December).

—— (2010a) 'Some criminals advocated "not up to the job"' *Law Society Gazette* (25 February).

—— (2010b) 'Purge of criminal legal aid firms planned' *Law Society Gazette* (25 March).

—— (2010c) 'High street firms fear for the future' *Law Society Gazette* (23 August).

—— (2010d) 'Law Society wins family tender challenge' *Law Society Gazette* (30 September).

Baldwin, J and McConville, M (1977) *Negotiated Justice* (London: Martin Robertson).

Banton, M (1964) *The Policeman in the Community* (New York: Basic Books).

Becker, HS and Geer, B (1957) 'Participant Observation and Interviewing: A Comparison' 16 *Human Organization* 28.

Bell, M (2005) 'A Woman's Scorn: Toward a Feminist Defense of Contempt as a Moral Emotion' 20 *Hypatia* 80.

Bettelheim, B (1983) *Freud and Man's Soul* (New York: Knopf).
Berkowitz, L and Knurek, DA (1969) 'Label-mediated hostility generalization' 13 *Journal of Personality and Social Psychology* 200.
Bevan, G (1996) 'Has there been Supplier-induced Demand for Legal Aid?' 15 *Civil Justice Quarterly* 98.
Billig, M (1996) *Arguing and Thinking* (Cambridge: Cambridge University Press).
Binder, A, Bergman, P, Price, SC and Tremblay, PR (2004) *Lawyers as Counsellors: A Client-Centred Approach* (Minnesota: West).
Black, G (1988) 'The plight of the criminal practitioner' *Law Society Gazette* (27 January).
Blank, G (2004) 'Toward a Sociological Theory of Choice' paper presented at the American Sociological Association (California: American Sociological Association).
Blumberg, AS (1967) 'The Practice of Law as Confidence Game: Organizational Cooptation of a Profession' 1 *Law and Society Review* 15.
Bocock, R (1981) 'British Sociologists and Freud: A Sociological Analysis of the Absence of a Relationship' 32 *British Journal of Sociology* 346.
Bogoch, B and Danet, B (1984) 'Challenge and Control in Lawyer–Client Interaction: A Case Study in an Israeli Legal Aid Office' 4 *Text* 249.
Bohner, G and Wanke, M (2002) *Attitudes and Attitude Change* (East Sussex: Psychology Press).
Boon, A (2005) 'From Public Service to Service Industry: the impact of socialisation and work on the motivation and values of lawyers' 12 *International Journal of the Legal Profession* 229.
Boon, A, Duff, L and Shiner, M (2001) 'Career Paths and Choices in a Highly Differentiated Profession: The Position of Newly Qualified Solicitors' 64 *Modern Law Review* 563.
Boston, J, Martin, J, Pallot, J and Walsh, P (1996) *Public Management: The New Zealand Model* (Auckland: Oxford University Press).
Bottoms, A (1995) 'The Philosophy and Politics of Punishment and Sentencing' in Clarkson, C and Morgan, R (eds), *The Politics of Sentencing Reform* (Oxford: Clarendon Press).
—— (2002) 'On the decriminalisation of English juvenile courts' in Muncie, J, Hughes, G and McLaughlin, E (eds), *Youth Justice: Critical Readings* (London: Sage Publications).
Bottoms, A and McClean, J (1976) *Defendants in the Criminal Process* (London: Routledge).
Bourdieu, P (1984) *Distinctions: A Social Critique of the Judgment of Taste* (Massachusetts: Harvard University Press).
—— (1987) 'The force of law: toward a sociology of the juridical field' 38 *Hastings Law Journal* 805.
Bourdieu, P and Wacquant, L (1992) *An Invitation to Reflexive Sociology* (Chicago: University of Chicago Press).
Braun, V and Clarke, V (2006) 'Using thematic analysis in psychology' 3 *Qualitative Research in Psychology* 77.
Brewer, MB (2007) 'The Social Psychology of Intergroup Relations: Social Categorization, Ingroup Bias and Outgroup Prejudice' in Kruglanksi, AW and Higgins, ET (eds), *Social Psychology: Handbook of Basic Principles*, 2nd edn (New York: The Guilford Press).
Bridges, L (2006) 'The Ethics of Representation on Guilty Pleas' 9 *Legal Ethics* 80.
Bridges, L, Cape, E, Fenn, P, Mitchell, A, Moorhead, R and Sherr, A (2007) *Evaluation of the Public Defender Service in England and Wales* (London: HMSO).
Bridges, L, Hodgson, J, McConville, M and Pavlovic, A (1997) 'Can Critical Research Influence Policy?' 37 *British Journal of Criminology* 378.

Brownlee, I (1998) 'New Labour – New Penology? Punitive Rhetoric and the Limits of Managerialism in Criminal Justice Policy' 25 *Journal of Law and Society* 313.
Brym, RJ and Lie, J (2007) *Sociology: Your Compass for a New World*, 3rd edn (California: Thomson Higher Education).
Bryman, A (2001) *Social Research Methods* (Oxford: Oxford University Press).
Buber, M (2008) *I and Thou* (London: Hesperides Press).
Burnard, P (2005) *Counselling Skills for Health Professionals* (Cheltenham: Nelson Thornes Ltd).
Burton, A (1994) 'The demise of criminal legal aid' 144 *New Law Journal* 1491.
Butler, J (1999) *Gender Trouble* (London: Routledge).
Cain, M (1983) 'The General Practice Layer and the Client: Towards a Radical Conception' in Dingwall, R and Lewis, P (eds), *The Sociology of the Professions* (London: Macmillan).
Cape, E (2004a) 'Overview: Is Reconciliation Possible?' in Cape, E (ed), *Reconcilable Rights? Analysing the Tension between Victims and Defendants* (London: Legal Action Group).
—— (2004b) 'The Rise (and Fall?) of a Criminal Defence Profession' *Criminal Law Review* 401.
—— (2006a) 'Rebalancing the Criminal Justice Process: Ethical Challenges for Criminal Defence Lawyers' 9 *Legal Ethics* 56.
—— (2006b) *Defending Suspects at Police Stations*, 5th edn (London: Legal Action Group).
Cape, E and Moorhead, R (2005) *Demand Induced Supply? Identifying Cost Drivers in Criminal Defence Work* (London: Legal Services Commission).
Carlen, P (1974) 'Remedial Routines for the Maintenance of Control in Magistrates' Courts' 1 *British Journal of Law and Society* 101.
—— (1976) *Magistrates' Justice* (London: Martin Robertson and Co).
Carstensen, LL, Gottman, JM and Levenson, RW (1995) 'Emotional behaviour in long term marriage' 10 *Psychology and Aging* 140.
Carveth, DL (1996) 'Psychoanalytic Conceptions of the Passions' in O'Neill, J (ed), *Freud and the Passions* (Pennsylvania: The Pennsylvania State University Press).
Casper, JD, Tyler, T and Fisher, B (1988) 'Procedural Justice in Felony Cases' *22 Law and Society Review* 483.
Chambliss, E (2010) 'Measuring law firm culture' in Sarat, A (ed), *Special Issue Law Firms, Legal Culture, and Legal Practice* (Bingley: Emerald Group Publishing Ltd).
Chapman, J (2002) 'Why Teach Legal Ethics to Undergraduates?' 5 *Legal Ethics* 68.
Choongh, S (1997) *Policing as Social Discipline* (Oxford: Clarendon Press).
—— (1998) 'Policing the Dross: A Social Disciplinary Model of Policing' 38 *British Journal of Criminology* 623.
Christie, N (1977) 'Conflicts as Property' 17 *British Journal of Criminology* 1.
Church, T (1985) 'Examining local legal culture' 10 *American Bar Foundation Research Journal* 449.
Cicourel, AV (1995) *The Social Organization of Juvenile Justice* (New Jersey: Transaction Publishers).
Cockcroft, R and Cockcroft, S (1992) *Persuading People* (Hampshire: Palgrave Macmillan).
Cole, G (1970) 'The decision to prosecute' 4 *Law and Society Review* 331.
Collier, R (2005) '"Be smart, be successful, be yourself . . .?": representations of the training contract and trainee solicitor in advertising by large law firms' 12 *International Journal of the Legal Profession* 51.
Cook, D (2006) *Criminal and Social Justice* (London: Sage).

Craib, I (1989) *Psychoanalysis and Social Theory* (Brighton: Harvester Wheatsheaf).
—— (1998) 'Sigmund Freud' in Stones, R (ed), *Key Sociological Thinkers* (Hampshire: Palgrave).
Crook, S (1991) *Modernist Radicalism and its Aftermath* (London: Routledge).
Cunliffe, AL (2004) 'On Becoming a Critically Reflexive Practitioner' 28 *Journal of Management Education* 407.
Cunningham, CD (1991–92) 'Lawyer as Translator, Representation as Text: Towards an Ethnography of Legal Discourse' 77 *Cornell Law Review* 1298.
Davies, J (2007) *The Criminal Advocate's Survival Guide* (Farnham: Carbolic Smoke Ball Co).
Davis, G, Cretney, S and Collins, J (1994) *Simple Quarrels* (Oxford: Clarendon Press).
Day, C, Kington, A, Stobart, G and Sammons, S (2006) 'The personal and professional selves of teachers: stable and unstable identities' 32 *British Educational Research Journal* 601.
Denzin, N (2009) *The Research Act* (New Jersey: Transaction Publishers).
Departmental Committee on Legal Aid in Criminal Proceedings (1966) *Report*, Cmnd 2934 (London: HMSO).
Department for Constitutional Affairs (2005) *A Fairer Deal for Legal Aid* (London: The Stationary Office).
—— (2006a) *The Carter Review of the Procurement of Criminal Defence Services: Market-Based Reform* (London: The Stationary Office).
—— (2006b) *Delivering Simple, Speedy, Summary Justice* (London: HMSO).
Devereux, A, Tucker, J, Moorhead, R and Cape, E (2009) *Quality Assurance for* Advocates (London: Legal Services Commission).
Duff, E, Shiner, M, Boon, A and Whyte, A (2000) *Entry into the Legal Professions: The Law Student Cohort Study Year 6*, Research Study 33 (London: Law Society).
Durkheim, E (1964) *The Division of Labour in Society* (Glencoe: The Free Press).
Dutton, DG and Corvo, K (2006) 'Transforming a flawed policy: A call to revive psychology and science in domestic violence research and practice' 11 *Aggression and Violent Behavior* 457.
Economides, K (2007) 'Anglo-American Conceptions of Professional Responsibility and the Reform of Japanese Legal Education: Creating a Virtuous Circle?' 41 *The Law Teacher* 155.
Ede, R and Edwards, A (2008) *Criminal Defence* (London: Law Society).
Edwards, A (2008) 'The Role of Defence Lawyers in a "Re-balanced" System' in Cape, E and Young, R (eds), *Regulating Policing* (Oxford: Hart Publishing).
Elliot, P (1972) *The Sociology of the Professions* (London: Macmillan).
Eraut, M (1994) *Developing Professional Knowledge and Competence* (Abingdon: Routledge Falmer).
Ericson, R and Baranek, P (1982) *The Ordering of Justice: a Study of Accused Persons as Defendants in the Criminal Process* (Toronto: Toronto University Press).
Evans, A and Palermo, J (2002) 'Australian law students' perceptions of their values: interim results in the first year – 2001 – of a three year empirical research assessment' 5 *Legal Ethics* 103.
Faulkner, D (1996) *Darkness and Light: Justice, Crime and Management for Today* (London: Howard League).
Felstiner, WLF (2001) 'Synthesising socio-legal research: lawyer–client relations as an example' 8 *International Journal of the Legal Profession* 191.
Felstiner, WLF and Sarat, A (1992) 'Enactments of Power: Negotiating Reality and Responsibility in Lawyer–Client Interactions' 77 *Cornell Law Review* 1447.

Fenn, P, Gray, A and Rickman, N (2007) 'Standard fees for legal aid: an empirical analysis of incentives and contracts' *Oxford Economic Papers* (12 June).

Fennell, P (1980) 'Solicitors, their Markets and their "Ignorant Public": The Crisis of the Professional Ideal' in Bankowski, Z and Mungham, G (eds), *Essays in Law and Society* (London: Routledge).

Fielding, N (2001) 'Ethnography' in Gilbert, N (ed), *Researching Social Life*, 2nd edn (London: Sage).

Flood, J (1994) 'Shark Tanks, Sweatshops and the Lawyer as Hero? Fact as Fiction' 21 *Journal of Law and Society* 396.

—— (2005) 'Socio-Legal Ethnography' in Banakar, R and Travers, M (eds), *Theory and Method in Socio-Legal* Research (Portland: Hart Publishing).

Flyvberg, B (1998) 'Habermas and Foucault: thinkers for civil society?' 49 *British Journal of Sociology* 210.

Fores, M and Glover, I (1978) 'The British disease: professionalism' *Times Higher Education* (24 February).

Fox, AT (2003) 'Medical Slang in British Hospitals' 13 *Ethics and Behavior* 173.

Francis, A (2005) 'Legal ethics, the market place and fragmentation of legal professionalism' 12 *International Journal of the Legal Profession* 173.

Francis, A and Sommerlad, H (2009) 'Access to legal work experience and its role in the (re) production of legal professional identity' 16 *International Journal of the Legal Profession* 63.

Freidson, E (1988) *Profession of Medicine: A Study in the Sociology of Applied Knowledge* (Chicago: University of Chicago Press).

—— (1994) *Professionalism Reborn* (Cambridge: Polity Press).

—— (2001) *Professionalism: The Third Logic* (Cambridge: Polity Press).

Freud, A (1993) *The Ego and the Mechanisms of Defence* (London: Karnac Books).

Freud, S (1989a) 'Formulations on the Two Principles of Mental Functioning' in Gay, P (ed), *The Freud Reader* (New York: WW Norton and Company).

—— (1989b) 'On Narcissism: An Introduction' in Gay, P (ed), *The Freud Reader* (New York: WW Norton and Company).

—— (1989c) 'The Ego and the Id' in Gay, P (ed), *The Freud Reader* (New York: WW Norton and Company).

—— (1989d) 'The Question of a Weltanschauung' in Gay, P (ed), *The Freud Reader* (New York: WW Norton and Company).

—— (1995a) 'The Dissection of the Psychical Personality' in Strachey, J (ed), *New Introductory Lectures on Psychoanalysis* (New York: WW Norton and Company).

—— (1995b) 'Explanations, Applications and Orientations' in Strachey, J (ed), *New Introductory Lectures on Psychoanalysis* (New York: WW Norton and Company).

—— (2009) 'Splitting of the Ego in the Process of Defence' in Bokanowski, T and Lewkowicz, S (eds), *On Freud's 'Splitting of the Ego in the Process of Defence'* (London: Karnac Books).

Fuller, L (1978) 'The Forms and Limits of Adjudication' 92 *Harvard Law Review* 353.

Galanter, M (2005) *Lowering the Bar: Lawyer Jokes and Legal Culture* (Wisconsin: The University of Wisconsin Press).

Garfinkel, H and Weider, DL (1991) 'Two Incommensurably Asymmetrically Alternate Technologies of Social Analysis' in Watson, G and Seiler, R (eds), *Text in Context: Contributions to Ethnomethodology* (London: Sage).

Garland, D (2001) *The Culture of Control: Crime and Social Order in Contemporary Society* (Oxford: Oxford University Press).

Garside, R (2010) 'Too good an opportunity to miss?' 79 *Criminal Justice Matters* 36.
Giddens, A (1986) *The Constitution of Society* (Berkeley: The University of California Press).
Gilboy, J and Schmidt, J (1979) 'Replacing lawyers: A case study of sequential representation of criminal defendants' 70 *Journal of Criminal Law and Criminology* 1.
Glucksmann, M (1974) *Structuralist Analysis in Contemporary Social Thought* (London: Routledge and Kegan Paul).
Goffman, E (1990) *The Presentation of Self in Everyday Life* (London: Penguin).
—— (1991) *Asylums* (London: Penguin Books).
Golding, R (1982) 'Freud, Psychoanalysis and Sociology: Some Observations on the Sociological Analysis of the Individual' 33 *British Journal of Sociology* 545.
Goriely, T (1996) 'The Development of Criminal Legal Aid in England and Wales' in Young, R and Wall, D (eds), *Access to Criminal Justice* (London: Blackstone Press Ltd).
Goriely, T, McCrone, P, Duff, P, Knapp, M, Henry, A, Tata, C, Lancaster, B and Sherr, A (2001) *The Public Defence Solicitors' Office in Edinburgh: An Independent Evaluation* (Edinburgh: Scottish Executive).
Gorz, Z (1999) *Reclaiming Work: beyond the Wage-based Society* (Cambridge: Polity Press).
Gottman, JM (1995) *Why Marriages Succeed or Fail: And how you can make yours work* (New York: Simon and Schuster).
Gray, A, Fenn, P and Rickman, N (1996) 'Controlling Lawyers' Costs through Standard Fees: An Economic Analysis' in Young, R and Wall, D (eds), *Access to Criminal Justice* (London: Blackstone Press Ltd).
Green, N and Mendell, P (2010) *Legal Aid and Access to Justice: Rational Decision-Making and the Cost of Doing it Badly* (London: Criminal Bar Association).
Griffiths, J (1970) 'Ideology in Criminal Procedure or a Third "Model" of the Criminal Process' 79 *Yale Law Journal* 359.
Grossman, BA (1978) *The Prosecutor: An Enquiry into the Exercise of Discretion* (Toronto: University of Toronto Press).
Habermas, J (1999) *Moral Consciousness and Communicative Action* (Massachusetts: The MIT Press).
Harker, D and Sandbach, J (2010) 'Reaching further' in Robins, J (ed), *Closing the Justice Gap* (London: Waterlow Legal and Regulatory Ltd).
Heinz, JP and Laumann, EO (1982) *Chicago Lawyers: The Social Structure of the Bar* (New York and Chicago: Russell Sage Foundation and American Bar Foundation).
Hekman, S (1983) *Weber, the Ideal Type and Contemporary Sociological Theory* (Oxford: Martin Robertson and Company).
Henry, S (1983) *Private Justice* (London: Routledge and Kegan Paul).
Heumann, M (1978) *Plea Bargaining* (Chicago: University Of Chicago Press).
Hillyard, P (2002) 'Invoking Indignation: Reflections on Future Directions of Socio-legal Studies' 29 *Journal of Law and Society* 645.
Hoggett, P (1996) 'New Modes of Control in the Public Service' 74 *Public Administration* 9.
Hood, C (1991) 'A public management for All Seasons?' 69 *Public Administration* 3.
Hopper, K (2008) 'Qualitative and Quantitative Research: Two Cultures' 59 *Psychiatric Services* 711.
Hostika, CJ (1979) 'We Don't Care about What Happened: We Only Care about What is Going to Happen: Lawyer–Client Negotiations of Reality' 26 *Social Problems* 599.
House of Commons Committee of Public Accounts (2010) *The Procurement of Legal Aid in England and Wales by the Legal Services Commission*, Ninth Report of Session 2009–10 (London: The Stationary Office).

House of Commons Constitutional Affairs Committee (2007) *Implementation of the Carter Review of Legal Aid*, Third Report of Session 2006–07, Volume II (London: HMSO).
Hoyle, C (1998) *Negotiating Domestic Violence* (Oxford: Oxford University Press).
Hucklesby, A (1997a) 'Remand Decision Makers' *Criminal Law Review* 269.
—— (1997b) 'Court Culture: An Explanation in the Variations in the use of Bail by Magistrates' Courts' 36 *The Howard Journal* 129.
Hughes, EC (1958) *Men and their Work* (Glencoe: The Free Press).
Hume, D (1969) *A Treatise of Human Nature* (London: Penguin Books).
Hynes, S and Robins, L (2009) *The Justice Gap* (London: Legal Action Group).
Iyengar, SS and Lepper, MR (2000) 'When Choice is Demotivating: Can one desire too much of a good thing?' 70 *Journal of Personal and Social Psychology* 996.
Jackson, J (2004) 'Putting victims at the heart of criminal justice: the gap between rhetoric and reality' in Cape, E (ed), *Reconcilable Rights? Analysing the Tension between Victims and Defendants* (London: Legal Action Group).
Jacob, JM (1999) *Doctors and Rules: A Sociology of Professional Values* (New Jersey: Transaction Publishers).
Johnson, E (1980–81) 'Lawyer's Choice: A Theoretical Appraisal of Litigation Investment Decisions' 15 *Law and Society Review* 567.
Johnson, T (1972) *Professions and Power* (London: Macmillan).
Joint Advocacy Group (2010) Consultation paper on proposals for a quality assurance scheme for criminal advocates (August).
Jourard, S (1971) *The Transparent Self* (New York: Van Nostrand Reinhold).
Jung, CG (2009) *Psychological Types* (London: Routledge and Kegan Paul).
Lacey, N (1994) 'Introduction: Making Sense of Criminal Justice' in Lacey, N (ed), *A Reader on Criminal Justice* (Oxford: Oxford University Press)
Larson, MS (1977) *The Rise of Professionalism* (Berkeley: University of California Press).
Law Society (2009a) 'As new report finds legal aid lawyers paid less than sewage workers, Law Society says NO to more fee cuts' *Law Society Press Release* (19 November).
—— (2009b) 'NAO Report shows lawyers are ready to walk as failing legal aid system crumbles' *Law Society Press Release* (30 November).
—— (2010) *Access to Justice Review* (London: Law Society).
—— (2011) *Criminal Litigation Accreditation Scheme* (London: Law Society).
Leicht, KT and Fennell, ML (2001) *Professional Work: A Sociological Approach* (Massachusetts: Blackwell Publishers).
Levine, MP (2000) *The Analytic Freud: Philosophy and Psychoanalysis* (London: Routledge).
Lewis, D (2003) 'Factory Issues' *Law Society Gazette* (26 September).
Lodziak, C (2000) 'On Explaining Consumption' 72 *Capital and Class* 111.
Lofland, J and Lofland, L (1995) *Analyzing Social Settings* (California: Wadsworth).
Lord Chancellor's Department (1995) *Legal Aid – Targeting Need: The Future of Publicly Funded Help in Solving Legal Problems and Disputes in England and Wales*, Cm 2854 (London: The Stationary Office).
—— (1998) *Modernising Justice* (Kent: Martin Pearce Associates).
—— (2000) *Criminal Defence Service: Establishing a Salaried Defence Service and Draft Code of Conduct for Salaried Defenders Employed by the Legal Services Commission* (London: HMSO).
—— (2001) *Code of Conduct for Employees of the Legal Services Commission who provide services as part of the Criminal Defence Service* (London: The Stationary Office).
Lukacs, G (1971) *History and Class Consciousness* (London: The Merlin Press Ltd).

Lynch, M (1982) 'Closure and Disclosure in Pre-Trial Argument' 5 *Human Studies* 285.
—— (1993) *Scientific Practice and Ordinary Action: Ethnomethodology and Social Studies of Science* (Cambridge: Cambridge University Press).
Kapardis, A (2003) *Psychology and Law: A Critical Introduction*, 2nd edn (Cambridge: Cambridge University Press).
MacDonald, S (2008) 'Constructing a Framework for Criminal Justice Research: Learning from Packer's Mistakes' 11 *New Criminal Law Review* 257.
MacKay, K (2001) 'Salaried services: a strategy in legal need' *Legal Action Group Policy* (December).
Maharg, P (2007) *Transforming Legal Education* (Hampshire: Ashgate).
Marcuse, H (1964) *One-Dimensional Man* (London: Routledge and Kegan Paul).
Mason, J (2006) 'Underhand dealings' *Law Society Gazette* (16 March).
Mather, L, Maiman, RJ and McEwan, CA (1995) '"The Passenger Decides on the Destination and I Decide on the Route": Are Divorce Lawyers "Expensive Cab Drivers?"' 9 *International Journal of Law and the Family* 286.
Maynard, DW (1990) 'Narratives and Narrative Structure in Plea Bargaining' in Levi, JN and Walker, AG (eds), *Language in the Judicial Process* (New York: Plenum Press).
McBarnet, DJ (1981) *Conviction* (London: Macmillan).
McCall, G and Simmons, J (1969) *Issues in Participant Observation* (New York: Addison-Wesley).
McConville, M (2002) 'Plea Bargaining' in McConville, M and Wilson, G (eds), *The Handbook of the Criminal Justice Process* (Oxford: Oxford University Press).
McConville, M and Baldwin, J (1981) *Courts, Prosecution and Conviction* (Oxford: Oxford University Press).
McConville, M, Hodgson, J, Bridges, L and Pavlovic, A (1994) *Standing Accused* (Oxford: Oxford University Press).
McConville, M, Sanders, A and Leng, R (1991) *The Case for the Prosecution* (London: Routledge).
McDonald, P (1982) 'The class of '81' – a glance at the social class composition of recruits to the legal profession' 9 *Journal of Law and Society* 267.
McGann, A (2005) 'The Problem of Consensus in Habermas and Rawls: Rethinking the Basis of Deliberative Democracy', Annual Conference of the American Political Science Association (Washington DC: American Political Science Association).
Meffre, P (2005) 'Self-Image' in de Mijolla, A (ed), *International Dictionary of Psychoanalysis* (Michigan: Thomson Gale).
Mille, A (2010) 'Moral politics, moral decline and anti-social behaviour' 4 *People, Place and Policy Online* 6.
Millerson, G (1964) *The Qualifying Associations: a Study in Professionalism* (London: Routledge and Kegan Paul).
Ministry of Justice (2009) *Legal Aid: Funding Reforms* (London: HMSO).
—— (2010a) *Restructuring the Delivery of Criminal Defence Services* (London: The Stationary Office).
—— (2010b) *Proposals for the Reform of Legal Aid in England and Wales* (London: The Stationary Office).
Montagu, A and Matson, FW (1983) *The Dehumanization of Man* (Berkshire: McGraw-Hill).
Moorhead, R (2004) 'Legal Aid and the decline of private practice: blue murder or toxic job?' 11 *International Journal of the Legal Profession* 160.

Moorhead, R, Sherr, A and Paterson, A (2003) 'What Clients Know: Client perspectives and legal competence' 10 *International Journal of the Legal Profession* 5.
Morison, J and Leith, P (1992) *The Barrister's World* (Milton Keynes: Open University Press).
Mouzelis, N (1995) *Sociological Theory: What went wrong?* (London: Routledge).
Mulcahy, A (1994) 'The Justifications of Justice' 34 *British Journal of Criminology* 411.
Mulcahy, L (2007) 'Architects of Justice: The Politics of Courtroom Design' 16 *Social and Legal Studies* 383.
Mungham, G and Thomas, P (1979) 'Advocacy and the Solicitor-Advocate in Magistrates' Courts in England and Wales' 7 *International Journal of the Sociology of Law* 169.
National Audit Office (2009) *The Procurement of Criminal Legal Aid in England and Wales by the Legal Services Commission* (London: The Stationary Office).
Nelken, D (1986) 'Beyond the Study of "Law and Society"?' 11 *American Bar Foundation Research Journal* 323.
Newman, D (2012) 'Still standing accused: addressing the gap between work and talk in firms of criminal defence lawyers' 19 *International Journal of the Legal Profession* 3.
Nichols, MH (1974) 'Kenneth Burke and the 'New Rhetoric' in Harper, NL (ed), *Human Communication* (New York: MSS Information Corporation).
Nicolson, D and Webb, J (1999) *Professional Legal Ethics* (Oxford: Oxford University Press).
—— (2005) 'Public rules and private values: fractured profession(alism)s and institutional ethics' 12 *International Journal of the Legal Profession* 165.
Office for National Statistics (2009) *2009 Annual Survey of Hours and Earnings* (Newport: Office for National Statistics).
O'Hagan, DPC (2008) 'Faceless Factories' *Law Society Gazette* (14 February).
Osborne, D and Gaebler, T (1996) 'How the Reinventing Government Movement in Public Administration was Exported from the US to other Countries' 56 *Public Administration Review* 247.
Packer, HL (1968) *The Limits of the Criminal Sanction* (California: Stanford University Press).
Parker, C (1999) 'Compliance Professionalism and Regulatory Community: The Australian Trade Practices Regime' 26 *Journal of Law and Society* 215.
Parsons, T (1964) *Social Structure and Personality* (New York: The Free Press).
Passmore, C (2010) 'The future is bright' in Robins, J (ed), *Closing the Justice Gap* (London: Waterlow Legal and Regulatory Ltd).
Paterson, A (1996) 'Professionalism and the legal services market' 3 *International Journal of the Legal Profession* 137.
Podmore, D (1980) 'Bucher and Strauss Revisited: The Case of the Solicitors' Profession' 7 *British Journal of Law and Society* 1.
Pope, L and Ferraro, K (2006) *Considerations When Adapting the Power and Control Wheel* (Montana: Collaborative Consulting).
Popper, K (2000) *In Search of a Better World* (London: Routledge).
—— (2005) *All Life is Problem Solving* (Abingdon: Routledge).
—— (2006) *Conjectures and Refutations* (Abingdon: Routledge Classics).
Potter, J (1996) *Representing Reality* (London: Sage).
Rae, D (1975) 'The Limits of Consensual Decision Making' 69 *American Political Science Review* 1270.
Rethinking Crime and Punishment (2005) *Victims and defendants' rights: can they be reconciled?* (London: Esmee Fairbairn Foundation).
Rhode, DL (2004) *Access to Justice* (Oxford: Oxford University Press).

Rintala, M (2003) *Creating the National Health Service: Aneurin Bevan and the Medical Lords* (London: Frank Cass Publishers).
Robins, J (2010) 'Rising to the Challenge' in Robins, J (ed), *Closing the Justice Gap* (London: Waterlow Legal and Regulatory Ltd).
Roosevelt, E (1947) *My day–14 October 1947* (New York: United Feature Syndicate).
Rose, N (2009) 'Straw's pay warning to legal aid lawyers' *Law Society Gazette* (12 March).
Rosenberg, MJ and Hovland, CI (1960) 'Cognitive, affective and behavioural components of attitudes' in Rosenberg, MJ, Hovland, CI, McGuire, WJ, Abelson, RP and Brehm, JW (eds), *Attitude Organization and Change* (Connecticut: Yale University Press).
Rutherford, A (2001) *Criminal Justice Choices: what is criminal justice for?* (London: Institute for Public Policy Research).
Sandefur, RL (2001) 'Work and Honor in the Law: Prestige and the Division of Lawyers' Labor' 66 *American Sociological Review* 382.
Sanders, A and Young, R (2006) *Criminal Justice*, 3rd edn (Oxford: Oxford University Press).
Sanders, A, Young, R and Burton, M (2010) *Criminal Justice*, 4th edn (Oxford: Oxford University Press).
Sarat, A and Felstiner, WLF (1986) 'Law and Strategy in the Divorce Lawyer's Office' 20 *Law and Society Review* 94.
—— (1988) 'Law and Social Relations: Vocabularies of Motive in Lawyer/Client Interaction' 22 *Law and Society Review* 737.
—— (1995) *Divorce Lawyers and their Clients* (Oxford: Oxford University Press).
Sarat, A and Schiengold, S (1998) 'Cause Lawyering and the Reproduction of Professional Authority: An Introduction' in Sarat, A and Schiengold, S (eds), *Cause Lawyering* (Oxford: Oxford University Press).
Scheffer, T (2007) 'File work, legal care and professional habitus – an ethnographic reflection on different styles of advocacy' 14 *International Journal of the Legal Profession* 57.
Schnall, S, Haidt, J, Clore, GL and Jordan, AH (2008) 'Disgust as Embodied Moral Judgment' 34 *Personality and Social Psychology Bulletin* 1096.
Schon, DA (1983) *The Reflective Practitioner* (New York: Basic Books).
Schwartz, B (2005) *The Paradox of Choice: Why More is Less* (London: HarperCollins).
Shermer, M (2010) 'I am a sceptic, but I'm not a denier' *New Scientist* (15 May).
Sherr, A and Webb, L (1989) 'Law students, the external market, and socialisation; do we make them turn to the City?' 16 *Journal of Law and Society* 225.
Shiner, M (2000) 'Young, gifted and blocked! Entry to the solicitor's profession' in Thomas, P (ed), *Discriminating Lawyers* (London: Cavendish).
—— (2010) 'Post-Lawrence Policing in England and Wales: Guilty, Innocence and the Defence of Organizational Ego' 50 *British Journal of Criminology* 935.
Simons, HW (1990) *The Rhetorical Turn* (Chicago: University of Chicago Press).
Skinns, L (2009) '"Let's get it over with": early findings on the factors affecting detainees' access to custodial legal advice' 19 *Policing and Society* 58.
Smith, R (2002) *Legal Aid: Models of Organisation* (Budapest: European Forum on Access to Justice).
—— (2010) 'Special delivery' in Robins, J (ed), *Closing the Justice Gap* (London: Waterlow Legal and Regulatory Ltd).
Solicitors Regulation Authority (2007) *Solicitors' Code of Conduct* (Redditch: Solicitors Regulation Authority).
Solomon, RC (1993) *The Passions: Emotions and the Meaning of Life* (Indianapolis: Hackett Publishing).

Sommerlad, H (1995) 'Managerialism and The Legal Profession: a new professional paradigm' 2 *International Journal of the Legal Profession* 159.

—— (1996) 'Criminal Legal Aid Reforms and the Restructuring of Legal Professionalism' in Young, R and Wall, D (eds), *Access to Criminal Justice* (London: Blackstone Press Ltd).

—— (1999) 'The implementation of quality initiatives and the New Public Management in the legal aid sector in England and Wales: bureaucratisation, stratification and surveillance' 6 *International Journal of the Legal Profession* 311.

—— (2001) '"I've lost the plot": an everyday story of legal aid lawyers' 28 *Journal of Law and Society* 335.

—— (2008) 'Reflections on the reconfiguration of access to justice' 15 *International Journal of the Legal Profession* 179.

Sommerlad, H and Wall, D (1999) *Legally Aided Clients and their Solicitors*, Research Study 34 (London: Law Society).

Spencer, M (2002) 'Public subsides without strings – Labour and the lawyers at the birth of legal aid' 9 *International Journal of the Legal Profession* 251.

Stein, JM (2001) *The Future of Social Justice in Britain: A New Mission for the Community Legal Service* (London: London School of Economics Centre for Analysis of Social Exclusion).

Strauss, A, Schatzman, L, Bucher, R, Elrich, D and Sabshin, M (1964) *Psychiatric Ideologies and Institutions* (New York: The Free Press).

Sudnow, D (1965) 'Normal Crimes: Sociological Features of the Penal Code in a Public Defender Office' 12 *Social Problems* 255.

Suseno, Y, Pinnington, AH, Gardner, J and Schulman, AD (2006) 'Social capital and knowledge acquisition in professional–client relationships' 13 *International Journal of the Legal Profession* 273.

Tata, C (2007) 'In the Interests of Clients or Commerce? Legal Aid, Supply, Demand and "Ethical Indeterminacy" in Criminal Defence Work' 34 *Journal of Law and Society* 489.

Tata, C, Goriely, T, McCrone, P, Duff, P, Knapp, M, Henry, A, Lancaster, B and Sherr, A (2004) 'Does mode of delivery make a difference to criminal case outcomes and clients' satisfaction? The public defence solicitor experiment' *Criminal Law Review* 120.

Tata, C and Stephen, F (2006) '"Swings and Roundabouts": do changes to the structure of legal aid remuneration make a real difference to criminal case managements and case outcomes?' *Criminal Law Review* 722.

Thomas, PA and Mungham, G (1983) 'Solicitors and Clients: Altruism or Self-Interest' in Dingwall, R and Lewis, P (eds), *The Sociology of the Professions* (London: Macmillan Press).

Thompson, EP (1977) *Whigs and Hunters* (London: Penguin).

Thomson, A (1992) 'Foreword: Critical Approaches to Law, Who Needs Legal Theory?' in Grigg-Spall, I and Ireland, P (eds), *The Critical Lawyer's Handbook* (London: Pluto Press).

Thornton, M (2006) 'The Dissolution of the Social in the Legal Academy' *Australian Feminist Law Journal* 3.

Tickle, L (2005) 'The Crucible of the Classroom' in Beijaard, D, Meijar, P, Morine-Dershimer, G and Tillema, H (eds), *Teacher Professional Development in Changing Conditions* (Dordrecht: Springer).

Tickle-Dengen, L and Rosenthal, R (1990) 'The Nature of Rapport and its Nonverbal Correlates' 1 *Psychological Inquiry* 285.

Tonry, M (2004) *Punishment and Politics* (Cullompton: Willan Publishing).

Torrance, J (1995) *Studies in Marxism and Social Theory* (Cambridge: Cambridge University Press).

Travers, M (1997a) 'Preaching to the Converted? Improving the Persuasiveness of Criminal Justice Research' 37 *British Journal of Criminology* 359.
—— (1997b) *The Reality of Law: Work and Talk in a Firm of Criminal Lawyers* (Aldershot: Ashgate).
Trigg, J (2010) 'Citizen power' in Robins, J (ed), *Closing the Justice Gap* (London: Waterlow Legal and Regulatory Ltd).
Tuitt, P (2005) 'Legal Practice and Modes of Dying: Bruno Latour, Technology and the Critical Legal Instance' 16 *Law and Critique* 113.
Turner, BS (1977) 'The Structuralist Critique of Weber's Sociology' 28 *British Journal of Sociology* 1.
Tyler, TR (1988) 'What is Procedural Justice? Criteria used by Citizens to Assess the Fairness of Legal Procedures' 22 *Law and Society Review* 103.
Vaillant, GE (1992) *Ego Mechanisms of Defence: A Guide for Clinicians and Researchers* (Washington, DC: American Psychiatric Pres, Ltd).
Van Maanen, J and Kolb, D (1983) 'The Professional Apprentice: Observations on Fieldwork Roles in two Organizational Settings' in Bacharach, SB (ed), *Perspectives in Organizational Sociology* (Greenwich: JAI Press).
Waddington, P (1999) 'Police (Canteen) Sub-Culture: An Appreciation' 39 *British Journal of Criminology* 287.
Wear, D, Aultman, J, Varley, J and Zarconi, J (2006) 'Making Fun of Patients: Medical Students Perceptions and Use of Derogatory and Cynical Humor in Clinical Settings' 81 *Academic Medicine* 454.
Weber, M (1949) *The Methodology of the Social Sciences* (Glencoe: The Free Press).
—— (1978) *Economy and Society* (Berkley: University of California Press).
Welsh, J (2003) *Advocacy in the Magistrates' Court* (London: Cavendish Publishing Limited).
White, LE (1990) 'Goldberg v Kelly on the Paradox of Lawyering for the Poor' 56 *Brooklyn Law Review* 861.
White, R (1975) 'The Distasteful Character of Litigation for Poor Persons' 3 *Juridical Review* 233.
White, S (2006) 'Unsettling Evidence and Lively Language: Reflexive Practitioner as Trickster' in White, S, Fook, J and Gardner, F (eds), *Critical Reflection in Health and Social Care* (Berkshire: Open University Press).
Williamson, H (1980) 'Defence and Mitigation in the Juvenile Court: The Role of the Solicitor in Juvenile Justice' in Bankowski, Z and Mungham, G (eds), *Essays in Law and Society* (London: Routledge).
Wolfradt, U, Hempel, S and Miles, JNV (2003) 'Perceived parenting styles, depersonalisation, anxiety and coping behaviour in adolescents' 34 *Personality and Individual Differences* 521.
Worrall, A (1990) *Offending Women* (London: Routledge).
Young, J (2003) 'Winning the fight against crime? New Labour, populism and lost opportunities' in Mathews, R and Young, J (eds), *The New Politics of Crime and Punishment* (Cullompton: Willan Publishing).
Young, K (1940) 'The Impact of Freudian Psychology on Sociology' 10 *American Journal of Orthopsychiatry* 869.
Young, R and Wall, D (1996) 'Criminal Justice, Legal Aid and the Defence of Liberty' in Young, R and Wall, D (eds), *Access to Criminal Justice* (London: Blackstone Press Ltd).
Zander, M (2007) *Cases and Materials on the English Legal System*, 10th edn (Cambridge: Cambridge University Press).

—— (2010) 'Foreword' in Robins, J (ed), *Closing the Justice Gap* (London: Waterlow Legal and Regulatory Ltd).
Electronic sources
BBC News (2003) 'Doctor slang is a dying art', BBC at www.bbc.co.uk (18 August).
Bloch, J (2009) 'Legal Aid: Worse than shovelling sh*t', *Family Lore* at www.familylore.co.uk (20 November).
Family Law Newswatch (2009) 'Legal aid lawyers paid less than sewage workers', *Family Law* at www.familylaw.co.uk (19 November).
Faulkner, N (2010) 'The best and worst paying university degrees', Love Money at www.lovemoney.com (14 May).
Keogh, A (2009) 'LSC disputes Crimeline BVT massacre figures', Crimeline at www.wikicrimeline.co.uk (7 June).
May, T (2010) 'Theresa May's Speech to the Police Federation', Home Office at www.homeoffice.gov.uk (19 May).
McPartland, C (2009) 'Legal aid lawyers earn less than sewage workers, claims Law Soc', *The Lawyer* at www.thelawyer.com (19 November).
Morrell, P (2006) 'Some Notes on the Sociology of the Professions', *Homeopath International* at www.homeoint.org/morrell (June).
Murphy, C (2009) 'Power and control: Lawyer–client relationship', *Speak Out Loud* at www.speakoutloud.net (27 June).
Newman, C (2011) 'Fact Check: Do legal aid reforms protect the needy?', The Fact Check Blog at www.channel4.com (20 December).
Rozenberg, J (2010) 'New legal aid cuts could restrict lawyer-client contact', BBC at www.bbc.co.uk (30 June).
Straw, J (2008) 'Punishment and Reform – Jack Straw's speech and cultural theory', Royal Society for the Arts at www.thersa.org (27 October).
—— (2009) 'Constitutional Continuity – Jack Straw speech at the London School of Economics', Ministry of Justice at www.justice.gov.uk (3 March).

Newspapers articles

Berlins, M (2009) 'Calling a lawyer's client a customer is plainly wrong' *The Guardian* (27 June).
Bowcott, O (2012) 'Legal aid cuts will save less than half government's forecast, study finds' *The Guardian* (9 January).
Doyle, J (2012) 'Hamza's failed bids to stay in UK cost us £1m: Justice Secretary orders immediate review following investigation' *The Daily Mail* (17 November).
Freeland, J (2006) 'It is worth fighting to save the least loved branch of the welfare state' *The Guardian* (11 October).
Gibb, F (2007) 'What do clients think of their lawyers?' *The Times* (6 December).
—— (2009) 'Jack Straw deplores "astonishing growth" of legal aid' *The Times* (3 March).
Hanman, N (2010) 'Legal aid cuts put access to justice at risk, say lawyers' *The Guardian* (17 August).
Helm, T, Asthana, A and Townsend, M (2010) 'George Osborne takes spending axe to prisons and legal aid' *The Observer* (16 October).
Hickley, M and Slack, J (2008) 'Liberals who push criminal rights drive me nuts, says Justice Secretary Jack Straw' *Daily Mail* (26 October).

Hirsch, A (2009) 'Peer Pressure' *The Guardian* (17 June).
Jowit, J (2012) 'David Cameron's "tough, but intelligent" initiative on crime runs into trouble' *The Guardian* (20 October).
Mansfield, M (2012) 'Justice can't be treated as a business enterprise' *The Guardian* (29 August).
Marquand, D (2001) 'The breath of renewal' *The Guardian* (20 March).
Morris, N (2008) 'More than 3,600 new offences under Labour' *The Independent* (4 September).
Rogers, S (2009) 'The Queen, Jonathan Ross, nurses and teachers. What do people get paid in the public sector?' *The Guardian* (17 November).
Rose, N (2010) 'Death by a thousand cuts for legal aid' *The Guardian* (18 May).
Rozenberg, J (2012) 'Chris Grayling, Justice Secretary: non-lawyer and "on the up" politician' *The Guardian* (4 September).
Tebbit, N (2012) 'Cameron can overcome Mitchell crisis by imposing some discipline' *The Observer* (21 October).
Walters, S and Owen, G (2012) 'Cameron: "It's time to mug a hoodie": PM promises to seek "retribution" against lawbreakers in new anti-crime crackdown following catastrophic week' *The Daily Mail* (20 October).
Watt, N (2010) 'Clarke plans to shut 157 courts' *The Guardian* (24 June).

INDEX

www.ingramcontent.com/pod-product-compliance
Ingram Content Group UK Ltd.
Pitfield, Milton Keynes, MK11 3LW, UK
UKHW021822170926
15199UKWH00092B/47

9 781849 464338